C000296188

# VIETNAM

## THE IRISH EXPERIENCE

Copyright © 2008 James Durney
All rights reserved. No part of this publication may be reproduced, transmitted, in
any form or by any means, without prior permission of the author.

Also by James Durney and published by Gaul House.

## The Mob.
The History of Irish Gangsters in America.

## Far From the Short Grass.
The Story of Kildaremen in Two World Wars.

## On the One Road.
Political Unrest in Kildare 1913-94.

## The Volunteer.
Uniforms, Weapons and History of the Irish Republican Army 1913-97.

## The Far Side of the World.
Irish Servicemen in the Korean War 1950-53.

## In the Shadow of Kings.
Social Housing in Naas 1898-1884.

Published by:
Gaul House, Naas. 045 896265.
www.jamesdurney.com


Printed by:
Naas Printing Ltd., Main Street, Naas, Co. Kildare
Tel: (045) 872092

Design and Layout:
Naas Printing Ltd

Cover Design: www.thinktank.ie

Cover Photograph:
Pat O'Leary, 101st Airborne, in the Ashau Valley, 1969.

*This book is dedicated to my wife, Caroline,*
*a child of the sixties.*

# VIETNAM

## THE IRISH EXPERIENCE

# CONTENTS

# ACKNOWLEDGEMENTS

More than 2,500 Irishmen and women served in Vietnam between 1964 and 1973; twenty-nine were killed in action, or died in accidents or of natural causes, while dozens more were wounded. Of those who returned, few escaped unscathed, and many carry emotional scars and memories that continue to revisit them to this day. This book is a tribute to them, and all those Irishmen and women, drawn by a twist of fate into a terrible war in a faraway land.

Many people helped with this book; some spoke about long ago events for the first time, while some family members helped put together the pieces of life that included their loved ones last moments. For everyone it was an emotional experience, for some it was too much to delve into. I would like to thank especially: John Hawkins, Enniscorthy, Co. Wexford; Ed Somers, Camolin, Co. Wexford; Tom Kelly, Dysart, Co. Roscommon; John Dullahan, Washington, DC; Clive Dennis, Dublin and Naas, Co. Kildare; John Barnicle, Dublin; Walter O'Shea, Tipperary, for permission to use his tribute to Ed Landers; Dan Danaher, Tralee, Co. Kerry; B/2501st webmaster, Cathy Jimerson; Clyde Crossguns, Pat O'Leary, John McCammon, Brian Scott and James Duke for their reminiscences on John Driver; Terry Toenges and Jay Peterson for their permission to use Jay's tribute to Peter Nee; Margaret Walsh, Athy Heritage Centre, Athy Co. Kildare; Noel and Anne Flood, Ardscul House, Kilmeade, Co. Kildare; Mike and Anne Flood, Long Island, NY; Jim Kirk, Long Island, NY; Michael Cahill, The Curragh, Co. Kildare; Terry Boone, Kansas City, Mo; William F. Lee, USMC (retired); Don Driver, Dublin, for stories of his brother John; Dan and Mary McGee, Ballyconnell, Co. Cavan, for Mike Smith's story; Sean McGovern, New York; Michael Coyne, Jenkinstown, Co. Meath; Gerry Duignan, Rinn, Co. Roscommon; Rory O'Connell, Greenwood, Indiana; Stanley Bancroft, Dromore, Co. Down; John J. Jennings, Long Island, New York; Gary Hart and Jim Gebhardt for their reminiscences on John Collopy; Joe Doherty, New York, for reminiscences on his brother Martin Doherty; Canice Wolahan, Dublin; Pat Landers, Youghal, Co. Cork; Liam Kane, Dublin; Martin Hennigar, Liscannor, Co. Clare; Sean Levins, Monsterboice, Co. Louth; John O'Sullivan, Carstown, Co. Louth; Pat Nee, Boston, Massachusetts; John Barrett, Lahinch, Co. Clare; Mario Corrigan, Local Studies, Genealogy and Archives Department, Newbridge, Co. Kildare; Joe Hennessy, Limerick, for his help and permission to use his essay on the exploits of Air America; John Wiren, President Air America Association; John Dobbin, Carrickfergus, Co. Antrim; Stan Hickey, Naas; Marc Leepson, Middleburg, Virginia; and last, but not least, Brian Durney, photographic technician and cartographer.

Special thanks goes to Declan Hughes, Irish Veterans Memorial, Ireland, who unselfishly made available all his research and his contacts from his painstaking years of work on Ireland's Vietnam veterans; Ann Roper whose groundbreaking RTE documentary The Green Fields of Vietnam highlighted Irish involvement in the Southeast Asia war; Ed Somers, Vietnam veteran and friend, who wrote the forward to this book and for his technical and military advice.

# FOREWORD

Before I left Ireland the only thing I knew about Vietnam was that the French Army had suffered a disastrous and humiliating defeat at Dien Bien Phu at the hands of a guerrilla force. But having served there for over a year with the 1st Battalion Royal Australian Regiment, that remote and mysterious country, has left its mark on my heart and soul forever.

The events I experienced there stand out in stark reality. The trauma of combat, loss of friends and sometimes the odd incredible flash of humour, have lent to my subsequent life a curious dreamlike quality. For infantry soldiers the war was hard and relentless. It is impossible for people who have never been in the mincing machine of war to understand what it must be like. Equally, veterans who have survived and made it home again, run into the same impossibility of understanding, that while they were struggling with a deadly enemy, life went on as normal.

Vietnam veterans in particular faced indifference and hostility. Many of them recoiled into isolation, carrying their burden of bitterness with them. War is pain, loss, waste and confusion, but, also, courage, sacrifice and a brotherly love that rises and transcends all. (Many a soldier sacrificed his own life to save others.)

James Durney has, in writing this magnificent book, given a voice to those whose stories have never been heard – the veterans and their families, suffering in silence. The brave Irishmen who died and now lie in isolated graveyards around the world, including Ireland. The wounded, suffering loss of limbs or other injuries. The ones who carry their own internal scars. (Maybe the hardest of all to bear.) The mothers, fathers, wives and other family members who suffered bereavement and loss without any recognition. For them this book will be a source of consolation and recognition of sacrifice.

The picture arising from these pages is one of Irishmen, serving under various foreign flags in a brave and humane manner, keeping alive the tradition of honour and respect accorded to the Irish soldier throughout history.

Edward J. Somers
Camolin
Co. Wexford
Spring 2008

# PROLOGUE

Every war has its own story to tell, but from the start the war in South Vietnam was different. In Ireland the conflict between American supported South Vietnam and communist North Vietnam is known as the Vietnam War. Some historians refer to it as the "Second Indochina War", the first being the 1945-54 conflict between the Viet Minh and the French colonial rulers. In the United States it is also known as the Vietnam War. In Vietnam it is known as the War against the Americans, for they have had a few other wars since, and many before. Whatever it was called, the war, and it was never officially declared a war, was a devastating soul-destroying conflict which left five million people dead, mostly Vietnamese. The United States lost 58,000 men, while Australia, one of its most important allies, lost 496 men. Of these American and Australian servicemen at least twenty-six were natives of Ireland. Few people here realise how many Irishmen fought and died in the green fields of Vietnam, but upwards of 2,000 served in the armed forces of America, Australia and New Zealand.

When the first large concentration of American troops arrived in Vietnam, after the Gulf of Tonkin incident, there were several Irish-born soldiers among them. However, they were not the first Irish soldiers to grace the battlefields of Vietnam. Irish soldiers had been in Vietnam, or Indochina as it was then known, long before the coming of the Americans. Some were members of the British Army who had occupied Indochina after the Japanese surrender, while others were members of the French Foreign Legion who fought the Viet Minh in the French-Indochina War. Others were serving members of the British and Commonwealth forces who were seconded to French units in Indochina.

One Irish-born special forces' operator, was a veteran of Korea and later Borneo and Malaya, and was part of a mixed Commonwealth unit assigned to the French at Hue and "was on the Perfume river long before any Americans arrived". Captain Robin Charley, of the Royal Ulster Rifles, a veteran of Palestine and Korea, was to be seconded to the French at Dien Bien Phu, but the enclave was over-run before his orders were finalised. In 1955 US Marines of the Seventh Fleet aided in the evacuation of 300,000 refugees from North Vietnam to the south. No doubt there was an Irish representative among the Marines.

Ironically, the nationalist and communist leader Ho Chi Minh was partly inspired by Irish freedom fighters. In 1913-7, when he lived and worked in London, as an assistant pastry chef in the city's Carlton Hotel, Ho is reported to have shown great interest in the Easter Rising. Of Terence McSwiney, who died on hunger strike after seventy-four days, Ho said, "A nation which has such citizens will never surrender." In 1923 Ho travelled to the USSR to study Marxism.

It was there during an anti-imperialist conference that he met Sean McBride, the IRA veteran who went on to become a co-founder of Amnesty International. Like many budding revolutionaries Ho read IRA leader Tom Barry's memoir *Guerrilla Days in Ireland* and studied his method of guerrilla warfare. Back in Indochina he would put these tried and trusted guerrilla warfare methods to the test and begin a conflict that spanned four decades. During WWII the Americans supported Ho and his guerrillas in their fight against the occupying Japanese. Two decades later Ho would be using these same guerrillas and tactics against the Americans and their allies. Unknown to him, some of Ho's enemies would be the sons and grandsons of the fighting Irish he had so admired.

# American Presence in Vietnam 1965-1975

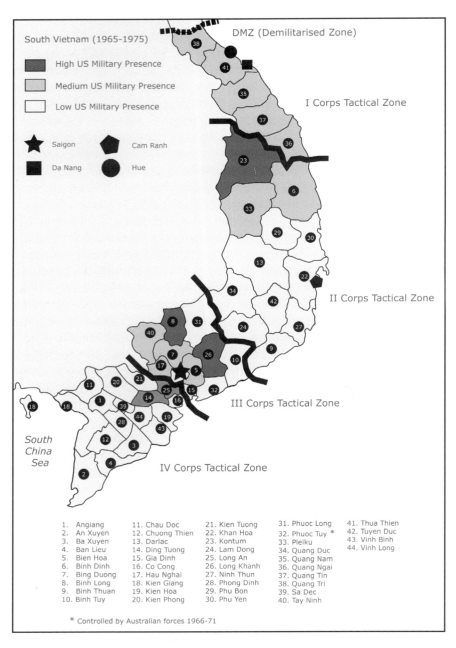

South Vietnam (1965-1975)

- High US Military Presence
- Medium US Military Presence
- Low US Military Presence

★ Saigon  ⬠ Cam Ranh
■ Da Nang  ● Hue

DMZ (Demilitarised Zone)

I Corps Tactical Zone

II Corps Tactical Zone

III Corps Tactical Zone

IV Corps Tactical Zone

South China Sea

| | | | | |
|---|---|---|---|---|
| 1. Angiang | 11. Chau Doc | 21. Kien Tuong | 31. Phuoc Long | 41. Thua Thien |
| 2. An Xuyen | 12. Chuong Thien | 22. Khan Hoa | 32. Phuoc Tuy * | 42. Tuyen Duc |
| 3. Ba Xuyen | 13. Darlac | 23. Kontum | 33. Pleiku | 43. Vinh Binh |
| 4. Ban Lieu | 14. Ding Tuong | 24. Lam Dong | 34. Quang Duc | 44. Vinh Long |
| 5. Bien Hoa | 15. Gia Dinh | 25. Long An | 35. Quang Nam | |
| 6. Binh Dinh | 16. Co Cong | 26. Long Khanh | 36. Quang Ngai | |
| 7. Bing Duong | 17. Hau Nghai | 27. Ninh Thun | 37. Quang Tin | |
| 8. Binh Long | 18. Kien Giang | 28. Phong Dinh | 38. Quang Tri | |
| 9. Binh Thuan | 19. Kien Hoa | 29. Phu Bon | 39. Sa Dec | |
| 10. Binh Tuy | 20. Kien Phong | 30. Phu Yen | 40. Tay Ninh | |

* Controlled by Australian forces 1966-71

## CHAPTER 1

# GOOD MORNING, VIETNAM

Vietnam is a country in Southeast Asia, situated in eastern Indochina –
bordering China, Laos, and Cambodia, as well as the South China Sea.
It is the most populous country among the mainland Southeast Asian countries. The name of the country comes from the Vietnamese Viet Nam, which
is in turn a reordering of Nam Viet – the name of an ancient Kingdom from
the ancestral Vietnamese that covered much of today's northern Vietnam
and southern China. Three quarters of the country consists of mountains
and hills and is crisscrossed with thousands of streams and rivers. The
waterways are a very convenient means of transport with major rivers like
the Red river in the north and the Mekong river in the south. The southern
provinces are affected by south-east monsoon wind, with hot weather all
the year round, two distinct seasons: rainy season from May to October, dry
season from November to April. The region has also two seasons: hot and
rainy season from May to October, cold and sunny season from November
to April. Vietnam has fifty-four different nationalities, but the ethnic
Vietnamese – Kinh – amounts to approximately eighty-six per cent. While
the majority of Vietnamese were Buddhists, there were many Roman
Catholics, though after the First Indochina War these were mostly concentrated in the South.[1]

Vietnam had been absorbed into the colony of French Indochina in 1883,
while the emergence of communists at the head of the Vietnamese
Revolution was through an accident of French politics. Ho Chi Minh and his
disciples were not originally communists but were mandarins, Vietnamese
nationalists, and the natural leaders of the people. The Vietnamese derived
their pre-colonial system of government from China and an emperor who
governed through a hierarchy of mandarins also ruled Vietnam. However,
French colonialism corrupted the Vietnamese mandarin class and they lost
the legitimacy of their claim to national leadership. The son of a Confucian
scholar-aristocrat dismissed for nationalist activity Ho Chi Minh joined the
French Socialist Party only because its more radical members advocated

independence for the colonies. Ho then became a founder of the French Communist Party when he was told the Third International also supported the people of the colonies. In 1941 Ho arrived back in Vietnam, after thirty years of exile, to form an alliance with non-communist groups and individuals in a national front organisation known as the Vietnamese Independence Brotherhood League (Viet Nam Doc Lap Dong Minh Hoi) or by its Vietnamese abbreviation – the Viet Minh.[2]

During WWII French Indochina was occupied by the Japanese. After Pearl Harbour American forces were involved in air and naval warfare with the Japanese in the skies and waters of Indochina. Even the harbour of Saigon had been raided and bombed by US carrier-based aircraft. (The first American killed in Vietnam was Flying Tiger John T. Donovan, shot down in 1942.) Over 200 Americans were also held as POWs in two Japanese camps in Saigon. When Japan surrendered in 1945, the French were not prepared to resume control of their Indochina colonies and protectorates. As previously determined at the Potsdam Conference, the British accepted the surrender of Japanese forces south of the 17th Parallel, and the Nationalist Chinese accepted the surrender of the Japanese north of the 17th Parallel. Because of the absence of an established government to assume control of Indochina, the Viet Minh, who had been trained and equipped, by the Americans to conduct guerrilla operations against the Japanese, were able to march into Hanoi, establish a government, and declare complete independence from France. On 4 September 1945 an American Office of Strategic Services (OSS) team led by Major Peter Dewey arrived at Tan Son Nhut airport to arrange for the repatriation and evacuation of the American POWs. Earlier difficulties had arisen when British Major-General Douglas D. Gracey,* commander of occupation forces in Indochina south of the 17th Parallel, objected to an American presence and sought to bar their participation. However, Admiral Lord Louis Mountbatten intervened, and Dewey's team were allowed to leave Ceylon for Saigon.

Until 12 September the American OSS team was the only Allied presence in Saigon. On that day a British Gurhkha division and a company of French paratroopers flew into Saigon. In the interim Dewey had made contact with the communist Viet Minh "Committee of the South", who believed that they could prevent the return of the French through negotiations and with Allied help – Russian, Chinese and American. Opposing the Committee was an assortment of nationalist groups who maintained that independence could not be supported by negotiations alone and fuelled that contention with rumours that the British planned to bring back French colonial rule.

---

* Douglas D. Gracey had family ties in Scotland and Ireland.

Fighting broke out between the many groups and on 26 September Major Dewey became the first American ground fatality when his jeep was shot up at a roadblock manned by Viet Minh, who assumed Dewey was French. (Gracey had established a provisional administration and freed French soldiers imprisoned by the Japanese. The French then began taking control of the cities of Vietnam within the British region.)

For the next few weeks British, French and departing Japanese forces battled the rising Vietnamese nationalist and communist groups. Hundreds of Viet Minh were killed in the attacks while the British lost forty men killed, the French and Japanese had somewhat higher fatalities. Most of the British casualties were Indian and Gurhka troops. The last British troops left in March 1946 as Gracey handed complete control over to the French. The French government began negotiations with both the Viet Minh and the Chinese for a return of the French army to Vietnam north of the 16th Parallel. The Viet Minh were willing to accept anything, including French rule to end the Chinese occupation. Ho Chi Minh and others had fears of the Chinese based on China's historic domination and occupation of Vietnam. The French negotiated a deal with the Chinese where pre-war French concessions in Chinese ports such as Shanghai were traded for Chinese assistance in Vietnam and landed a military force at Haiphong in early 1946. Negotiations then took place which talked about a future for Vietnam as a state within the French Union. These talks eventually failed and the Viet Minh fled into the countryside to wage guerrilla war. In 1946, Vietnam gained its first constitution and a new name, the Democratic Republic of Vietnam (DRV).[3]

In December hostilities broke out in Hanoi between the Viet Minh and the French. Ho Chi Minh appealed to the US for support, but the Americans were decidedly silent and Ho was forced to evacuate the capital in favour of remote mountain areas. Guerrilla warfare ensued with the French in control of most everything except very remote areas. Vietnamese nationalists and communists united to force the French out, thus beginning the First Indochina War. Most of the fighting took part in the north of the country where the communists were stronger. In 1948, seeking a post-colonial solution, the French re-installed Bao Dai as head of state of Vietnam under the French Union. The Viet Minh quickly denounced the government and stated that they wanted "real independence, not Bao Dai independence". Victorious Communist China and the Soviet Union recognised Ho Chi Minh as the legitimate ruler of Vietnam and sent him more and more supplies and material aid, while the Americans reluctantly began supplying the French. The escalating guerrilla war continued until the humiliating French defeat at Dien Bien Phu in 1954. This defeat led to the end of eight years of fighting with a ceasefire between the French and the Viet Minh. The Geneva Cease-Fire Conference split Vietnam into communist North and non-communist South along the 17th Parallel – the traditional dividing line through most of Vietnam's previous history. South Vietnam and its chief supporter, the United States, were not signatories to the 1954 agreement but did agree to respect its conditions. In 1955 a referendum approved the formation of a republic in the South with the Catholic and anti-communist leader Ngo Dinh Diem as president. The free elections scheduled by the Geneva Conference for 1956 were blocked by Diem who refused to countenance a combined election for the reunification of Vietnam on the grounds that the election would not be free in the North and that the North, with its larger population, would automatically outweigh the vote in the South.

The North was content to wait, expecting to achieve reunification through an economic collapse in the South. However, with American economic and military aid, South Vietnam became a comparatively peaceful and prosperous state. The politburo in Hanoi decided to reactivate the Viet Minh organisation, overthrow the Southern government and reunify the country under communist rule. When the country was divided 800,000 refugees had fled south while 80,000 had moved north. Many of these committed communists were sent home again to link up with pockets of Viet Minh still in the South. There was no need for a build-up phase and in 1959 the Second Indochina War went straight into the guerrilla warfare phase.[4]

Working among the mainly Catholic 800,000 refugees from northern Vietnam was an Irish-American physician, Thomas Anthony Dooley, who would have a huge influence on America's anti-communist policy in Southeast Asia. Tom Dooley had arrived in the summer of 1954 as part of a US military operation to assist refugees fleeing northern Vietnam. The Geneva Cease-Fire allowed a one-year period in which people could cross freely into the region under the control of the government they preferred, either the communist north or the non-communist south. Dooley worked in the refugee camps established in Haiphong, a port city in the north where refugees gathered for transportation to the south. Edward T. Donnell writing in *The Irish Echo* said: "He soon caught the attention of Lt Col Edward G. Lansdale, a top CIA official in Vietnam who saw in Dooley an ideal symbol of American goodwill and anti-communist idealism. It also helped that Dooley was Catholic, since American Catholics had become, by the mid-1950s, a key foundation of American anti-communism and South Vietnam was a largely Catholic country with a Catholic president. Through Lansdale, Dooley also came to the attention of the International Rescue Committee (IRC) and the American Friends of Vietnam (AFV), two key groups in the so-called "Vietnam Lobby" that were eager to focus American anti-communist efforts in the small southeast Asian nation."

Led by influential men like Cardinal Francis Spellman and Senator Joseph McCarthy American Catholics had embraced anti-communism in the 1940s and 1950s "with an unmatched intensity and passion". (It was no mistake the President Kennedy was also a Catholic and an anti-communist.) American Catholics saw in it a moral, and patriotic, obligation to defend the world against a "Godless Communism" that already held in its grip the Catholic nations of Eastern Europe and threatened to spread globally. Dooley, with a little help from his friends, wrote a book about his experiences in Vietnam, which became an instant bestseller. *Deliver Us From Evil: The Story of Vietnam's Flight to Freedom* contained gripping and heartrending stories of the efforts of Dooley and his team of US Navy personnel to care for countless battered and tortured refugees fleeing communist rule in northern Vietnam, and confirmed the American public's view of communism as an inherent evil ideology and the obligation of the United States to thwart its spread by any means necessary.[5]

Cardinal Francis Spellman's Vietnam stance was also in accordance with the wishes of the Pope. Malachi Martin, a former Jesuit who worked at the Vatican during the years of the escalating US commitment to Vietnam, said the Pope wanted the United States to back Diem because the Pope had been influenced by Diem's brother, Archbishop Thuc, and was concerned about communism making more gains at the expense of the Catholic Church. He turned to Spellman to encourage American commitment to Vietnam. Spellman with another Catholic and anti-communist, President John F. Kennedy, helped form a pro-Diem lobby in Washington. The rallying cries were anti-communism and Catholicism. Through their connections, they soon had a high-powered committee, which was a lumpy blend of intellectuals and conservatives, and included many prominent politicians and militarists.[6]

Shortly after the French defeat in Vietnam an alliance was organised under the Southeast Asia Collective Defence Treaty (SEATO) by representatives of Australia, France, Great Britain, New Zealand, Pakistan, the Philippines, Thailand, and the United States, to oppose further communist gains in Southeast Asia. The Eisenhower administration had formulated what became known as the "domino theory" which maintained that if communists succeeded in Vietnam other countries such as Laos, Cambodia, Thailand, Burma, Malaysia and Indonesia would fall like a row of dominoes. This would give them a geographically strategic advantage, from which they would be able to threaten Japan, Formosa, the Philippines, Australia and New Zealand. (The treaty was supplemented by a Pacific Charter, affirming the rights of Asian and Pacific peoples to equality and self-determination and setting forth goals of economic, social, and cultural cooperation between the member countries.) The civil and military organisations established under the treaty had their headquarters in Bangkok, Thailand. SEATO relied on the military forces of member nations and joint manoeuvres were held annually. SEATO's principal role was to sanction the US presence in Vietnam, although France and Pakistan withheld support. With American advisers already present in South Vietnam, and SEATO in the background, the US Armed Forces were gradually sucked into the escalating conflict.[7]

With South Vietnam in danger of collapsing Diem found a ready ally in President Kennedy, a fellow Catholic and Cold War hardliner. In May 1961, following a visit to the country by Vice- President Lyndon B. Johnson, Kennedy sent 400 American Green Beret "Special Advisers" to Vietnam to train South Vietnamese soldiers. Kennedy believed that allowing South Vietnam to fall to the communists would be a political disaster, especially after his criticism during the 1960 race for the White House when he had claimed the US was losing the arms race to the Soviet Union. Kennedy concluded that Vietnam was a test of his government's credibility and resolve in the global struggle against communism. By 1962 there were 12,000 American advisers in South Vietnam. (The first US advisers arrived in 1955.)[8] Drawing on their Korean experience the Americans had built up the South Vietnamese Army into a conventional force with artillery and tanks to meet an expected communist invasion. However, the Viet Minh, now called the Viet Cong (a term invented by the Americans from an abbreviation of 'Vietnamese communists'),[9] had an underground movement in the population and military support from village squads and regional and regular units and were using guerrilla tactics. The ARVN was too cumbersome for guerrilla warfare and the Americans began training them in counter-insurgency tactics. On December 11 1961 direct US aid to South Vietnam began as two US Army helicopter companies arrived in Saigon. The following February the Americans began the instigating of a strategic hamlet programme based on the successful British New Village scheme in Malaya.[10] The Americans, anxious to show that this was a combined effort, asked for non-combat military assistance from their SEATO allies to which Australia duly responded. In May 1962 a group of thirty experienced officers and warrant officers formed the Australian Army Training Team – Vietnam (AATTV) and arrived in Saigon in July. The AATTV integrated with its American counterparts to undertake training of ARVN units in the art of jungle warfare.[11]

Canice (Ken) Wolahan was one of the first Irishmen to arrive in Vietnam with the American military. Born in Rathfarnham, Dublin, Canice wanted to see the world and with this in mind decided to join the US Navy just after leaving school. However, the US Embassy told him that he would first have to make his way to America. Using his aunt's address in Cleveland the eighteen-year old, even though he was not a US citizen, was accepted into the US Navy in December 1963. From Cleveland, in Ohio, he flew to San Diego, California, to commence basic training at the Naval Training Centre. At the Recruit Training Command the navy recruit undergoes his transition from civilian to military life; learns the history, tradition, customs and regulations of the US Navy; and receives instruction in naval skills, physical fitness and subjects which will provide basic information throughout his period of naval service. Naval personnel have to spend time on both land and sea. After qualifying as a Basic Seaman, Canice was sent for further specialist training in Logistics and Supply Support Systems, again in San Diego, after which he found himself on his way to Saigon, in South Vietnam. In June 1964 Canice was assigned to Headquarters Support Activity based at Cholon, Saigon.

When he learned he was going to Vietnam Canice read up on the country and its history, which was very confusing. He found that the French still dominated much of the civilian social scene. The old colonial attitude prevailed and the French would not allow US servicemen into their clubs. With his Irish accent and Irish passport Canice easily passed for one of the many Irish who worked for foreign companies like Esso, or in the British Embassy. However, his haircut always attracted attention. He recalled that the British Embassy celebrated St Patrick's Day with a party and had Guinness and Irish Whisky for the guests. His nickname was "Irish" and he met quite a number of fellow countrymen in his travels around the country, including a Fr. Murray, serving as a chaplain in the USAF. "Fr. Murray did a lot of good work not just for the troops but also for any Vietnamese in need," Canice said.[12]

In 1963 the mutual disenchantment between President Diem and the American administration had escalated with the Buddhist crisis, which was badly mishandled by Diem and his family. Diem, a Catholic, had removed Buddhists from several key government positions and replaced them with Catholics. Buddhist monks protested against Diem's intolerance for other religions and the measures he took to silence them. In a show of protest, Buddhist monks began setting themselves on fire in public places. Diem reacted by raiding the pagodas. The Vietnamese and Americans began to look for ways of getting rid of Diem. With the tacit approval of the United States Diem was subsequently overthrown and murdered to be replaced by General Duong Van Minh. However, Minh was ousted in a subsequent coup by General Nguyen Khanh, who himself was later succeeded by Air Vice-Marshal Nguyen Cao Ky.[13] "There were five coups while I was in Vietnam,"

Canice Wolahan said. "There was a constant state of change." There were regular anti-government riots; fighting between Catholics and Buddhists. One day he saw a crowd running towards something in the streets of Saigon, an unusual occurrence because crowds generally ran away from something rather than towards it. With several other Americans, Canice decided to see what the commotion was. A Buddhist monk calmly poured petrol over himself and lit a match. "He stayed squatting there, praying, while he burnt to death. He never cried out. He just keeled over. He went up in a ball of flame. As he did this the Buddhist Monks were chanting around him."[14]

In 1964 the American supply system for the growing war effort was under the command of the US Navy though all services were involved. "We were based mainly in Cholon," Canice said, "a Chinese district on the outskirts of Saigon. Supplies came into the country by sea and air and were stored and distributed throughout South Vietnam by road convoy, boat where possible, plane, and increasingly by helicopter." Everything was gung ho at the beginning, but things began changing during the following years. Discipline was at a high level, the seasoned professionals – still referred to as advisers – were replaced by draftees." Drugs were always freely available, but in those early years the career servicemen frowned upon their use and rarely indulged. Most servicemen were content with a few beers. Canice Wolahan found South Vietnam a fascinating country. He was assigned to logistics and supplies and his duties were varied allowing him to gain first hand experience of the Vietnamese way of life. At this time US servicemen in many instances were still using WWII and Korean War weapons. He was armed with an M14 and Browning automatic. (The M16 followed two years later.) Saigon – the "Paris of the Orient" – resembled a large southern French city. The influx of American dollars was creating a booming economy. It could also be a dangerous place. Saigon and Cholon were the scene of a deadly terrorist campaign waged by the Viet Cong against American and government targets. Grenades were thrown into crowded bars and restaurants; suitcase bombs thrown under buses; bombs planted in hotels, restaurants and bars frequented by US servicemen, and bombs even placed at the exit points to catch those fleeing bomb scenes. "You could never be too cautious," Canice said. "You were a foot taller than everyone else and stuck out like a sore thumb. You could never let your guard down. You could not identify friend from foe but they could identify you. If the cab driver suddenly jumped out of his car to check something, you quickly followed. You took no chances and didn't trust anyone. At one time there was a spate of knifings of lone Americans coming home at night, so you didn't travel alone. The first and last months were the most dangerous. The first month because you were naive and knew nothing; the last month because you had survived for so long and you could get careless, cocky, let your guard down." He remembered a few friends were killed, a good few injured. But it was an interesting posting. Though a war was raging times were not too bad. You could live well and eat well. Many of the US servicemen had their uniforms and civilian clothes tailored. This included suits, shirts, and even shoes. The US troops had nothing but the best in terms of food, drink, and medical supplies. When you could eat out, the menus in top class restaurants were priced in French, English, Chinese and Vietnamese. Prices started at the dearest, which was in English, and worked their way down to the cheapest, in Vietnamese, so if you knew a little Vietnamese you could eat cheaper.

On Christmas Eve 1964, Bob Hope and his USO troupe arrived at Ton San Nhut Airbase. They were in-country to do their annual Christmas tour for the troops and were en route to their billet at the Caravelle Hotel in central Saigon. Canice Wolahan was assigned to the Bop Hope Show for the duration as a security officer. However, the cue card man, Barney McNulty, was late getting the cue cards off the plane. Canice recalled that the cue cards were more important than anything else as without them the show could not go on. During the show a cue man was always present at the front of the audience to hold up the jokes and punch-lines for the ageing short-sighted entertainer.[15] The delay with the cue cards ultimately saved many lives when a Viet Cong truck loaded with 300 pounds of TNT exploded in the hotel parking lot of the Brinks Hotel, which was very close to the Caravelle Hotel and housed a large number of American military personnel in its Bachelor Officers' Quarters. Two Americans and thirteen Vietnamese were killed and one hundred and seven others wounded. A later investigation revealed a Viet Cong document indicating that Bob Hope was the target of the attack. His opening comment at his next show was: "I want to thank you for your welcome to Saigon. As I came into town, I saw a hotel go the other way."[16] Canice drove past the area shortly after the bomb went off and witnessed the scene of carnage. "There was mass hysteria, bits of people lying all over the place, both military and civilian. When I eventually got back to my own quarters, close by, I found the front wall inside my wardrobe and all my possessions destroyed."[17]

Canice Wolahan completed his Vietnam tour in July 1965 as the war continued to escalate. He returned via the Middle East and Europe, stopping off in Ireland for a visit home, and then went back to the US. Canice served on board the USS *Caválier*, a troop transport, as a Supplies and Logistics Petty Officer and when he received his honourable discharge left the navy and returned home to Ireland to study economics. After a year in Vietnam Canice had no illusions about the war. "It was not a popular war. Even when

I returned in 1965 it was not a popular war. Protests had already started and guys going over there subsequently realised this before they left."[18]

As South Vietnam slipped into chaos President Kennedy was also assassinated and succeeded by his Vice-President Lyndon B. Johnson. Johnson appeared less cautious about direct US involvement in the war than Kennedy had been. He declared that he would not let South Vietnam go the way of China.[19] During a previous tour of Asian countries Johnson had visited Diem in Saigon and assured him that he was crucial to US objectives in Vietnam. Johnson had no mandate to deal with the escalating war, but this was partly rectified by the Tonkin Gulf incident, as a result of which Congress gave the President full powers in the Tonkin Gulf Resolution. On 2 August 1964, three North Vietnamese PT boats fired torpedoes at the USS Maddox, a destroyer located in the international waters of the Tonkin Gulf, some thirty miles off the coast of North Vietnam. The attack came after six months of covert US and South Vietnamese naval operations against North Vietnam. A second, even more highly disputed attack, was alleged to have taken place on 4 August, but was found to be that inexperienced crewmen had simply responded to sonar and radar anomalies. President Johnson accused the North Vietnamese of another blatant attack on a US ship and he convinced Congress to pass the Gulf of Tonkin Resolution which, authorised the President to "take all necessary measures to repel any armed attack against forces of the United States and to prevent further aggression". The resolution passed unanimously in the House, and by a margin of 82-2 in the Senate. The Resolution allowed the President to wage all out war against North Vietnam without ever securing a formal Declaration of War from Congress.[20]

By this stage the Viet Cong were on the verge of victory. Whole ARVN units were being engaged and defeated and the North Vietnamese had begun to infiltrate regular army units into the south. Only the intervention of the regular armed forces of the United States could now prevent the collapse of the Saigon regime and the unification of Vietnam by Ho Chi Minh and his followers in Hanoi. After securing his re-election President Johnson was faced with the alternative of a complete collapse of American policy, and the difficult extrication of 20,000 Americans, or of committing US combat troops to the war. In February 1965 American and South Vietnamese aircraft launched the first bombing attack on North Vietnam and in March US Marines landed on the beaches of Da Nang.[21] Twelve years after the end of the Korean War America was again at war in Asia.

CHAPTER 2

# THE GREEN MACHINE

As America geared itself up for war in Southeast Asia many thousands of young Irish emigrants were eligible for the draft. Most Irishmen received call-up papers within six months of their entering the United States. When issuing an immigration visa to an Irish national of military service age, the United States Embassy in Dublin informs him that if he fails to register for military service within six months of his arrival in America or if he pleads the 1950 Treaty of Friendship, Commerce and Navigation to ensure exemption, he may not, if he ever leaves the United States be allowed to re-enter. Most emigrants took their chances and registered. Few thought they would be asked to fight a war. Fewer still thought they would die in a war far from their new home.

Rates of emigration from Ireland to the US after 1945 varied widely, as the Irish economy alternated between cycles of stagnation and prosperity, and as American immigration laws were reformed. Between 1949 and 1956, the Irish Republic's national income rose by only one-fifth of the rate for western Europe overall. Between 1955 and 1957, Ireland was the only country in the western world where the total volume of goods and services consumed actually fell. Unemployment reached a record 78,000 in 1957, a year in which 54,000 people emigrated. Apart from the natural course of hopping across the water to Britain, America remained the first choice of Irish emigrants. They arrived in their thousands to traditional Irish areas like New York, Boston, Chicago and San Francisco. The combined metropolitan areas of Boston, Chicago and New York were home to between 54 and 58 per cent of all Irish emigrants to the US in the twentieth century.[1] Little had changed since the mid-nineteenth century when the country's most rural southern and western counties – Cork, Kerry, Galway, Mayo, Tipperary and Limerick – alone provided nearly half of southern Ireland's emigrants. By the mid-1950s, Cork, Kerry, Galway, Mayo, Donegal and Limerick provided 55 per cent of the emigrants from the Irish Republic. All these counties had large rural populations, poor quality land divided into numerous small land-holdings and few large towns. At the start of the 1960s the population of the twenty-six counties was smaller after forty years of independence than it had been during the days of British rule. In all, between 1946 and 1961, over 500,000 people left Ireland – more than half of them women. Most went to Britain but 68,000 emigrated to America. In the 1940s 26,967 Irish emigrated to America, followed by 57,332 in the 1950s. Another 37,461 Irish emigrants arrived in the US in the 1960s, but the figure fell to 6,559 in the 1970s. The drop in the demographic significance of the Irish-born in the US was precipitous. In 1900, the Irish-born were 2.13 percent of the US population, but in 1960 the Irish-born were only 0.05 percent. (In 1965 the US Congress passed a new law, overturning the old national origins quota system in place since the 1920s. Under the new system, Ireland's quota increased slightly from 17,000 to a maximum allowable figure of 20,000. But the rules of admission changed, with preference given to potential immigrants who either had close family ties to US citizens or possessed skills needed in the US. Most Irish people in the 1960s and 1970s could not meet either of these qualifications. At the same time, the Irish economy was exceptionally strong in these two decades.)[2] Irish emigrants holding American green cards were eligible for conscription to the US armed forces and soon many were heading to Southeast Asia.

For some Irish, it was by emigrating to Australia that brought them to Vietnam. After WWII there was a considerable labour shortage in Australia and out of desperation for the country's future Australia introduced the Assisted Passage Programme. Between 1945 and 1972 an estimated one million British people, and many Irish resident in the UK, left struggling post-war Britain to seek a new life in Australia. (Citizens of the Republic of Ireland born before 1949 were eligible as they too were British citizens.) The British and Australian governments arranged their transportation by ship to Australia while only paying nominal travel costs (£10) – the "ten-pound system". Like America, once legally in Australia, men became eligible for conscription to the armed services and were called upon to perform two years continuous full-time service in the Regular Army Supplement, followed by three years part-time service in the Regular Army Reserve.[3]

During the early morning of 7 February a Viet Cong attack against the US military compound at Pleiku in the Central Highlands left nine Americans dead, 128 wounded and 127 aircraft destroyed or damaged. Three days later another VC attack on the American compound in the coastal city of Qui Nhon left twenty-three US soldiers dead and another twenty-two wounded. Public indignation over these casualties grew in the United States and on 6 March it was announced in Washington that two battalions of Marines were being sent to South Vietnam to serve as security troops for the Da Nang airbase, which was felt to be particularly vulnerable, thereby freeing ARVN troops for combat duty. On 8 March 1965 3,500 men of the 9th Marine Expeditionary Brigade waded ashore at Da Nang ostensibly to guard the airfield. To their great surprise they were not met by armed resistance, but by pretty Vietnamese schoolgirls who festooned them with flowers. Secretary of State Dean Rusk, when questioned, said that the Marines would shoot back if fired upon. When the commitment began the US Marines were well-trained, organised and equipped for orthodox operations. The Marines, and most Americans, assumed the situation would be resolved in a few months, never realising that it would be many years.

The bay of Da Nang above the airbase was an excellent harbour formed by the Hai Van Peninsula on the north and a sprawling promontory known as Mon Ky (or Monkey) Mountain to the south. The city of Da Nang, formerly the old French colonial city of Tourane, had a population of about 200,000 — more than half of them refugees and other displaced persons. The Marines had been warned that the refugees in Da Nang had been heavily infiltrated with Viet Cong, and that they would possibly come under hostile fire. But when the men from Battalion Landing Team 3/9 came ashore a crowd of local dignitaries and civilians greeted them instead. The real reason for the high-profile amphibious assault was to send a very public message to the North Vietnamese — and their Russian and Chinese allies — that America was not prepared to stand idly by and watch their South Vietnamese ally fall to the communists. The deployment of the rest of the brigade went off with little incident except some desultory small-arms fire at incoming C-130 transport planes. The high ground around the airbase was quickly secured but the Marines faced a bigger problem in defending the military region known as I Corps.

I Corps Tactical Zone, within which Da Nang airbase was located, consisted of 10,000 square miles of variegated territory, about one-sixth of the total land area of South Vietnam. It encompassed a population of 2,755,800 in five provinces, six cities and 549 major villages. Its upper boundary touched the border of North Vietnam; its eastern edge running along the China Sea; west was the common border with Laos; while the southern boundary were the peaks of the Annamite mountains. Historically, the long, high stretch of the Annamites had always separated the region from the rest of Vietnam not only geographically but culturally as well. From the west, valleys and ridges served as infiltration routes for communists attacking coastal population zones, and these same hinterlands served as enemy rear and staging areas. I Corps was a rural area, which included the Central Highlands and the Montagnards, an indigenous, largely Christianised tribal people who differed in a number of culturally significant ways from other Vietnamese. They would become the most loyal of America's allies during the coming war.[4]

By 12 April the Marine strength in the Da Nang area had reached about 5,000. Among the Marines arriving in Vietnam was Patrick Nee, a tough teenager from South Boston. Pat Nee joined the US Marine Corps in 1962 when he was seventeen. He was born in Galway Hospital and spent his first six years in Rossmuc, Connemara, Co. Galway, and another two years in Galway City, where the family lived in Courthouse Lane (now Druid Lane). His father was an ex-Irish Army soldier who left for America when employment – precarious at the best of times in 1950s Ireland – steadily got worse. Paddy and Julia Nee wanted the best for their children and Paddy emigrated to Boston in 1951. He saved up the fare for the rest of the family to join him the following year when Pat Junior was eight. The Nee family moved to South Boston, or "Southie," that most insular of Irish-American neighbourhoods. Coming from Connemara the Nees were all Gaelic speakers, but that was the norm in Southie at the time. Paddy Nee immediately got a job in the Labourers Union. When he showed up for work at the union hall in South Boston, the first to be called were the Gaelic speakers, then the children of Irish immigrants. As Pat Nee said, if you didn't fall into these two categories then you were out of luck, because back then "the Irish ruled Southie". As a teenager Pat began hanging around with the Mullens, a local street gang, brawling, thieving and hi-jacking along the South Boston waterfront. Many of the Mullens were ex-servicemen – the gang was named after a WWI veteran, James Joseph Mullen – and Pat Nee remembered sitting for hours listening to the "older Mullens" telling war stories from WWII and Korea. Three of his older friends were highly decorated combat Marines from the Pacific fighting and they made a big impression on Pat. When he was seventeen Pat Nee decided a stint in the Marines would get him back on the straight road, and besides it was a tradition in Southie dating back to the Civil War. He headed to the nearest USMC recruiting station with two other friends, also members of the Mullens. His father had to sign his papers, as he was still underage. Pat Nee became a US citizen on 1 July 1962 and left for Parris Island, South Carolina, a week later.[5]

The United States Marine Corps has a unique culture of pride that makes it one of the world's premier fighting forces. Men "join the Marines because they want to be the best". Mike Flood, who served in Vietnam in 1968-9, said, "When I was going to Vietnam I wanted to be with the best, so I joined the Marines."[6] The US Marines have a special espirit de corps and has a long line of proud traditions – they are always first to fight, they never leave their dead and wounded behind, officers always eat last. The Marines code is

"Semper Fi"– "always faithful." James Bradley wrote, "the Army has Army officers and soldiers, the Navy has naval officers and sailors, the Air Force has Air Force officers and airmen – but the Marines have only Marines". Basic training for marines is widely recognised as the most demanding recruit training in the world.[7] Pat Nee described his basic training as "twelve weeks of pure hell."[8]

"In 1962 I decided to join the Marines with two good friends, Jerry Shea and Louie Lentini. My mother Julia (Grealish) became a US citizen first so my brother (Seán) and myself could become US citizens. I went to Parris Island and graduated in the top seven of my platoon (PLT 350). Served with 2nd Marine Division for a while, did a 'Mediterranean Cruise' (with the 6th Marine Brigade) in the summer of 1963. I remember JFK being killed – that was a bad day … Transferred to 1st Marine Brigade in Hawaii … Had a great time. A small group of us had a small house two blocks from Waikiki Beach, where I learned to surf." In January 1964 Pat Nee was posted to Hawaii to the 3rd Battalion, 4th Marine Regiment, where he excelled as a 106mm recoilless rifle gunner. When he heard of the escalating war in Southeast Asia Pat volunteered for duty in South Vietnam.[9]

Pat Nee landed in Vietnam with the 3/4 Marines in April 1965. He was nineteen. "Our ship headed up the Perfume River (north of Hue) and even though we were in friendly territory, this was a full assault landing; we were locked and loaded, ready to hit the beach. I remember feeling my gut tight with anxiety. The emerald green foliage that shielded the river's banks seemed to ooze tropical sounds. New smells – pungent, powerful aromas – overwhelmed our olfactory senses, heightening the intensity of what was about to happen. Some Marines looked like they might be praying. We were just kids, and what we'd seen of what we were about to do came from film of assault landings during World War II. Finally the command came to hit the beach. But instead of being met by a volley of bullets, as my memory serves me there was a South Vietnamese band playing the Marine Corps hymn by way of welcome."[10]

The 3rd Battalion marched to Phu Bai to secure the airport and "settle in". Here they set up battalion areas for command and operations. "We dug a 360-degree defensive perimeter around the airport and erected razor-sharp wire to keep out the Viet Cong. In the event that the VC were crafty enough to cut through the wire our boys had a little welcoming party wait-ing. First they laid wire connected to trip flares. The instant the flares fired into the air it took away Charlie's protective cover of darkness. Immediately the perimeter would convert from midnight black to an umbrella of day-light. And if the VC got past the flares, there'd be another trip wire several feet inside the perimeter attached to claymore mines laid every fifty yards.

Claymores spray 3,200 pieces of razor-sharp US steel at 2,800 feet per second. Anything in a 180-degree arc within an area of fifty yards would be reduced to mash. Or at the very least, it wouldn't be walking away."10

"My childhood friend, Jerry Shea, ended up in Battalion Recon, attached to my outfit. We were only 100 yards apart in Phu Bai, but it still took us a month to find each other." While Pat never met any other Irishmen in Vietnam he found his allies – "Aussies and South Korean troops very good, the ARVN not so hot". He didn't like the VC, but thought the "NVA good fighters". He found the weather was another enemy – "either too hot, 115 degrees, or too wet, monsoon season.11 During the day we'd build little shelters we could call home, protection from the sun and cover from the rain. Monsoon season started in October. It was like being underwater twenty-four hours a day: for six to eight weeks you'd be wet from head to toe. Your boots and socks would rot. I had trouble with the skin on my feet turning wrinkly white and peeling off. The continuous sheets of rain turned the earth into a rancid shit field."12

The 3rd Battalion was responsible for security around Phu Bai, which housed an Army radio intelligence station and an auxiliary airfield. In May the 3rd Marine Division opened another enclave in southern Quang Tin province and called it Chu Lai. Despite having almost an entire 22,000-man division on the ground the Marines were still restricted to close-in patrols of the three airbases at Da Nang, Phu Bai, and Chu Lai. The infantry commanders wanted to at least push out the perimeter so that the airfields themselves would be out of enemy mortar and artillery range. The ARVN commander near the Marine enclaves did not want the Marines to patrol aggressively as he was not sure the leathernecks were ready to do battle with the experienced Viet Cong units operating in the area. He also did not want the heavily armed Marines patrolling densely populated areas.13

Pat Nee recalled his first night patrol was filled with "nothing short of breathtaking fear". But when the patrol came under fire everything he was taught in training at Parris Island just kicked in. "We had no idea what to expect. My fixed position was in a foxhole about forty yards from the woods line. I'd just dug two little holes below the sandbags, placing my hand grenades in one and my illumination grenades in another. Although the air around me was pitch black, I wanted to know exactly where my frags were if things got busy. Out of nowhere I heard the distant rat-tat-tat of a Russian AK-47 cutting through the night. It must have been a hundred yards from my position. Instantly I heard return fire from our guys. I sat up on the edge of my foxhole watching the tracers run across the black blanket covering the jungle."14

Pat Nee had several close calls while in Vietnam – a truck he was travelling in ran over a landmine and was blown up, but apart from loss of hearing for a short time, he was uninjured – "not a scratch on me"; on jumping out of a helicopter he slipped down a hill, while a buddy was impaled on a punji stick and paralysed; and on a night ambush one Marine's alarm clock went off, causing the patrol to hastily abandon ambush positions. He recalled that everything happened in combat so fast he was only nervous afterwards.[15] The 3rd Battalion redeployed during December 1965 to Camp Schwab, Okinawa, and Pat Nee arrived back in the US in January 1966

After eight months in Camp Elmore, Norfolk, Virginia, his term in the USMC was up and Pat received an honourable discharge in October 1966 and returned to Boston. Back home in Southie Pat tried to live a straight life but after his brother, Peter, was killed he was sucked back into organised crime activities which would ultimately see him gun-running for the Irish Republican Army and working with Boston's most notorious gangster, James J. "Whitey" Bulger. Pat's brother, Peter, was twenty-two when he was shot dead in April 1969, just two months after returning from Vietnam. Peter, a year younger than Pat, was born in Rossmuc, Co. Galway, and had served two tours of Vietnam (1967-8 and 1968-9) with the USAF Strategic Air Command. Ironically, another Irish-American who was decorated for valour with the Marines in Vietnam shot him dead during an argument.[16] Two other brothers, Michael and Seán, were also servicemen: Michael served one tour with the Army in Vietnam (1970), while Seán served overseas in Germany.[17] Michael would later write home from Phu Bai that he was sitting in a trench that the Marines had originally dug back in 1965 when Pat was serving there.[18]

On 6 May 1965, the 3rd Marine Division opened the Marine Compound at the Da Nang Airbase. The Division, which had been stationed in Okinawa since 1956, operated in Vietnam from this time participating in operations from Da Nang to Phu Bai to Quang Tri/Dong Ha Combat Base. On 7 May the designation of the Marine units in I Corps was changed from the 9th Marine Expeditionary Force into III MAF – Third Marine Amphibious Force, in case the Vietnamese might take exception to the term 'Expeditionary' which evoked memories of the colonial days of the French Expeditionary Corps. By the end of May three months of defensive operations had resulted in almost 200 casualties, including eighteen Marines dead. The feeling was growing among the Marines that if this was what constituted a static defensive role, they did not like it. Even the Commandant of the Marine Corps, General Wallace M. Green, told the press that his Marines were not in Vietnam to "sit on their ditty boxes," they were there to "kill Viet Cong." On 1 July a VC demolition team slipped through the ARVN perimeter security at Da Nang airbase and struck the parked aircraft with mortar and rocket fire and explosives destroying or damaging three C-130s and three F-102s. As a direct consequence President Johnson announced that the country's military forces would be increased from 75,000 to 125,000 almost immediately, that the draft quota would be increased from 17,000 to 35,000 a month, and enlistment programmes would be stepped up.[19]

More US troops soon followed, initially to protect other US installations, but US military commanders viewed this initial "enclave" strategy as ineffective. From 8 June American troops were officially permitted to begin "offensive patrolling," which was soon broadened to include "search and destroy" missions. Search and destroy missions were sweeps through the countryside in an attempt to perform the Army's traditional objective: "find, fix and finish the enemy". US troops were based in heavily fortified camps. They would board helicopters at these bases, head out into the country and set down in some predetermined point. From there they would march ("hump") to another predetermined point in an attempt to pin down and destroy the Viet Cong. These tactics were badly flawed, as the lighter equipped VC, and later NVA, could easily escape the heavier equipped Americans and their allies. The enemy could also stay just long enough to inflict morale-damaging casualties on the Americans and then disappear into the jungles and mountains.[20]

By June there were more than 50,000 American soldiers in Vietnam, including nine battalions of Marines and Army paratroops. Although the Johnson administration was being vague in public about the decisions it was reaching, more American battalions were clearly on the way. They were arriving just in time. The Saigon government had been preparing to evacuate all five northern provinces along the Central Coast – the whole of the I Corps zone where the Marines now held the airfield at Phu Bai as well as the port and airbase at Da Nang. The Saigon generals were beginning to panic and were uncertain whether they would be able to defend the remnants of the Central Highlands they still held long enough to shift the burden to the Americans. It was clear the regime would not survive into 1966 without an American rescue. With the arrival of more American combat troops the United States Army and Marine Corps would provide the muscle to stop the communists until the Johnson administration turned the Saigon regime into a government whose leaders were not fundamentally corrupt men and reorganise their army into a functioning force capable of defeating the communists.[21]

In August of 1965, the 62nd Engineer Battalion deployed to Vietnam. It was the first engineer battalion to ship out for the big build-up. To accommodate the huge numbers of American and allied troops arriving in Vietnam to fight the war the engineers would have to construct ports, jet-capable airfields, supply and repair depots, base camps, hospitals, communications systems, and other elements of the elaborate support structure needed.[22] Martin Hennigar was a platoon sergeant with the 62nd Engineer's A Company. Born in Limerick in 1935 Martin had emigrated in late 1958 to New York. He was living in Bay Ridge, Brooklyn, when he was drafted in July 1959. He was inducted at the Armed Forces Induction Centre, Whitehall Street, Manhattan – the old induction centre for WWI and WWII. After basic training in Fort Benning, Georgia, "I was sent to Fort Leonard Wood in Missouri," Martin said, "which is the Engineer Training Centre. I also came back there between my tours in Nam as an instructor." With a background in engineering and as an honour graduate he was given a choice of overseas duty, so he put in for duty in Germany. Instead Martin was sent where "his MOS (Military Occupation Specialty) was needed" – Korea. He sailed from San Francisco on a troopship with 2,000 other men on Christmas Eve 1959. "I'll never forget it," Martin said. "Going under the Golden Gate Bridge on Christmas Eve. The convicts were waving at us from Alcatraz. We felt they were better off than us. We must have looked the most miserable group of people ever." He spent thirteen months in Korea as an engineer retrieving mines left over from the war of 1950-3. On his return to the US he was given a month's leave and travelled home to Limerick. In 1964 he became a US citizen. While stationed in Fort Tilden, Rockaway, Queens, Martin re-enlisted for a further three years, most of which he spent in France and Germany. His next stop was Vietnam. Officially no one in the 62nd Engineers knew where they were going and were only told their destination while at sea. The Battalion left San Francisco by troopship in August, was detained for a time in Oakland and then sailed for South Vietnam, stopping at Hawaii, Japan and the Philippines before arriving in Cam Rahn Bay on 20 September. The 62nd's first mission was to construct a 10,000-foot airstrip and cantonment at Phan Rang, fifty miles south of Nha Trang.

"Vietnam," Martin remembered, "was a good place not to be. Snakes, tigers, and monsoons. You were wet all the time, either with sweat or rain." On their first indoctrination he remembered the advice about snakes. "There are a 100 different types of snakes in Vietnam. Ninety-nine of them are poisonous, the other big son-of-a-bitch will choke you to death." The job of the engineers was to build roads and bridges and lay and take up mines and "anything else that backed up the infantry. We were always there to support the infantry." Martin Hennigar was working on a temporary runaway when the legendary John Wayne, on a USO visit to South Vietnam, arrived for an overnight stay in the area. The Duke, dressed in fatigues and jungle hat, got off an airplane, a few feet from Martin, to be greeted by Lt Bill Carpenter, Distinguished Service Cross winner and Army football player. Martin remembered that the Duke looked as big and imposing in real life as he did on the cinema screen.[23] John Wayne was a supporter of the US involvement in Vietnam and prompted by the anti-war atmosphere and social discontent in the America in 1968 made a movie, *The Green Berets,* to help counter that. The Duke had entertained the troops in Vietnam, and wanted *The Green Berets* to be a tribute to them.[24]

As his first tour ended Martin Hennigar "was in a processing centre, a big mess hall, in the chow line, when this guy taps me on the shoulder and asked me was I Martin Hennigar and did I recognise him. Turned out it was Larry Feehan, from Limerick, who went to school with my younger brother. Larry was only arriving in-country. I got him a pass and we went out on the town in Saigon." Martin Hennigar returned to the US and a month's leave home in Limerick. Based back at Fort Leonard Wood he was an instructor in demolitions, but the Army had more dangerous plans for him. Nine months later he was sent back to Vietnam for another tour, this time with the 577th Engineer Battalion who were in-country since July 1966. While "out in the field a helicopter came in with mail and food and an officer told me I had to go back to HQ in Nha Trang. Back at HQ another officer told me 'You're a lucky guy. Congress just changed the law. Anyone in-country within twelve months shouldn't be here. However, there's a catch. You have to go on a month's leave.' I choose to go to Ireland. Another officer said, 'It has to be the continental USA.' The other guy said, 'It says anywhere. He can go to Ireland. Go back out and pick up your shit in the field and be back here tomorrow.'"

Martin went back to the US and then flew to Ireland. He arrived back in Shannon airport, his second time there in six weeks. While his family were shocked to see him so soon, they were delighted he was home again. Back home in Limerick Martin's friends told him he was crazy to go back to the US where he would be sent back to Vietnam again. Martin returned after his month's leave and despite his protests was sent back again to Vietnam, "just in time for Tet – not a nice time to be in Vietnam".[25] Violence could come quick in Vietnam even to construction troops and the 35th Engineer Group News Bulletin printed this article in their 15 February 1968 issue: "Tuy Hoa. Company A of the 577th Engineer Battalion (Construction) has been personally commended by LTC Jack C. Aherns, commander of the Phu Hiep Airfield for their quick retaliatory measures in repulsing a Viet Cong attack on the base. The airfield defence perimeter is nearly a mile from the Engineer Battalion's own cantonment. Within ten minutes after the perimeter came under fire, the defences were more than tripled. The attackers were driven off by a relentless return of fire from the engineers machine guns and other smaller weapons. The gunfire was so intense that the Viet Cong attack was thwarted and the airfield has never again come under attack, even though the communists have still been operating in the area and have harassed other units." After this incident a village outside the perimeter was investigated and the bodies of several women and children were found in a schoolhouse. The Viet Cong had killed them before or during the attack and took away their own dead during the night.[26]

Martin was wounded some weeks before his tour was completed. "Our truck ran over a mine. Five of us were in a three-quarter ton truck going back to base camp at Tuy Hoa. When we left the airbase we called ahead and said we were on our way back. When we didn't arrive they knew something was up. We had to be off the roads by six o'clock. After six anything on the road would be fired on because the VC moved at night. When we didn't arrive back in time they came looking for us. A helicopter picked us up." Martin received shrapnel wounds to the left side of his head and spent a few weeks in hospitals in Vietnam and the US. Martin Hennigar left Vietnam on 5 September 1968. "I came through it alright," he said of his experiences.[27]

Martin Hennigar was well thought of by the men under his command and by his superiors. His commanding officer in Company A, Captain Lawrence Gralla, had this to say in his letter of recommendation, "The personnel in this company are the most safety conscious, neatest and hardest working of any in the 35th Engineer Group and it is partly due to your effort... It is through the fine support and assistance of a non-commissioned officer like yourself that has enabled Company A to achieve the fine reputation that it has."[28] Martin served a total of eleven years and nine months in the US Army and left in 1970. "I had a choice to stay in or get out, but I left then and went back to New York. As a veteran you were allowed so many points and I got a job with the New York City Transit Authority Power Distribution Department." Martin worked for twenty-two years with the NYC Transit Authority. He returned to Ireland in 2001.[29]

On 14 August 1965, as the troop build-up continued, a four-month involuntary extension of duty was announced for all USMC/USN enlisted personnel. In Vietnam Marines and Navy personnel would serve a thirteen-month tour while Army troops served twelve months. Army, Marine Corps and Air Force units were arriving in Vietnam as fast as they could be dispatched. By August there were four Marine regiments in-country: 3rd Marines, with its 1st and 2nd Battalions at Da Nang and the 3rd Battalion, 4th Marines, attached and stationed at Phu Bai; 9th Marines, with its 2nd and part of the 1st Battalion guarding the area south of Da Nang; the rest of the 1st was on the airbase itself; 4th Marines at Chu Lai, with its 1st and 2nd

Battalions and 3rd Battalion, 3rd Marines attached; 7th Marines, also at Chu Lai with its 1st Battalion; the 2nd Battalion was at Qui Nhon and the 3rd was at sea with the Fleet Special Landing Force.

On line with the new point of view regarding offensive actions, III MAF Headquarters decided to engage the Viet Cong in a major battle, to take place in the area south of Chu Lai, where intelligence indicated that the 1st Viet Cong Regiment, some 1,500 men, was gathering for an attack on the air strip. By chance two large fresh American units were in the area, and they became the basis for Operation Starlite, the first regimental-size American attack force since the Korean War. The attack began on 18 August 1965 with a three-pronged assault: a river landing from the north, helilift on the west and an amphibious landing on the beaches on the southeast. On the morning of 18 August the amtrac (armoured amphibious tractors) of the 3rd Battalion, 3rd Marines came ashore on the beach at An Cuong. As the Marines advanced towards the thatched huts of the nearby hamlet they walked into a wall of Viet Cong machine gun fire and exploding mortar shells. It took supporting fire from an offshore light cruiser before the advance could continue. A pitched battle developed as the Marines surged forward into the VC trenches and bunkers and took on the enemy in hand-to-hand combat. After several hours of savage fighting, the hillside was secured.

Later that day an amtrac force with three tanks, on its way to re-supply the men of Company I, 3rd Battalion, 3rd Marines, became lost in a maze of trails and stumbled into a devastating VC ambush. A hastily dispatched force from Coy I was also hit as it tried to relieve the pressure on the knocked-out column and a savage battle ensued. The Marines held off the attack and both sides suffered heavy casualties.[30]

Irish-American Robert E. O'Malley, of Company I, was the first Marine recipient in Vietnam of the Medal of Honour – America's highest decoration – for conspicuous gallantry in the fighting that day. Cpl Robert Emmett O'Malley raced across an open paddy field and jumped into a trench where he single-handedly killed eight Viet Cong with his rifle and grenades. He then led his squad to assist another, beleaguered unit. After helping to evac- uate wounded comrades, he went back to the scene of the heaviest fighting. Ordered, finally, to an evacuation point by an officer, "O'Malley gathered his besieged and badly wounded squad, and boldly led them under fire to a helicopter for withdrawal," his Medal of Honour citation reported. "Although three times wounded in this encounter, and facing imminent death from a fanatic and determined enemy, he steadfastly refused evacua- tion and continued to cover his squad's boarding of the helicopters while, from an exposed position, he delivered fire against the enemy until his wounded men were evacuated. Only then, with his last mission accomplished, did he permit himself to be removed from the battlefield."

Robert Emmett O'Malley was born on 3 June 1943, in New York City, to parents from Ireland. His father was from Rossanrubble, Co. Mayo, and his mother from Co. Kerry. He lived in Woodside, Queens, a distinctly Irish neighbourood. (Of New York City's five boroughs, Queens had, and probably still has, the largest concentration of Irish and Irish-Americans, with about one-third of the city's total.) Robert O'Malley enlisted in the US Marine Corps on 11 October 1961. He was promoted to sergeant in December 1965. President Johnson decorated him at a White House ceremony on 6 December 1966. In addition to the Medal of Honour, Robert holds the Purple Heart, the Navy Unit Commendation, the Good Conduct Medal, the National Defence Service Medal with one Bronze Star, and the Vietnam Service Medal.[31]

On 8 December the *Irish Times* reported: "LBJ praises the O'Malley spirit. John O'Malley of County Mayo and President Johnson joined with a governor, a senator, the US Defence Secretary and the Joint Chiefs of Staff to honour a young man of twenty-three whose only problem is deciding where he goes from here. 'He wants to loaf,' said John O'Malley of his son, the first Marine to win the Medal of Honour in Vietnam. 'And it's a pretty poor country if it can't support one bum.' There was an Irish crinkle in the face of the short, squat, father of five, including four sons who have followed each other into the Marines. 'I wonder what it is that makes men of this quality and I wonder what a man can say in the face of such bravery,' said the President, before draping the medal around the neck of a man who had single-handedly killed eight VC in close combat in Vietnam eighteen months ago."[32]

The battle Robert O'Malley had fought in, Operation Starlite, the first major American engagement of the war, had been a great success. The Marines had inflicted 614 VC killed, broke up a probable attack on Chu Lai, and rendered a VC regiment unfit for combat, for the loss of forty-five dead Americans. The key to the Marines' victory was undoubtedly the weight of firepower they were able to call up – artillery, heavy mortars, naval gunfire and air strikes – a way of fighting that would win the Americans many a pitched battle in the years to come. But the Viet Cong had learned lessons, too. They had neither the men nor the weaponry to face the Americans in large, fixed-location, set-piece battles. Their guerrilla warfare could not hope to match the sheer destructive power of American technology, so they would rarely meet the Americans on their terms. In the villages and paddy fields, or deep in the forests of the Central Highlands, the Americans would have to fight on *their* terms.[33]

## CHAPTER 3

# A RUMOUR OF WAR

Like all wars, Vietnam began with a series of threats that soon escalated into military action. Days before US ground troops landed in Vietnam US jet bombers struck military targets in North Vietnam. Then US Marines stormed ashore at Da Nang, ostensibly to guard the airbase, but in little over a month President Johnson had declared Vietnam a "combat zone." Commander of US Forces in Vietnam, General William Westmoreland, fearing for the success of the American involvement, asked for US troop strength to be increased from 50,000 to 200,000. In the first week of May 3,500 men of the 173rd Airborne Brigade arrived in Vietnam, the first US Army combat unit to join the conflict.[1] With the 173rd Airborne was a young Irish emigrant, Tom Kelly.

Tom Kelly, from Dysart, Co. Roscommon, emigrated to America in 1963 after working for five years on building sites all over England. When he was sixteen he had moved to England. "We laughed at the work on the building sites in England," Tom recalled. "It was nothing to the hardship in Ireland on the farms. We worked barefoot ploughing and harrowing.[2] When I left Dysart, my boyhood home in south Roscommon, in the west of Ireland, (it) was an economically starved backwater, an insignificant dot on a very large map. The country had struggled through the war years – or the 'Emergency,' as it was known here. Leaving the boreens of Roscommon at sixteen, and all the villages and simple farming folk I had grown up amongst, was more than a difficult journey of fear and trepidation at what the future might hold. It was almost the equivalent of stepping from one world into another, more extraordinary, 'future world.' Moving from an age of turf and donkey, to atomic power and, only a few years on, men aiming for the moon and stars."[3] From England Tom Kelly emigrated to the US and went to live with his brother in New Jersey, working on an electric assembly line. "We knew we were eligible for the draft," he recalled. "It was part of emigration." Tom registered for the draft and received his call-up papers the following year. After basic training in Fort Dix Tom volunteered for the paratroopers "for the extra money. Anything that was an extra dollar the hand was up. It meant a lot of extra training – advanced infantry training, airborne school, and from there to the all-volunteer 173rd Airborne Brigade. Other Irish became part of other units, and other branches of the Service. Irish women serving were scattered throughout the length and breadth of the military, in a variety of roles, and of course to a Combat Infantryman, in that most important of all roles – the Nurse … I probably didn't mind all that much. Being young, energetic, inquisitive, I wanted to see what the American army and travel was about. We didn't even know Vietnam existed." Tom Kelly soon got his wish for travel and excitement. He was posted to California from where he sailed to Okinawa and the 1st Battalion, 503rd Regiment, 173rd Airborne Brigade, who were preparing to go to Vietnam.

The 173rd Airborne Brigade was activated on the island of Okinawa on 26 March 1963 and Tom Kelly joined them as a replacement in April 1965. From its beginning, the 173rd proved to be an aggressive and unique unit led by Brigadier General Ellis W. Williamson who established realistic training throughout the Pacific region and made thousands of parachute jumps in a dozen countries. The Nationalist Chinese paratroopers on Taiwan called the 173rd the "Sky Soldiers" while on Okinawa the 173rd was called the "Fire Brigade" meaning that it was available to be dropped in any of the Southeast Asian countries if needed. To call Reveille, the officer commanding the 2nd Battalion, 503rd Regiment, erected a number of very large speakers from which the theme song to *Rawhide* – a popular Western series on American television – was blasted all over their camp. Every morning, men were rousted from their bunks by the blaring words, "Head 'em up, move 'em out, Rawhide", and the entire 173rd Airborne Brigade soon became known as "the Herd."

Between 3-12 May 1965 the 173rd Airborne Brigade arrived by transport planes in the Republic of South Vietnam. The 1st and 2nd Battalion of the 503rd Parachute Infantry Regiment arrived first along with the 3rd Battalion of the 319th Artillery. They were well supported by their own Support Battalion and Troop E, 17th Cavalry, and D Company, 16th Armour. Later the 1st Battalion, Royal Australian Regiment and an artillery battery from New Zealand were attached to the Brigade – making the 173rd Airborne the only multi-national combat unit in the war. The major portion of the 173rd landed at Bien Hoa Airfield in May 1965. Bien Hoa was the second largest airbase in South Vietnam and the 173rd found an area that had been battered frequently by Viet Cong guerrilla raids and shelling attacks. In the combat operations to follow, the paratroopers made their superb training pay off. Although trained as paratroopers, the soldiers of the

173rd reached these new battlefields primarily by helicopter. They also introduced the use of small, long-range patrols (Lurps). These small patrols would usually be infiltrated by helicopter deep into the enemy rear where they would operate independently for weeks at a time. Initially, the 173rd was assigned to defend the Bien Hoa Airbase. The brigade routinely conducted sweeps up to fifteen kilometres around the base, with company size operations often being the norm. The Brigade operated in the four provinces around Saigon (Xuan Loc, Long Khanh, Phuoc Long and Phuoc Tuy), but, in its role as a "Fire Brigade" also fought in the Central Highlands (Pleiku/Kontum).[5]

"We never saw a road, tank, or mechanised vehicle," Tom Kelly said. "We never used roads. If there was road we went off it. We trained on Okinawa in jungle warfare so we were strictly jungle. I was a point man for most of my tour. The climate was very severe. We had a lot of casualties due to heat exhaustion. There was no such thing as body bags in the jungle. You just wrapped them (the dead) in their ponchos. Normally we would be out of sight, have moved on, but it was quite gruesome to know they were not far away from you in their ponchos. You would go out with ten or twelve in the squad, but come back with very little." Tom Kelly was soon promoted to squad sergeant because most of his comrades had become casualties.[6] Bravo Company lost ten men killed in an ambush on 7 July 1965 and another twelve on 10 October. On 7 July the lead elements of Company B stopped to read a sign by the side of the road. It was written in Vietnamese and as the troopers clustered around their interpreter, the message – 'All Americans read this die' – exploded with devastating results. Simultaneously the VC opened up from camouflaged trenches and bunkers. The lead platoon was decimated. Six men were killed instantly and another nineteen were seriously wounded. For more than 200 yards the road was a scene of unbelievable carnage. The VC broke off contact as US artillery rained in on their positions.[7] "When I took over the squad all the others were gone," Tom said. "It was hard to live up to what they thought of me. I was Irish and they thought I could walk on water. They thought if they did what I did they would survive, but I had men didn't last twelve hours … Some died in my arms. My radio operator was killed when a barrage went down along the line. I was holding the phone while he was blown to bits. That was a little too close for comfort." On one occasion in November the 1/503rd fought off human waves from three VC battalions. Fighting was savage, with hundreds of enemy casualties. During these operations Tom recalled, "Three best friends got the Medal of Honour."[8] That was no mean feat as the Brigade received a total of twelve Medals of Honour for their six years in South Vietnam.[9]

The US Army at the time was the best equipped in the world. The standard infantryman was equipped with steel helmet, full combat battle dress, flak jacket, lightweight jungle boots, full webbing, water bottle, M1 or M14 (later M16) automatic rifle and spare ammunition bandolier. At full strength American rifle companies fielded 121 men plus six attached personnel. A company consisted of three platoons and a command post. Each platoon had three twelve-man squads and a platoon command post (CP). A squad consisted of seven riflemen, an M-79 man, an M-60 machine gunner and an assistant gunner (the assistant gunner carried an automatic rifle), an RTO (also carried an automatic rifle) and the squad leader. Platoon CPs consisted of the platoon leader, usually a 1st lieutenant, a platoon sergeant, a medic (attached) and an RTO. The company CP was headed by a company commander and had three RTOs. Attached to the main CP were the company medic, an artillery forward observer (usually a lieutenant) and a Kit Carson scout, a Vietnamese interpreter-scout-liaison.[10]

On 28 June, two battalions of the 173rd Brigade, reinforced by the 1st Battalion, Royal Australian Regiment, launched an assault and block operation near Ben Cat, the district capital. This was an area known as the "Iron Triangle" – an area of sixty square miles, defined by the Saigon river to the southwest, the Thi Tinh river to the east and the Than Dien forestry reserve to the north. Anchored on the villages of Ben Cat, Phu Hoa Dong and Ben Suc, the Iron Triangle had earned its reputation long before US forces arrived in Vietnam. It had been a refuge for guerrillas for nearly twenty years and defied every attempt to conquer it. It was given its name in 1963 when Peter Arnett, an Associated Press correspondent, who was the first to notice that with respect to enemy concentration, it resembled the Iron Triangle of the Korean War. Before the Americans had arrived the ARVN had made sporadic forays against it without result.[11] When Prime Minister Robert Menzies announced that Australia would commit ground troops to the American cause the 1st Battalion, Royal Australian Regiment was the first unit chosen for duty in Vietnam. 1 RAR had been on home soil less than four years after completing a two-year tour of duty in Malaya in November 1961. 1 RAR comprised only volunteer soldiers. An advance party arrived in May 1965 and was followed by the main strength of the battalion on 8 June when the troopship, former aircraft carrier HMAS *Sydney*, with attendant destroyers HMAS *Duchess* and *Parramatta*, anchored off Cape St Jacques near Vaung Tau, south-east of Saigon. *Sydney's* cargo of men, supplies and equipment were unloaded into landing craft or lifted ashore by US helicopters. From the port area of Vaung Tau, a former beach resort for the French colonialists, the troops were moved to the area's airfield and flown to Bien Hoa, their new home for the next twelve months.[12]

Ed Somers was twenty-two, already an army veteran, when he arrived in Vietnam with the 1st Battalion, The Royal Australian Regiment. Edward Somers was born in Davidstown, Enniscorthy, Co. Wexford. There was no military history in the family, apart from two great uncles killed in New Ross during the 1798 Rebellion, and a distant relative Sgt James Somers, Inniskilling Fusiliers, awarded the Victoria Cross at Gallipoli. Growing up in rural Ireland Ed had a deep interest in Irish history and read everything he could find on war and conflict. He learned to use firearms and hunt in the wild countryside. He dreamed of adventures in far off places, but it was the harsh reality of life in rural Ireland, which sent Ed across the Irish Sea when he was seventeen. "Things were very poor in Ireland at the time," he recalled, "and people were leaving the country at a hell of a rate." He worked in Breewood Hospital for a year and in 1960, when he turned eighteen, joined the British army at Aldershot. After completing basic training Ed was posted to the Royal Army Service Corps as a driver. "For a young lad it was a great time," he said. "Long convoys all over England; cross-country driving at night; being attached to famous regiments like the Irish Guards or the Argyll and Sutherland Highlanders." Ed was posted to Cyprus for a six-month tour and experienced his first taste of combat. When his three-year term was up Ed returned to Ireland. "Ireland was in the grip of a deep economic sleep. Farming was the only real industry, carried on in the old fashioned way." He tried his hand at farming, then a milk delivery and when that didn't pay either he set his sights on Australia. "I heard a lot about Australia," he said, "read a lot about Australia. To me it seemed at the time to be the last frontier. The year I left –1963 – 80,000 people emigrated." Ed Somers bought a £500 one-way plane ticket to Australia. He arrived in Sydney and went into an employment exchange, where he was fixed up with work in Tasmania. Ed spent a year working as a farm manager in Tasmania for Dick Thomas, who had served with the Australian Special Forces in WWII. On hearing of the American intervention in South Vietnam and with tales of Thompson's jungle fighting ringing in his ears, Ed flew to Melbourne to enlist.

"I heard about the war starting in Southeast Asia and reckoned I just wanted to get in on it. I knew that it was going to be an exciting place. I liked the idea of going into the jungle and testing myself. I wanted to go. I was looking forward to it. I wanted to experience what it was like to be in combat and under fire. I was not afraid. When you are young you don't care. I had no commitments; my family didn't even know that I was there. I heard about the Australian soldier, how good they were; the comradeship; the sort of laid-back attitude they had in a military sense. I flew to the mainland and joined up. I didn't know where Vietnam was, but it didn't matter. There was a war there, that's what mattered. I joined the 1st Australian Battalion and finished training in time to go with them to Vietnam. They were a great battalion to be with. 1st Battalion RAR was formed as a pen-tropical battalion. It was an elite battalion, hard to get into; the selection code for it was very hard. Most members were experienced soldiers, veterans of Korea, Borneo, and Malaya. Its main expertise was jungle fighting and jungle survival and they prided themselves on long distance marches through bush and jungle. A new recruit coming into the battalion would find he was not fully excepted until he proved himself. The officers and sergeants were of superior quality. They were eager to get to Vietnam to try out their skills."[13]

Due to the financial and other advantages gained by going overseas there was no shortage of volunteers among regular soldiers of the Australian Army for duty in Vietnam. Dan Danaher, Tralee, Co. Kerry, was also serving with 1 RAR and on his way to South Vietnam. Dan was born in Nenagh, Co. Tipperary, in 1940, but his parents moved to Tralee when he was two years old. Dan had left home for Dublin when he was seventeen. In the capital he played football for the Dublin Minors before he left for England. While working as a bus driver in cold, wintery London he had seen an advertisement for surfing and bought a plane ticket to Australia. Sydney at the time had little work options and was not what he expected so Dan joined the Australian Army. He went through six months basic training with Ed Somers at Wagga Wagga in New South Wales. Dan was sent to 5 Platoon, 1 RAR, as an infantryman, while Ed went to 6 Platoon, also as an infantryman.[14]

In late May Ed Somers and Dan Danaher sailed for Vietnam on board the aircraft carrier HMAS *Sydney* with the bulk of 1 RAR. "It took fourteen days," Ed Somers said. "On the way we learned Vietnamese; we played rugby; we played all sorts of games on deck. We would release a couple of hundred balloons – we had coconut mats – lie down and just shoot at them. One day this balloon was about 500 yards away. This officer ordered me to shoot it. I fired and at the same time the balloon burst, probably accidentally. I became known as a great shot and later when a great shot was required I was sent for." The HMAS *Sydney* arrived at a beach at Cape St Jacques and "we were disembarked from the ship by landing craft, much like you see in the movies, D-Day and all that. We were met by Vietnamese kids selling bottles of Coca-Cola from bicycles. How they knew we were coming was a mystery." Ed remembers the local people cheering the Australian troops when they arrived. "We drove along in these big American trucks. Kids and people came out shouting, and cheered and welcomed us just like the liberation of France. We thought, 'This is it. This is what we came out here to do.' We flew to Bien Hoa, which was to be our base. We became part of the American 173rd Brigade. The immediate task was to protect the Bien Hoa airbase."[15]

At Bien Hoa, north-east of Saigon, soldiers of 1 RAR were absorbed into the US 173rd Brigade; they did not operate as a separate entity. As well as the Americans they were also to work closely with South Vietnam's 3rd Corps Headquarters. The principal duty of the 173rd Brigade was the defence of Bien Hoa's huge airbase, the country's third largest after Tan Son Nhut at Saigon and Da Nang in the north. The Australians had their own area within the base and soon discovered that Vietnam was not going to be as soft a posting as Malaya or Singapore. Viet Cong guerrillas regularly came down the river in small boats until they were close enough to mount mortar attacks on the airbase.[16] "The (local) people were terrified," Ed said, "and our mission was to protect them. It wasn't all blood and bombing. As well as combat we did a lot of humanitarian work. It was as much a humanitarian effort. We would regularly bring food and medical supplies to the villages. We would send out small medical patrols to villages about fifteen miles away to look after people who had absolutely no medical facilities. The Battalion furnished and built a school with the help and donations of the Australian public. We also helped local orphanages, and another time we brought 500 cows that the Australian Government had shipped out so that the people could start a dairy farm."[17]

1 RAR operated in a fifty-mile corridor that stretched from the Cambodian border right across to the coast. For the first couple of months not much happened, except constant patrolling, with little sign of the enemy. 1 RAR went to Vietnam with some WWII weaponry, with unsuitable boots and uniforms, and with unreliable combat equipment and obsolete personal gear. However, half way through their first year they had been equipped with modern weaponry and appropriate uniforms and other equipment.

They were fortunate to have several months initially in which they were not called on to participate fully in operations.[18] "When the Battalion started patrolling they were effective and far-reaching. With American support most battles the Battalion fought were won, in fact all were won, by the Battalion. The Battalion gained a name within the Brigade for reliability and thoroughness in carrying out missions," Ed Somers said. "The further deeper we probed into enemy territory, the more resistance they put up and we began to lose men. The Americans couldn't understand why the Australians were never to be seen. We were always in the bush. It was very interesting being in the bush. That's where we spent most of our time, looking for the Viet Cong. But they seemed to have the upper hand nearly all the time. Sometimes we would be so far into the bush that it could take six days to walk out of it. You were in there totally on your own. You were there with a rifle and a pack and that's it."[19]

"In Vietnam our tactics were quiet, cautious," Dan Danaher said. "The Americans took four times the casualties we took. You never learn anything about war until a guy is trying to kill you. Then you learn by experience."[20] Australian training dictated a stealthy approach to jungle fighting rather like that of the Viet Cong, whereas the Americans tended to barge around the jungle inviting trouble. The Americans derided the Australian tactics saying that while the Aussies were creeping around the jungle the enemy was making use of established trails and thus neither ever came in contact with the other. Australian units tended to have a much lower casualty rate in proportion to the Americans, so they claimed there was wisdom in their tactics. The Australians also had the advantage of being a small, cohesive force in which standards of training and discipline could be maintained at a relatively uniform level. The Americans with their vast army of more than a half a million men found maintaining such standards very difficult if not impossible.[21] At first the typical American soldier in Vietnam was a career regular but as the US troop commitment grew, the non-volunteer GIs, caught by the draft, began to arrive in large numbers. Some only had sixteen weeks of basic training before arriving overseas, while the Australians would have six months training. Often this was the difference between life and death.

It was early August before Ed Somers encountered his first fire-fight, as 6 Platoon were engaged by the Viet Cong force who had been following them all day. "We were patrolling and had paused to check our compasses and maps to see where we were. The group of Viet Cong had been actually trailing us and when we paused, they attacked. We came under very heavy rifle fire from the back. And I still remember the first shots. The crack of a bullet pass close to your ear and to see somebody lying there with blood coming out of them, to see somebody badly wounded, screaming in pain. That was the first battle we were in." Three VC were wounded, with one suspected killed, but the bodies quickly disappeared and the blood trails were lost. On sweeping through the area a large mine was discovered. The speed of the contact had not allowed the VC to detonate it in time. For the next two months 1 RAR were on constant patrols. Apart from the hardships of the jungle there was always the constant fear of attack. "You could be just patrolling quietly and there could be a sniper's telescope focused on your chest. Or you could be just about to trip a mine or set off a booby trap or fall into a punji pit. The danger was there all the time and you'd be a fool if you thought, I'm going to survive this. And you would never let yourself get captured alive. So you always carried a hand grenade for personal use. It's like being a good hunter. You don't let the sniper get you if possible. Or you don't fall into the pit. Or you look out for the string across the path with the grenade attached to it." The Viet Cong used ingenious ways to inflict casualties with booby traps and punji pits. "The object (of the punji pit) was to wound rather than kill. A wounded man takes a lot of time, a lot of effort; a lot of time getting him out. The minute someone is wounded he has to be got out."[22]

The Australians sold captured enemy weapons and exchanged their Aussie bush hats, always popular with the Americans, to troops in the bases and in rear echelon areas. Originally the Australians were also denied alcohol on the base and again had to buy or barter for beer from the Americans until the ban was replaced with an official allocation of two cans of Australian beer per man per day. "In my platoon there were several Irishmen," Ed Somers said. "And scattered throughout the battalion there were other Irishmen. So somebody said there's an Irish guy up in B Company (173rd Airborne). I heard the Americans were looking for weapons. I said, I'd go up to the American 1st Battalion and see can I sell these (weapons). This was where Tom Kelly was. The three battalions sat on three hills; Tom's was half a mile away from mine. So Tom and I became particular friends. I got to know Tom well and because the Americans had really good steaks in their cookhouse, I always went up there, especially if we had a few weapons to sell."[23] Ed and Tom became good friends, going on leave together on one occasion. They also fought together. In the run-up to Christmas, operating southeast of Bien Hoa on the Courtenay Rubber Plantation, the 1st and 2nd battalions of the 503rd along with the 1st RAR began saturation patrolling. On the morning of 18 December the recon platoon of the 2/503rd encountered a defended VC trench system supported by numerous machine guns. Tom Kelly's B Company smashed into the enemy from a different direction and overran the enemy position resulting in sixty-two VC killed. Ed and Tom were back at the base for Christmas celebrations where the Americans as usual pulled out all the stops so their troops could have a sumptuous Yuletide feast and the Australians had a bicycle race with a "Le Mans" start using captured VC bicycles.[24]

By the end of 1965, the ground war in South Vietnam was the main focus of American strategy and General Westmoreland saw the build-up of troops as the answer to the deteriorating situation. His first concern was to protect Saigon, his second to "pacify" the countryside. Saigon was to be ringed by huge base camps as the US 1st and 25th Infantry Divisions arrived. The sites chosen were, not surprisingly, close to areas of Viet Cong domination and intense activity. Before establishing these camps the area had to be swept and secured. On 7 January 1966 over 8,000 soldiers of the 1st Infantry Division, the 173rd Airborne Brigade, and the Royal Australian Regiment were airlifted from Phu Loi to Cu Chi district in an operation codenamed "Crimp." Here, the allied troops would face a new and more frightening element in Vietnam warfare – tunnel fighting.[25]

"Crimp was a rude awakening," Ed Somers said. "Before that, most operations were only small skirmishes, quick five-minute battles. After that the operations got heavier and harder."[26] 1 RAR were helicoptered into the notorious Ho Bo woods just west of the infamous Iron Triangle to act as a blocking force on the northern perimeter. It was an area covered with light scrub, rubber plantations and secondary growth.[27] Both Ed Somers and Dan Danaher were with B Company as it helicoptered into the LZ. Apart from odd sniping the landing was unopposed. As the second helicopter flight approached the LZ and landed armed helicopters strafed the Company. Although fire fell within inches of the men, no one was hit. The Aussies took sniper fire, tripped booby traps, endured several casualties from punji sticks, but saw little of the Viet Cong. 4 Platoon lost its first man, hit by a sniper, while they killed two VC in separate incidents. Arms caches, bunkers and tunnels were discovered, but again few sightings of the VC were made. The men were puzzled. That night puzzlement turned to outright confusion as the Viet Cong consistently penetrated the Australians perimeter. Unknown to the Australians they were actually sitting on top of a large Viet Cong bunker system. The VC were underneath and all around them. When the men responding to automatic fire from within the perimeter returned fire they hit their comrades on the outer edge of their area. Private Desmond Penn was hit by friendly fire in the confusion and Ed Somers dragged him in as bullets flew in all directions. However, Pte Penn was seriously injured and died shortly after being medivaced by chopper. Ed had great praise for the American helicopter pilots who came in to take out the Australian wounded. One particular pilot landed in the pitch darkness guided by two flash lamps, overloaded the helicopter with wounded and then returned for a second dust-off to get the remainder of the Aussie wounded out. "The real heroes that night were the dust-off pilots. They were coming down in the dark not knowing what was on the ground. We only had torches to guide them in. We might just as easily have been Viet Cong, that was a trick they tried now and again. This unknown pilot deserved a medal."[28]

The next day things got worse. When Private Delaney was wounded by a sniper two medics were shot dead while going to his aid. The sniper was spotted shooting from behind an anthill, but when a LAW rocket blew that away, there was no sign of the sniper. There was only one conclusion. The VC had gone underground. A network of tunnels was located and the engineers called in. Two American engineers arrived with a specially adapted commercial air blower and began pumping smoke and CS gas into some of the tunnel openings to make them inhabitable and also to expose other openings. Eventually, at least three-quarters of a mile of communication tunnels, bunkers, and underground chambers were found. Two Australian engineers – called tunnel ferrets by the Aussies, and tunnel rats by the Yanks – decided to go down and take a look for themselves. However, some of the smoke stayed underground and when Corporal Bowtell got stuck in a narrow opening he soon realised that lingering smoke had expelled most of the oxygen in the tunnel. He shouted for help, but by the time Sapper Jim Daly got to him, Bowtell was already unconscious. Several attempts were made to rescue the engineer, but the men returned retching and reeling from the effects of the gas and smoke. Eventually a decision was made to dig down to him directly from the surface. Dan Danaher said, "They started to dig straight down. It took about two hours to dig the hole and by the time they got down to him, put a rope around his leg and pulled him out he was dead."[29] Dan had been posted as an infantryman but after two months became a radioman, or signaller, so "at least I knew as much as the officers what was going on".[30]

When Operation Crimp ended on 14 January, Australian deaths in Vietnam had doubled from eight to sixteen. By this time the two American battalions of the 173rd had lost over 170 dead. The tunnels the allies had discovered turned out to be a huge complex that was part of the Viet Cong's Military Region IV headquarters.

While fighting in the tunnels of Cu Chi was still a thing of the future important lessons had been learned. The Australian engineers' assessments were probably the most accurate and the most prescient, but, despite their success the Aussies were never again to be so involved in the tunnels of Cu Chi.[31] It was times like these that Ed Somers asked himself the same question many soldiers before him asked: "'What the hell am I doing here?' We were just after one hell of a battle. The rain was pouring down and you couldn't tell whether the noise was from the guns or the thunder. A lot of our lads had been wounded or killed. At one point I remember sitting on the edge of a hole and wondering what the hell am I doing here. But we felt we were there for a purpose. We were to protect the people in the South from the communist invaders from the North. We were welcomed by the people in the areas that we were in, so we felt we were doing a good job. We felt we were there as saviours."[32]

From 19-26 February B Company was engaged in night ambushes and defence of a new Engineer Base Position. On the night of 23 February sporadic machine gun fire erupted around B Company's positions. Groups of VC were spotted and engaged as mortars rained down on the base. One American engineer was killed and several wounded as the gunfire and mortars continued for some time. The next morning eight dead and two wounded Viet Cong were found outside the perimeter. Dan Danaher was on ambush position that night. "We were protecting the engineers. After an ambush we killed about ten Viet Cong," Dan said. "The next morning these American engineers arrived and started taking pictures. One of them put his boot on the chest of a dead VC while another took his picture!"[33]

"We must have spent nine months in the jungle," Dan said, "and three months in the base. We got a day off once a month in Saigon. In Saigon I carried a .45 in a shoulder holster under a loose shirt, because I got a gun pulled on me once."[34] With the coming of the war and the influx of the US military, which set up its headquarters and largest bases in and around Saigon, the Pearl of the Orient became a fortified American city. Thousands of bars and strip joints sprang up to entertain the troops. Generals moved into the old French villas and the plush hotels became officers' clubs. The black market flourished and corruption reached up to all levels.[35] "We also got a 'week's rest' doing security on a hotel where the Australian brass (the command structure of the Australians) stayed. We also had one-week security duty at Ton Son Nhut, one section at a time. The Australians had their radio installations there with a direct line from Canberra to Vietnam. The ARVNs were on the perimeter, while American units were all around – MPs, air force police. Eight of us were guarding the Australian contingent. One day when we were coming off duty this Yank called us over, 'Hey, Aussie, come over here and have a beer.' We went over to this American tent. They had three dustbins full of beer on ice. We thought it was Christmas. Around two o'clock in the morning this big black guy appeared with a jeep and started giving out M16s like lollypops. I asked him what was going on and he said, 'It's a red alert.' What's a red alert, I asked. 'Red alert means the base is under attack,' he said. So I asked him where the weakest part of the perimeter was, because the VC always attack at the weakest point. 'Perimeter!' the guy said, 'I don't know where the motherfuckin' perimeter is.' He was a staff sergeant in the air force police and had a driver and he didn't know where the perimeter was, so I said we'll go back to our own position, which had sandbags and an M60. One of the American guys, an air force guy we were drinking with, said to me, 'What'll I do if they get in here. They got in here last year.' I said, 'Fire a few rounds with your M16, then throw a grenade. That will give you a head start – then run like hell.' I felt sorry for these guys. They only had tents, no gunpits, and were unused to the frontlines. They couldn't even defend themselves they were that pissed. We went back to our own position. We had our own enclosed area with sandbags and an M60, but in the end nothing even happened."[36]

From 9-22 March 1966 both the 503rd and 1 RAR were involved in Operation Silver City, which was aimed at locating and destroying a local VC Headquarters in Long Khanh Province. The 173rd Airborne, including elements of the 1 RAR, conducted a heliborne assault near the Song Be river in War Zone D to initiate Operation Silver City. The first few days of the operations consisted of thorough screening of the area, leading to the discovery of vast quantities of food, munitions, bunkers, tunnel systems documents, and several large VC base camps. 1 RAR's task was to secure the 173rd Brigade LZ and crossing point over the Song Be river then secure brigade headquarters and the logistic and fire support base. (Fire Support Bases mounted 155mm howitzers, 105mm howitzers and mortars, which extended range to the limits of an operational area.) This it did by perimeter defence and patrolling in depth. A few days later the two American battalions went back into the bush while the Australians were left back at the base. Tom Kelly was with his battalion, the 1/503rd. On 16 March the 501st VC Battalion attacked the 2/503rd Task Force from all directions. The attack was planned to coincide with a daily programme that involved three rifle companies being absent from the base on deep patrolling. However, the three companies were delayed in moving out and the battalion was complete when the VC attacked. The troopers held their perimeter while inflicting heavy losses on the guerrillas. The 1st Battalion, 503rd, was directed to reinforce the 2nd Battalion during the battle and ran straight into an ambush. Numerous tactical air strikes were initiated with great effectiveness to relieve pressure on the 173rd. The VC battalion was nearly annihilated by this time and chose to break contact rather than tackle two battalions of paratroopers. Four hours after initial contact, all the VC were routed or destroyed. 302 VC bodies were found on the battlefield, but American casualties were also heavy – eleven dead and about thirty wounded.[37] One of the seriously wounded was Sgt Tom Kelly. He said, "One of the last battles we were in we lost contact with Ed Somers and in this engagement we got chewed up. Sergeant Butler was our platoon sergeant. He was a coloured sergeant – we had a kind of good relationship. He relieved me once on his own and he lost his life in the effort. He just gave me that bit of luck. I was very enamoured for that." (Sergeant Earle James Butler, was one of the eleven paratroopers killed that day.) Tom Kelly remembers very little of that day and how he managed to survive. To him it's like trying to reconstruct a nightmare and he still carries the scars, both physically and mentally.[38]

On that same day, 16 March, Ed Somers noticed sudden increased activity around the base hospital. "It was a quiet day. Around two o'clock in the afternoon … I was in the B Company area and walking towards battalion headquarters. I noticed a lot of choppers flying very low, long lines of them. It was most unusual. Normally one or two because people got killed everyday; someone wounded everyday. I went to our command post, where we had radios and listened in on the radio. All the guys were clustered around the radios. A call came over the radio for blood, for anyone not on duty to get down to the hospital to give blood. As each helicopter came in badly wounded people were taken off. Blood dripped off the choppers. As one took off another landed. There were two helicopter pads. They were just lifting bodies out, throwing them out. People who were already dead were stacked to one side. The ones that could be saved were brought straight into the operating theatre, a big long tent. The floor was slippery with blood. Absolute hell was the only way you could describe it. All this was happening and you said to yourself for what? The wastage of young lives; you are talking lads between nineteen and twenty lying there with the blood running out of their ears and mouths; faces pale with shock, screaming for their mammy; 'Mammy where are you', 'Help me mother'.

"We gave as much blood as they wanted. I said to a sergeant, 'What about B Company?' This was Tom's company. I was told, 'They got the brunt of it.' He didn't want me in the operating theatre. He said look outside, he's probably in the heap of bodies. I was looking for a nametag. Americans carried nametags on all their uniforms. So there was a pile of bodies to one side. Still had their big boots (on), big muddy boots covered in blood and mud. So I started to look for Tom. Because knowing him and knowing his squad, they would have been in the thick of it. He was shorter than most of the guys. I was looking for a small man with a big heart. After a while I just gave it up. I couldn't do it anymore. As I walked away from there, I just assumed … I just knew Tom was dead. He had to be in that pile of bodies." As Ed Somers walked away he passed a pile of equipment, which had been removed from the ambush site. He took a helmet from the pile – a memorial to his friend Tom Kelly.*

Ed doesn't remember much more about the rest of that day. "All I remember is I didn't find Tom."[39] After that the whole thing changed for

---

* In 1998, more than thirty years later, the Irish Veterans Memorial Project (IVMP) brought a replica of the Vietnam Memorial Wall to Ireland. Tom Kelly and Ed Somers both contacted the IVMP. Ed asked "if anybody called Kelly was on the wall. He (Declan Hughes) said he had been talking to a Kelly just a short while before, and he gave me the phone number. As soon as I rang I knew it was Tom, his voice hadn't changed a bit, and he recognised me immediately, too. I said 'Airborne' and he replied 'All the way.'" A few days later Tom travelled down to Camolin to meet with Ed, and they are still the best of friends. On the occasion of the meeting Ed presented Tom with the helmet which he picked up over thirty years before.

him. The early sense of excitement and adventure was gone. "We still felt we were doing a bloody good job, that we were good soldiers and that we had the upper hand, but from then on it just became a matter of survival." Ed Somers finished up his tour with the Regimental Police, as "security for the colonel – a plum job".[40] He left Vietnam in June 1966 when 1 RAR was rotated and replaced by another Australian battalion. Ed captures the atmosphere of what it felt like for thousands of soldiers as their time in Vietnam ended and they made the trip home to the 'World.' He wrote: "We were a bemused little group as we discarded our mud-stained old uniforms, had showers and a general clean up. With clean gear, clean boots and freshly washed we became new men. The weapons that had served us well were packed in bundles with the rest of the kit, ready for loading. The sun grew hot and we settled down to wait for transport. No one spoke much. There was a fear that the spell might be broken. Finally a couple of big brown U.S. Army buses arrived, covered in dust. Their windows shielded up with wire-mesh to stop hand grenades were a reminder that the war also extended into the towns and cities.

"The trip from Bien Hoa to Tan Son Nhut airbase was quick and easy. Soon we were entering one of the busiest airports in Southeast Asia. Big, medium, small aircraft were everywhere. Parked, taxing, taking off, landing. The constant roar of the jets was interspersed with the whopping of chopper blades. We stood in amazement looking at all this energy and motion. This was a different world from the quiet deadly jungle that we had been accustomed to. The enormity of the war was brought home to us. This was big business. Corporate America in full battle gear; what chance had the little men in the jungle against all this? A sergeant appeared with our boarding passes and we were led to our freedom bird – a beautiful silver Qantas 707. We started to board. It was cool and subdued in the aircraft. Soft music played. The stewardesses seemed like people from a different planet. They looked so clean and fragile." As the airplane took off, "a mighty cheer rang out 'Australia, here we come!'" Coincidentally, this Qantas 707 was the same plane that had brought Ed Somers from London to Sydney back in 1963.

"Looking out over the silver wings as we gained height we could glimpse the dark green jungle and serpentine rivers. God, it looked so peaceful down there. Hard to imagine right now patrols were sneaking along; ambushes taking place; dust-offs being called; B52 strikes ripping the earth apart; artillery firing; bombs and napalm; booby traps; punji pits and tunnels, all part of the war's fabric. Then the coast was cleared the first beer was handed around. The second. This was more like it. Someone began to sing. The usual Australian humour came to the surface. It became one big flying party." The plane stopped off in Manila, then Darwin and finally Sydney. There were only a few NCOs and drivers of the buses and army trucks waiting to greet the arriving troops. "This was where we had left for Vietnam over a year ago. Was it possible that life had gone on as usual all the time we had been away? That this traffic, clean cars, bright traffic lights, all the life of the city had continued to function as we lived on the edge of life. It seemed strange; nobody took any notice of us. Did they not know who we were, or what we had been doing? Of course not." At the army barracks "we were greeted with politeness and it seemed, some degree of awe". Their kit was taken away and Ed felt the loss of his rifle the most. "My friend of the black dark, wet terrifying nights; of scorching hot days; of deep mouldy jungle trails; wide rivers; dusty plains; of journeys by truck, helicopter, airplane, APC and long marches through all kinds of terrain. My friend was gone."[41]

In Sydney 300,000 locals lined the streets for a ticker-tape parade to welcome the "First" home. The strength of such welcome home gestures would wane over the following years, but at this time the majority were in favour of the Vietnam involvement. The Battalion marched in columns six deep, among them Dan Danaher. The battalion had been instructed, in the event of protestors getting among the ranks, not to break stride but to simply push them out of the way. The commander of B Company, which also included Dan, was marching about ten yards in front of the leading column of troops. Suddenly a woman, smeared with red paint broke away from the spectators on the pavement, dashed out onto the street and embraced the CO. The officer, despite being smeared with paint, ignored her and continued marching.[42]

Ed Somers saw out his term in the Australian army, assisting with training recruits for duty in Vietnam. In 1967 when he was discharged Ed returned to Camolin, Wexford.[43] Dan Danaher left the Australian army in 1967, but signed up for five years in the Reserve, which meant he could be called back to the colours at any time. However, Dan said, "Australia is a big country and they would have had a hard time finding me". He returned to Ireland in 1971 and went back to Australia in 1973. He then travelled to America and stayed for ten years returning to Ireland in the 1990s.[44] Tom Kelly also left Vietnam in June 1966, when his wounds healed, and returned to the US. He took advantage of the educational opportunities available to veterans and found work in the telecom industry. He returned to Ireland in 1970.[45]

## CHAPTER 4

# UNDER THE RED DUSTER

In early 1965 when Irishmen like Tom Kelly, Dan Danaher and Ed Somers were arriving in South Vietnam with the American and Australian armed forces, another young Irishman, Michael Cahill, was running the gauntlet of US ships and planes in the hostile Gulf of Tonkin on his way into North Vietnam. Michael Cahill was born in Dublin in 1946, the son of a medical practitioner. When his father, Michael, wound up his local medical practice two years later and joined the Irish Army the family moved to the Curragh, Co. Kildare. When he was eighteen Michael, following in the footsteps of his maternal uncle, Jack Hartnett, who had served in the Merchant Navy in WWII, headed for London and joined the British Merchant Navy as a cadet. In 1965 Michael Cahill was serving as Fourth Officer onboard the SS *Ardrossmore,* a 10,000 ton steamship operating out of Hong Kong under the British ensign – the Red Duster. He was one of two Irishmen on board – the other was Paddy Stapleton, from Little Island, Co. Cork. *Ardrossmore's* officers were British and Irish, and the crew mainly Chinese. The captain was an Englishman, Derek Blair. The SS *Ardrossmore* was named after Rossmore Stud, near the Curragh, and bought off the Irish government by the British Merchant Navy.[1]

In most seafaring countries, the merchant marine, or Merchant Navy, is a fleet of ships used for commerce that sometimes complements the navy. The merchant fleet of the United Kingdom became known as the Merchant Navy after World War I, when the title was granted by King George V in recognition of the part played in the war. The Merchant Navy is the whole fleet of British ships used for carrying cargoes and passengers. The cargoes may be raw materials such as grain, minerals or oil, or they may be manufactured goods. The duties of a merchant seaman are to take the ship from port to port in safety, avoiding shipwreck, fire, collision and any other dangers. Apart from the apprentices, all the officers and crewmembers (ratings) are signed on as seamen. They sign a paper called "the articles of agreement" (generally known as the Ship's Articles) which outline their duties as well as their rate of pay and the food to which they are entitled. At the beginning of a voyage the Ship's Articles are signed in the presence of a government official called the shipping master and at the end of a voyage the crew "sign off" in the presence of a government official. The 1960s was a golden era for the British Merchant Navy, when half the world's cargo ships were registered under British flags.[2]

In 1964, after service in the Mediterranean and the Persian Gulf, Mike Cahill found himself in the South China Sea. He took a keen interest in the politics of the countries he visited. "I sat on a fence and looked, and learned," Michael said. It was all a learning experience to the young impressionable Irishman. He had dinner with Lin Biao, the Chinese Communist leader – because of "work on behalf of the Chinese and Vietnamese people" – and was dined onboard the Motor Vessel *Ishma*, a Russian merchant ship responsible for bringing much of the arms from Russia to Haiphong, in North Vietnam. "When first in China, Mum used to send me out the *Leinster Leader*, (a local paper in County Kildare) but I never got it, as it was confiscated – deemed 'capitalist propaganda'." As American ground troops entered South Vietnam Russia and China stepped up their supplies of materials, both military and civilian, to North Vietnam. "At the time we were on time charter consignment from China," Mike said, "and we had come down from northern China to Hong Kong dry dock in 1965 – early May 65. We were informed on arrival in Hong Kong that we were going into a war area. Some of the office people from Hong Kong – Queens Road, in Hong Kong – came down to the ship to see us to inform us that we were travelling into a war area. If we wished we could fly home directly, if we didn't want to serve. We all agreed to go into Haiphong in North Vietnam. We arrived on the 25th of May 1965 in the early part of the war. It was our first incursion into the Gulf of Tonkin. We were paid our war bonuses by the Chinese Communists. When we finished our voyage and came back out of the Gulf of Tonkin, we were paid from entering, to leaving, the Gulf of Tonkin. One-hundred and thirty per cent war bonus. That was paid in cash in Hong Kong dollars by the Chinese when we went back to China again. Once the script was so old it wasn't recognised in Hong Kong. (At the time sixteen Hong Kong dollars were equal to one-pound sterling.)

"The first few runs into Vietnam were uneventful, really quiet, no action, and then we went up to Campha. It was a port near the Chinese border and we had no tugs or anything and I distinctly remember we were kedging the ship in on the starboard anchor. I was on the seaboard telegraph on the bridge operating the telegraph* and I looked over my shoulder and I saw

---

* The telegraph is used for passing orders from the bridge to the engineer who controls the ship's engines.

them (US planes) coming in on us. Now you must remember we had the British flag painted on the hatches and on the side of the ship. In the beginning in Vietnam we had armed guards onboard when we were in port. The captain decided that if fire was given from our vessel towards the American aircraft they were quite entitled to turn around and blow us out of the water. So he asked our guards on board, and the relevant authorities, to disarm the men on board. They were certainly welcome on board, but no firearms to be brought aboard the ship in case of them opening fire on incoming American aircraft, which would endanger our position somewhat more than it would normally do."[3]

On 2 March 1965 100 US jet bombers hit targets in North Vietnam as America began its graduated bombing campaign – Operation Rolling Thunder. The object of Rolling Thunder was to slow down the supply of arms and men from North Vietnam and to threaten the communists into a negotiated settlement. A month later Rolling Thunder was extended to cover non-military targets in North Vietnam, sparking off the first anti-war protests when 15,000 students demonstrated in Washington. On 22 November the Chairman of the House Armed Services Committee, L. Mendel Rivers, called for the bombing of Haiphong and Hanoi, saying it was "a folly to let the port of Haiphong and military targets of Hanoi remain untouched while war supplies being used against our troops are pouring into port". Operation Rolling Thunder raged on for three years, becoming one of the most costly bombing campaigns in history. In more than 300,000 sorties over North Vietnam, the Americans dropped 860,000 tons of bombs, killed 52,000 civilians and lost 922 of their own planes.[4]

After witnessing American planes bombing targets around Campha, Mike Cahill "left Campha and went back out to North Korea. We loaded coal in Hungnam, North Korea, and arrived back in Haiphong to unload. We were ashore drinking one night and there was an altercation in the Seaman's Club and I inadvertently hit a Vietnamese, for which I was subsequently arrested. I surrendered myself the next day, on the advice of the shipmaster of the vessel. I was put on trial. After a debate and such – I had my armed guard and stenographer there, and three senior officers – the local army commander, local navy commander and local air force commander.

They asked me my excuse, why I hit this individual? I explained to him that I was drunk and I was Irish. So, they accepted the excuse, and barred me from coming ashore again. I signed some articles for them, some paperwork for them. Believe it or not, some time later on, in the *Peking Monthly News*, there was a big statement and at the bottom was my signature saying the Americans were using biological warfare in Vietnam. So we let it settle at that. We didn't mind. I suppose I was lucky to get away with what happened.

"A week before that incident happened we were brought ashore to a field outside Haiphong. In that field were three recovered American aircraft. There was an Intruder, a Skyraider and a Seahawk, I believe. They had the ID in a glass case of one pilot – his photograph ID. (Michael could not recall the name of the pilot, but only that he was twenty-two years of age.) And in that case, they also had an old rifle, a bolt action rifle, Second World War type and a statement that a rice farmer in the paddy fields had shot down one of the jet-propelled American aircraft from the American 7th Fleet." Most of the *Ardrossmore's* trips to Vietnam were to Campha and Haiphong. All the essentials for the North's war machine came from Russia and Hanoi's other communist allies; the bulk arriving by sea. Freighters just happened to be the most convenient means of transport. Located in the delta of the Red river, about 100 kilometres from Hanoi, Haiphong served as the primary seaport for the northern region of the country and was subjected to heavy bombing by the Americans due to its status as North Vietnam's only major port.

The shipyards and the industrial section of the city were devastated, rail connections with Hanoi were disrupted, and thousands of homes were destroyed. The harbour was finally mined by US naval planes in May 1972, and effectively sealed until the mines were swept by American forces after the cease-fire agreement in 1973.[5] "The Americans put it out on *Reuters* that they would give us two weeks warning before they mined all the harbours in Vietnam," Michael Cahill said. "We had our photographs taken over a dozen times from Orions, USAF coastal aircraft, flying out of Thailand. All western crewmen had their names on the CIA's files."

In between its trips to Haiphong and Campha in North Vietnam the SS Ardrossmore made one voyage to Cambodia. "At the time Sihanouk was barely holding onto his power base. We were there for two weeks and back up to China again. One time we passed this US battleship. She was firing her big guns into South Vietnam as we approached, for some ground support in the Iron Triangle or the Mekong Delta. These shells could travel fifteen miles. I could hear the shells first and then literally see them flying through the air," Michael said. "When we discharged cargo in Hong Kong and Bangkok from Vietnam we used to meet American soldiers on local leave and had to be very careful what we said. All in all, we did twelve incursions into Vietnam.

They (North Vietnam) had stuff for export. Civilian stuff. We made a stipulation to China we would not carry firearms on the blockade runners but there was one time Captain Derek Blair and I went down the hold and we opened a few boxes to have a look. Completely done on the quiet. Nobody saw us. We just checked the boxes that looked like they were carrying arms, labelled agriculture machinery. There were 12.7mm guns in them, but we could say nothing. They were going to Haiphong from the Chinese."[6]

China's involvement in the Vietnam war began in the summer of 1962, when Mao agreed to supply Hanoi free of charge with 90,000 rifles and guns. After the launch of Operation Rolling Thunder, China sent engineering battalions and supporting anti-aircraft units to North Vietnam to repair the damage caused by American bombing, which freed North Vietnamese army units to go to the South. Between 1965 and 1970 over 320,000 Chinese soldiers served in North Vietnam; the peak year was 1967 when 170,000 were there. Soviet friendship began in earnest after Premier Kosygin visited Hanoi in early 1965. During his visit, American bombers attacked targets in North Vietnam, the first waves of Operation Rolling Thunder. On his return to Moscow, Kosygin pushed for increased military and economic assistance for Vietnam. Shipments of high tech Surface-to-Air (SAM) missiles and jet aircraft where rushed to Vietnam.

Throughout the war, Soviet military material was shipped to North Vietnam in increasingly large numbers. Military aid in 1965 amounted to 200 million dollars, which increased to over 500 million dollars by 1967. Initially, this aid was tailored for defensive purposes in the North. It consisted primarily of anti-air weapons to protect against American bombers. American intelligence discovered the first SAM site in April of 1965 and the first American plane was downed by a SAM missile in June of that year. Besides missiles, large numbers of anti-aircraft guns, radars, and jet aircraft were provided. The influx of aircraft doubled the size of the Air Force of the Vietnamese People's Army to a high of 200 planes. The flow of arms, advisers and agents to and from Vietnam relied heavily on Soviet shipping. Some supplies could come through China by rail, but this route, while taking only a week, was limited by the Chinese, who dictated what could be transported and when. Shipments were mostly undisturbed, but were sometimes delayed or stolen. Because an air corridor through China was denied, nearly eighty per cent of Soviet material came by sea through Haiphong. Soviet officials were increasingly concerned that the US would blockade Vietnam and orders were given to supply convoys to shoot their way through if needed. A possible blockade was not the only danger faced by merchantmen. Frequent bombings of Vietnamese harbours endangered the ships anchored there.[7]

"I remember one day, Paddy Stapleton and I were sitting in the Seaman's Club in Haiphong and a North Vietnamese Army colonel came in," Michael

Cahill recalled. "He must have been very well known, because they all recognised him straight away. He was some kind of a war hero, probably fought with Giap at Dien Bien Phu. He would have been that age. And he asked for the two Irishmen. Of course he knew there were two Irishmen on this ship and he just wanted to speak to us and we happened to be there and he was informed of that and that's why he came down. My vaccination certificate on the ship were UN, my cholera and my typhoid, yellow fever, everything was UN documentation, signed by my father in the hospital in the Curragh. I had a British seaman's discharge book, an Irish passport, an Irish seaman's ID card and UN documentation. This fellow was kind of puzzled. Now this man sat down between Paddy and I and ordered a beer. He asked Paddy where he was from. Paddy said, 'Cork.' (Paddy Stapleton's father, Jim, was also an officer in the Irish Army.) This man spoke absolute, grammatically correct English. He had been educated in Oxford University, in England, and he looked at us and asked me how did I have this UN vaccination coverage with the same name as mine on the bottom of a UN paper. I said, 'He's my father.' He said something to us that rocked me on my heels. Speaking as a socialist, himself like, is the way he put it, 'Our beloved General Giap has a great affinity for the Irish nation because he considered Michael Collins the greatest ever guerrilla warfare tactician he had ever come across.'" Mike Cahill was impressed with the compliment and admiration of the Vietnamese colonel.

After over a year of duty in Southeast Asia Michael Cahill went home on leave. "After I left the SS *Ardrossmore* I was on leave over in Ireland and she did a run into North Vietnam again, into Haiphong. There was an incursion by American aircraft from the 7th Fleet. The Chinese merchant ship that was in at the time was armed with 12.7 heavy machine guns. She opened fire (on the planes), but she also opened fire on the SS *Ardrossmore* ... hit the *Wakasa Bay* ... and I believe a Russian merchant ship, the MV *Ishma,* was hit as well. Consequently, to this, the SS *Ardrossmore* was in the South China Sea and the crew mutinied. The officers gathered with the master, Captain Derek Blair, on the bridge. Captain Derek Blair had to produce his firearm. The ship was boarded by the Royal Navy and eventually all the officers were sent home. I came back out to Hong Kong in the latter part of 1966 and I was asked did I want to join the *Ardrossmore* again. Having done two years and three months on her, I said no. I consequently, went to Bangkok and joined the Motor Vessel *Ribot* and went off to South Africa and various other parts and I never again visited Vietnam after that."

Michael Cahill's Vietnam experiences made a profound impression on him and left him with a great affinity for the Vietnamese people. "Vietnam, to me, was an experience. A great experience, actually. I found the

Vietnamese a lovely people," he said, "as generous and as honest and as open as you would get anywhere. But I do believe the Americans forgot one thing, as did the French at Dien Bien Phu, as did everyone else. The Vietnamese people, and their counterparts in Cambodia and Laos, had been at war for 700 years and I believe these people negated to look at that properly. They could never dampen the spirits of the Vietnamese. The Vietnamese loved their country. They practically beatified Ho Chi Minh and General Giap." Michael Cahill retired from the Merchant Navy after twelve years at sea. He lives in County Kildare.[8]

Another Irishman, John Dobbin, also served with the British Merchant Navy in the Vietnam theatre. John Dobbin served on board a Singapore-based tanker supplying petroleum to American bases. Born in 1930 John lived in the harbour town of Carrickfergus, Co. Antrim. He joined the British Merchant Navy in 1948 and travelled all over the world, retiring in the 1990s. John came from a seafaring family: his grandfather, Charles Spence, was a seafarer all his life and served in the Royal Navy during WWII; his uncle, James Spence, served as a master on foreign going and Russian convoys during WWII and was later Harbour Master of Carrickfergus for many years. John's twin brother, Harry, also served in the Merchant Navy for many years as a bosun. John Dobbin served as a chief steward in and around South Vietnam for eight months in 1967-8, sailing on UK registered Shell tankers – SS *Achatina* and SS *Partula*.[9]

John wrote: "On arrival at Cam Rahn Bay, in Vietnam, with a full cargo of jet fuel for American Air Force bases, we anchored close to shore across from the base, which was located under a cliff, which was carved out to house the pilots. It also contained accommodation for personnel and was like a small village. Above was the actual airbase, which was used for air strikes."[10] In addition to having two10,000 foot runways, Camh Rahn Bay had an excellent deep-water port and, due to its relatively secure location, was the site of large munitions and petroleum, oil, and lubricants storage site. From this location the 12th Tactical Fighter Wing carried out close air support, interdiction, and combat air patrol activities over both North and South Vietnam and Laos.[11]

"As soon as we dropped anchor two American Air Force officers arrived to check our cargo and to monitor cargo, which was pumped into small tankers of 200 tons to be transferred to holding tanks ashore. This was continuous until all our cargo was ashore. We then had to up anchor and proceed upriver to Saigon to take bunkers as they were not available to Cam Rahn Bay." The crew were fitted out with American issue helmets and protective gear to thwart Viet Cong snipers, who operated on both sides of the river. "We made this round trip three times and fortunately no one was hurt. On arrival back at Cam Rahn Bay, we again anchored and another ship came alongside – so we were back again as a supply ship. The American Air Force was kept busy dropping hand grenades to ward off Viet Cong frogmen from ships anchored in the bay. The electric power for the airbase was generated by five (American) T2 tankers beached at high tide and re-fuelled by other tankers. We served eight months before returning to Singapore for home leave."[12]

In 1980 John Dobbin was serving on board the newly built SS *Ebalina* as a stores catering officer. "We left the port at Chiba (new tonnage) round for Singapore light ship for cargo – Chiba was in Japan where the ship was built – when we picked up some boat people in the China Sea during Hurricane Anna."[13] In the years following the Vietnam War, over one million refugees fled the war-ravaged countries of Vietnam, Cambodia and Laos. Those Vietnamese who took to the ocean in tiny overcrowded ships were dubbed the "boat people." The survivors sometimes languished for years in refugee camps. The luckier ones were taken in by countries like the United States, Australia, Canada, Britain and Ireland.[14] On the way to Singapore, from Chiba, the *Ebalina* picked up some Vietnamese boat people whose sampan was facing difficulty during Hurricane Anna in the China Sea. There were nineteen people on board the small sampan – nine men, six women and four children. All the boat people were brought safely onboard and dropped off in Singapore. John later received a letter from one of the women who went on to Montreal. (Canada accepted over 50,000 boat people.) In April 2002 – in one of John's proudest moments – Belfast Lord Mayor Jim Rodgers, in recognition of its service, bestowed the freedom of the city on the Merchant Navy. "I have a veterans medal from Vietnam." John wrote. "I also received the Freedom of Belfast when I was a member of the Merchant Navy Association.* I also met the late Lord Gerry Fitt, who was also a merchant seaman during the Second World War." John Dobbin is now retired and living in Carrickfergus.[15]

---

* The Merchant Navy Association was formed to seek more recognition and respect for seafaring veterans, life at sea and British maritime history. According to the MNA: "This was in the minds of many seafarers, at that time, who felt that after nearly fifty years since the end of WWII little or nothing was understood of the Merchant Navy and the suffering and sacrifice of thousands of wartime merchant seafarers." The MNA has introduced medals for all the various campaigns since WWII, including a Vietnam Medal for men who served between 1960 and 1972.[16]

CHAPTER 5

# OTHER DAYS MAY NOT BE SO BRIGHT

By the autumn of 1965 America was firmly committed to a ground war in South Vietnam. The Vietnam War would display a full spectrum of violence, from individual terrorism and guerrilla fighting to conventional land combat with extensive sea and air components. In June the 1st Infantry Division, the Big Red One, began deploying to South Vietnam to form a US Army corps to subdue the Viet Cong in the eleven-province region around Saigon. In the mid-1960s, US divisions were organised differently than they had been in World War II and Korea. Each division had three brigades, which were "task organised." The concept was utmost flexibility. A brigade, depending on the operation, could have anywhere from two to five battalions along with organic and attached supporting units. The first unit of the Big Red One to deploy to Vietnam was the 2nd Brigade. "When the USNS *Gordon* sailed under the Golden Gate Bridge and steamed into the Pacific Ocean on June 25, 1965, few of the 4,000 American troops crowded onto its decks knew their destination, at least officially. Since late April, when the commanders of the 1st Infantry Division received orders to prepare a brigade for overseas deployment, the unit's home base at Fort Riley, Kansas, had been buzzing with rumours and feverish activity. In early June flatcars loaded with equipment and supplies began leaving for the West Coast on a regular basis. Several weeks later the soldiers of the division's 2nd Brigade departed by rail and plane, arriving at the Oakland Army Terminal on June 21 in full combat gear. By then there could no longer be any doubt. For the first time since World War II, the division known as the 'Big Red One' was going to war. The destination: Vietnam. After eighteen days at sea, the soldiers caught their first glimpse of Southeast Asia, as the *Gordon* approached the sheltered deep-water harbour at Cam Ranh Bay on July 12." The 1st Battalion disembarked here to provide security for the vast new port facility under construction. The rest of the brigade task force then moved south, landing at the port city of Vang Tau two days later. From there the 2nd Battalion, 16th Infantry and the 2nd Battalion, 18th Infantry were airlifted to Bien Hoa Airbase, where they immediately assumed responsibility for the defence of a portion of the perimeter.[1] John Freeman, from Lough Glynn, Co. Roscommon, arrived in Vietnam with Company C, 2nd Battalion, 16th Infantry. He had joined the US Army on 3 January 1964 while living in Chicago.[2]

The Big Red One's first operation began on 22 July 1965, when Company B, 2nd Battalion, 16th Infantry, conducted a search of the area around the base camp at Bien Hoa. The division's initial operations were confined mostly to patrols and small-scale sweeps of the areas surrounding their camps and made no significant contact with the enemy until mid-November.[3] In Vietnam John Freeman proved himself a good soldier, was awarded the Combat Infantryman Badge, and had an interesting encounter with the peculiarities of American immigration law. He was taken out of Radio Communication because of security clearance, as John was not yet a US citizen. Back in the United States John Freeman applied for citizenship with a recommendation written on his behalf by his commanding officer in Coy C, Captain Robert Canady: "Specialist Fourth Class Freeman served under my command from June 1965 to December 1965 in the Republic of Vietnam. During this period he demonstrated a high degree of moral and physical courage under the most adverse conditions. His personal integrity and loyalty to the principles of our great democracy were unwavering. Specialist Fourth Class Freeman, while functioning in an official capacity, did much purchasing on the civilian market for the Army. His exemplary conduct, honesty and integrity in dealing with the Vietnamese people did much to enhance the American image in this country. In my somewhat brief, but close relationship with Specialist Freeman, I have found this individual to be highly industrious, sincere, and with character above reproach. If the occasion should arise, I would be honoured to sponsor John A. Freeman in his position for citizenship, for I feel that he would be an asset to our economy and a credit to our great country." John Freeman, however, had to abide by the formula – three years in the service, or five in the country. He was discharged from the army on 2 January 1970.[4]

The newly formed 1st Cavalry Division was ordered to Vietnam on 28 July 1965. The 1st Cavalry Division (Airmobile) was the first military organisation in history to take full advantage of the helicopter as a vehicle to manoeuvre troops and bring firepower to bear. The 1st Cavalry Division was organised into a 16,000 man airmobile division with a total of 434 helicopters. Troops would be flown into action by helicopter, escorted by rocket-firing gunships, and with cargo-carrying CH-47 Chinooks to lift in artillery and ammunition. Most of the troops trained for more than a year at Fort Benning to get their roles right and in July 1965 the experimental division was given the colours of the 1st Cavalry Division. Within ninety days of becoming the Army's first airmobile division the "Air Cav" were prepared to enter combat, the ultimate test of its capabilities. Beginning on 14 August an advance party of 1,030 officers and men left Robbins Airforce Base on board C124s and C130s. They arrived at Nha Trang between the 19 and 27 of August, establishing a temporary base camp near An Khe, thirty-six miles inland from the coastal city of Qui Nhon. The remainder of the division was transported by sea, which took another month.[5]

The troops of the Air Cav would fly to the assault point in agile transport versions of the Huey gunships, called "slicks." There were "escort gunships" to shepherd these "slick ships" carrying the assault force and other "aerial rocket" Hueys with dozens of rockets in side-mounted pods to back up the riflemen once they were on the ground. Each battalion had an Air Force lieutenant attached as a forward air controller to put the heavier ordnance of the fighter-bombers where it would count. A large new cargo helicopter, the CH-47 Chinook, lifted the artillery to wherever the guns were needed. The Chinooks could move an entire battery of six 105mm howitzers twenty miles over roadless country and have the battery firing again within an hour after the first gun had been picked up. Advanced navigational systems enabled the Chinooks to keep the artillery and the troops supplied with almost unlimited quantities of ammunition and other sustenance of war at night or in bad weather.[6]

Airmobility produced a functional efficiency in the deployment of forces which previous warfare had never matched. The helicopter made it possible for entire battalions to be hop-scotched into action. The quicker infantrymen could be moved, the fewer infantrymen would be needed. However, the endless deployment, and redeployment from fight to fight was tough on troops. It was the task of the North Vietnamese Army (NVA) from sanctuaries in Laos and Cambodia to keep US forces occupied. (The first NVA regulars were committed to South Vietnam in May 1965 in response to the American commitment.) Their supplies came in from China and by ship from Russia and eastern Europe. The movement of troops and supplies to the front down the Ho Chi Minh Trial was slowed by US bombing, but never halted. Enough always got through to maintain the war at the pace at which the North was dictating. In early 1966 major battles occurred at Ia Drang and Dak To on the Cambodian border which suited the American concept of war with major units engaged and enormous firepower brought to bear. The communists suffered huge losses and "body counts" proclaimed American victories. But the communists learned valuable lessons and were reluctant to meet the Americans head on. They knew they could never defeat the Americans in a conventional war and resorted to engagements when and where they were strongest.[7]

Intangible things had also been invested in the creation of the Air Cavalry. The troops and their sergeants and officers knew and trusted one another. Most had organised and trained together for more than a year at Fort Benning as the experimental 11th Air Assault Division. The pilots of the different helicopter formations had learned to play their individual roles and to synchronise their movements in a complicated ballet. The experimental division was given the colours of the regular 1st Cavalry Division and additional battalions to bring it up to strength for service in Vietnam.[8] There were several Irishmen serving with the 1st Cavalry, including John Driver, from Ringsend, Dublin, and Christy Nevin, from Balla, Co. Mayo. Both would be killed in action in Vietnam: Christy Nevin in February 1966 and John Driver on his second tour of duty (with the 101st Airborne) in April 1969.

John Driver, along with his friend, Cornish-born Rick Rescorla, were to become two legends of the US 7th Cavalry. Both had similar backgrounds, having both served with the British Army in Cyprus, and later as soldiers in Rhodesia. Sergeant John Driver had a "very enjoyable sense of humour" and was a "favourite" among the troops. They were both courageous, fearless, and when not in battle had a tremendous sense of humour. Rick Rescorla* could sing all the favourite Irish ballads, including *Garryowen, Sergeant Flynn* and *The Wild Colonial Boy*. The 7th Cavalry, General George Armstrong Custer's old unit, was steeped in Irish traditions and customs. Even the regimental tune was the Irish fighting song Garryowen. During the Plains Indian Wars the 7th Cavalry was made up of at least one-third Irish immigrants. Carlow-born Lieutenant Myles Keogh, who died with his commander at the Battle of the Little Big Horn, is credited with introducing *Garryowen* to the regiment, which became a favourite of Custers.[9]

John Driver was born in Ringsend, Dublin, in 1936, the second eldest of six children. As a youngster growing up in Dublin John Driver had a big interest in the military. He was never interested in playing "cowboys and Indians" – John preferred war games. He loved John Wayne war movies and

---

\* As Vice President for Security at the World Trade Center Rick Rescorla led a large group of children down fifty-seven flights of dark, smoke-filled steps to safety, after terrorists exploded a bomb in the basement of the WTC building in 1993. On 11 September 2001 he once again led 2,700 people to safety, after terrorists flew two planes into the Twin Towers. After getting thousands out, Rick Rescorla went back up to get seven more people in wheelchairs and was never seen again.

went to see them all at the local cinema. John finished school in Westland Row in May 1952 and joined the British Army the following year when he was seventeen. It did not take the British Army long to recognise John Driver's soldiering talent. Not long after being presented with his parachute wings, John found himself in the Malayan jungle battling communist guerrillas. Quickly rising through the ranks to sergeant John served for eight years in many hot-spots, including Malaya, Cyprus, Egypt and Aden. When he was home on leave his younger brother, Don, would ask him was it bad out there? "Ah, yeah," John would say, and according to Don, "that was that. He'd never say anymore about it."[10]

With his friend, Rick Rescorla, John Driver joined the Rhodesian Army and was soon engaged in that country's civil war. He left the Rhodesian Army three years later with the rank of Platoon Sergeant. Rick Rescorla also left Rhodesia and emigrated to America, while John was home in Ireland. He wrote his Irish friend telling him he had joined the American Army. John headed off to the United States in February 1964 and within a week had joined the US Army at Fort Dix, New Jersey. At one point in his training he was awarded the title of "Fort Dix Infantry Trainee of the Week," although such a title might have been a little embarrassing to the much military experienced twenty-seven year old. His experience and background assisted John's rapid rise through the ranks and within a year he was a sergeant and was selected for attendance at the Seventh US Army Non-Commissioned Officers Academy in Germany. On completing his time at the Academy, he was designated as the "Distinguished Graduate" and received two prestigious awards, the "General George S. Patton Junior Award for Excellence" and the "General Douglas MacArthur Award for Leadership." In a letter to John's mother on 11 October 1965 the Commandant of the Academy, Lieutenant Colonel Emmett B. Lyle stated: "The ability to achieve distinction in competition with fellow soldiers is commendable; the ability to accomplish this in competition with the finest soldiers in Europe is an accomplishment from which you may draw real pride and satisfaction. This Academy judges its graduates not only in the light of academics, but predominately in the development of essential, practical characteristics vital for those who will lead other men. Your son has made a fine contribution to himself, his army, and his country."[11]

Within weeks John Driver would be testing these skills out on the battlefields of South Vietnam. John's tour was tough and brutal. He took part in about 200 missions against VC and NVA forces and described his experiences to an *Evening Press* reporter, in Dublin, in late 1966: "It's a dirty war. I went on these missions two or three times a week, often as many times a day. It's a game of hide-and-seek trying to track the Viet Cong down. The big difficulty is knowing who your enemy is — it's a war of nerves and booby traps." In 1966, while on operations in Bong Song valley in the Central Highlands, John was injured by a booby trap consisting of sharpened bamboo stakes, which pierced his buttocks and legs. He was evacuated to hospital by helicopter but found himself back in action barely a week later, recovered from his wounds. As a result of these wounds he was awarded the Purple Heart, which he received from President Johnson. (The medal is routinely awarded for wounds and posthumously for death.) He also received the Air Medal, the citation for which reads: "for distinguishing himself by meritorious achievement while participating in sustained aerial flight support of combat ground forces in the Republic of Vietnam during the period 21 November 1965 to 1 June 1966. During this time he actively participated in twenty-five aerial missions over hostile territory in support of counter-insurgency operations. During all of these missions, he displayed the highest order of air discipline and acted in accordance with the best traditions of the service. By his determination to accomplish his mission in spite of the hazards inherent in repeated aerial flights over hostile territory, and by his outstanding degree of professionalism and devotion to duty, he has brought credit upon himself, his organisation, and the military service."[12]

According to the 2nd Battalion surgeon, Captain William Shucart, one of the most highly regarded officers in the 2/7th Cavalry: "The guys who taught me most about the Army were Lieutenant Rick Rescorla, an Englishman, and Sergeant John Driver, who was an Irishman. Driver did tunnel-rat work; he would drop down in there and yell: 'Anybody home?' He didn't throw smoke in first, like everyone else. After his (first) tour, he went back and did OCS, then returned to Vietnam as a lieutenant and got killed. Driver had his own rules of war, and he tried to teach them to me. You know, when you clean a weapon the first rule is always clear the chamber. Not Driver. His first rule was always check to make sure it's your weapon, so you don't end up cleaning somebody else's weapon. He and Rick taught me a lot about being in the infantry. I would march with them to see what life was like."[13] Colonel Hal Moore also had great praise for Driver and Rescorla, saying both men were "two of the most heroic, dedicated and respected combat leaders who have ever served in the US Army during Vietnam or any other war".[14]

The American fighting man had come across tunnel complexes in previous campaigns in the Pacific and Korea but the tunnels of Vietnam were unique. The Viet Cong tunnel network was a labyrinth of underground arms factories, hospitals and hiding places. After initial bruising experiences it became clear to the Americans — ARVN troops never ventured down into a tunnel to explore it or engage the Viet Cong – that they would have to develop a new military skill in tunnel warfare. The Tunnel Rats were GIs of legendary skill and courage. Armed only with knives and pistols, they fought against a cruel and cunning foe inside the booby-trapped blackness of the tunnels. Only the very brave and foolhardy ventured into the tunnels. John Driver was such a person.

On 10 October the 1st Cavalry joined with ARVN marines to attack 2,000 NVA troops in the Central Highlands, in an operation that lasted four days. Several days later NVA troops launched a major assault on an ARVN/US Special Forces Camp at Plei Me, but were repulsed when reinforcements from the 1st Cavalry and ARVN arrived. With the camp secured General Westmoreland decided to seize the advantage and send in the 1st Cavalry to "find, fix and defeat the enemy forces that threatened Plei Me".[15] For all their training the men of the 1st Cav had yet to be tested in combat. The troops had only seen a few skirmishes during their two months in Vietnam and there were concerns about the shock of them suddenly encountering a large force of veteran NVA or VC.[16] On 1 November 450 men of the 1st Battalion, 7th Cavalry, under the command of Lt Col Hal Moore, were dropped by helicopter into a small clearing in the Ia Drang and were immediately surrounded by 2,000 NVA soldiers. Three days later, two and a half miles away, the 2nd Battalion was chopped to pieces. Together, these actions at the landing zones X-Ray and Albany constitute one of the most savage and significant battles of the Vietnam War and set the tone of the conflict to come.[17]

The two-day battle at LZ X-Ray was the first major engagement between US troops and North Vietnamese Army regulars. Heavily outnumbered the 1st Cavalry held on with the help of sustained fire support from artillery, gunships and massive B-52 bomber strikes. It was the bloodiest battle of the war to date and ended with a victory for the 1st Cavalry, as the decimated NVA 33rd Regiment retreated into the jungle. Seventy-nine Americans were killed and 121 wounded. As the NVA withdrew the 2nd Battalion, 7th Cavalry, was ordered to move overland some two miles northwest to a jungle clearing called Landing Zone Albany. Unknown to them the NVA had staked out all the clearings in the area, and its 8th Battalion, 66th Regiment, which had been held in reserve during the fight at LZ X-Ray, was alerted to their approach. Strung out for 550 yards along the line of march, the NVA sprang the ambush as the column reached the edge of LZ Albany. The 400 men of the 2nd Battalion were both surprised and outnumbered. The NVA forces included both the 550-man 8th Battalion and remnants of the 1st and 3rd Battalions, 33rd Regiment, which had retreated from LZ X-Ray the previous day. When the battle ended the next morning, 155 Americans had been killed and another 124 wounded. After several days of intense combat the NVA broke contact and headed for their sanctuaries across the Cambodian border or into the depths of the jungle. When the Air Cavalry returned to their base at An Khe they had lost 300 men but had accounted for 1,200 of the enemy.[18]

Thanksgiving was begun in its customary style, but General Westmoreland arrived to give the troops a pep talk and as the indoor mess halls were not completed the troops stood in the rain watching their hot turkey dinners turn into "cold Mulligan stew".[19] The Christmas period was marked by a truce, originally proposed by the Viet Cong. Hoping to persuade the communists into peace talks, America accepted the truce and refrained from bombing until 31 December. On 26 December US and ARVN forces abandoned efforts to extend the Christmas truce in ground warfare after extensive Viet Cong attacks. A glimmer of hope that the war in Vietnam might end in a negotiated peace faded. When the air raids restarted they drew ever closer to Hanoi and Haiphong – targets which the US had earlier avoided. On the ground, Korean, Australian and New Zealander troops joined US forces in the bloodiest search-and-destroy missions to date, centering on Operation Masher/White Wing. Beginning on 24 January, allied troops joined up across corps boundaries and for more than forty days swept across the Binh Dinh province. The 1st Cavalry Division joined Operation Masher in the An Lao Valley on the coastal edge of the Central Highlands. (The operation was later renamed "White Wing" after President Johnson complained that the codename "Masher" was a bit tactless.) Joining up with Marines from I Corps, already engaged in Operation Double Eagle in the Quang Ngai province, the 1st Cavalry Division, along with ARVN and Korean forces, swept through Binh Dinh in six weeks of almost continuous fighting. By now five US Army formations – the 173rd Airborne Brigade, the 1st Brigade of the 101st Airborne Division, the 1st Infantry Division, the 1st Cavalry Division (Airmobile) and the 3rd Brigade of the 25th Infantry Division – had been deployed to Vietnam. They were responsible for the security of existing bases and lines of communication, and for taking the war to the enemy in the war zones north of Saigon and in the Central Highlands.[20]

• • •

Vietnam may have been America's war but its northern neighbour, Canada, was heavily involved – for and against. Canada helped supervise ceasefires and was involved in secret missions, weapons testing and arms production, and also harboured American draft dodgers. Several thousand

Canadians volunteered to fight in Southeast Asia, while many more who lived and worked in the US were drafted. Ninety-three Canadians are officially listed as killed in action and seven as missing in action.[21] One of those missing in action is Irish-born James Sylvester Byrne. He was born in Dublin in 1929 and emigrated to Canada where he joined the Royal Canadian Army and saw service in Korea. A married man he lived in Aylmer, PQ. A serving sergeant with the Royal Canadian Army Service Corps, James Byrne was attached as a peacekeeper to the International Commission for Supervision and Control. On 18 October 1965 a Boeing 307, the F-BELV, of the ICSC, en route from Saigon to Hanoi went down over Laos. Thirteen crew members and passengers were lost, including Sergeant James Byrne. The F-BELV was on the last leg of its twice-weekly flights stitching together the offices of the ICSC throughout Indochina. It left Saigon earlier that day, touched down at Phnom Penh briefly went on to Vientiane and was en route to Hanoi, its last destination for the day. It would retrace the same route the next day.

Piloting the F BELV was Captain Henri Domerque, an experienced pilot. He was working for Paris based *Compaigne International des Transports Civil Aeriens* (CITCA). Also on board were three crew members and nine passengers – five Indians, three Canadians and one Pole. The Canadians were Sgt James Byrne, RCASC; Cpl Vernon J. Perkin, Royal Canadian Hussars; John D. Turner, a foreign service officer and Canada's senior representative on the ICSC delegation in Hanoi. The International Commission for Supervision and Control in Vietnam was set up to enforce the Geneva Accords of 1954. Communist Poland, anti-communist Canada, and neutral India each supplied one-third of the personnel; India supplied the chairman. ICSCs with the same composition were set up to supervise the implementation of the Accords in Laos and in Cambodia.

Wattay Airport Vientiane tower cleared the F-BELV's flight for take off. Fifteen minutes later, Captain Domerque radioed Gialam Airport, Hanoi, confirming departure from Vientiane. He reported the flight would cross the border with Vietnam (Muong Xen) at 3.55pm and would be over Phu Ly, south of Hanoi, at 4.44pm. Arrival at Gialam was expected at 4.58pm. One minute later, Gialam's air traffic control confirmed receipt of message and cleared the flight for arrival as scheduled. That was the last was heard of the plane. When the aircraft did not arrive, Gialam tried to contact it but there was no response. Hanoi authorities assumed, when the plane did not arrive that it hade returned to Vientiane. The Control Commission office in Hanoi radioed Vientiane shortly after 6.00pm that the plane was "unable to land" at Hanoi but that clearance had been obtained for it to land at 9.00am the next morning.

ICSC officials back in Vientiane were puzzled by the message and late that evening they prepared a reply questioning the report, noting the aircraft had not returned to Vientiane. Though intended for immediate transmission, the message was not sent until morning because of ionosphere interference with radio transmissions. Between 5.00pm on 18 October and mid-morning on the following day, Hanoi believed the aircraft had returned to Vientiane, while Vientiane believed that it was on the ground in Hanoi. The next morning ICSC authorities in Vientiane realised their message of the previous evening had not been sent and that there might be a problem. A "flash" message was sent at once requesting an immediate investigation. By noon, the confusion was over and all parties accepted that the F-BELV was missing. Information from all sources was quickly combined and ground and air searches organised.

Over the next days more than twenty-five aircraft searched between Vientiane and the Vietnamese border. The search area was south towards Paksane and north to the Plain of Jars, but north Vietnamese authorities did not allow ICSC search aircraft to fly over F-BELV route in Vietnam. It was ten days before the ICSC was allowed to resume flights to Hanoi. The Vietnamese authorities advised that it's own forces were carrying out searches. Search operations were also limited over areas controlled by Communist Pathet Lao* forces in Laos. The search continued until 16 November and in January 1966 the ICSC unanimously accepted the conclusion that the "aircraft met with an accident after it left Vientiane airport at 15.05 hours on October 18, 1965 and that all passengers on board F-BELV are dead". The conflict of the next decade passed the F-BELV by and it was quietly forgotten.

However, the ICSC continued efforts to determine the fate of the F-BELV until the Commission was disbanded in 1972. In both 1973 and 1974 Canada again raised the issue. In early 1975 Hanoi replied that no trace of the plane had been found, despite intensive searches. The Vietnamese advised that the investigation was complete and that the aircraft could not have crashed in Vietnam. A similar inquiry was made to Laos without a response. Other inquiries were made in late 1977 but no new information emerged. In early 1996, Canada asked the US Department of Defence to review the F-BELV disappearance. The request went to the POW/MIA

---

* Pathet Lao ("Land of Laos") was a communist, nationalist political movement, formed in Laos in 1950. The group was ultimately successful in achieving paramount power in Laos, following a civil war lasting from the 1950s to 1975. The group was always closely associated with Vietnamese communists. During the civil war, it was effectively organised, equipped and even led by the army of North Vietnam.

Office. In April the Americans replied that its records indicated a plane with characteristics similar to the F-BELV crashed in a location 14.5 miles south of the F-BELV flight path, west of the Laos-Vietnam border south of Muong Xen. It stated that there were also reports from refugees from the area indicating that a four-engined aircraft crashed in mid October 1965. This information was given to the government of Laos in June 1996 requesting that efforts be made to verify the crash report. A piece of a fuselage was brought back and inspected by Boeing, who claimed it was not part of the plane in question. However, the French government owned the plane and could have reworked that section of fuselage so there was no hard evidence that the plane was not the one in question. That was all the help the Laotian government gave. They consider the area around the crash site to be restricted because of its military importance. James Byrne was the first Irishman to die in Southeast Asia and in 2008 is still officially listed as Missing.[22]

* * *

The provinces of Binh Dinh and Quang Ngai on the Central Vietnamese coast had been hotbeds of resistance since the French Indochina War. In 1965 two North Vietnamese regular army regiments arrived in this important base area, combining with VC main force units already there to form the Third Division. MACV was determined to do what it could to break up the enemy base area and troop concentration. Against a division-sized North Vietnamese-Viet Cong force, planners calculated the need for a 20,000-man attack. Towards the end of January 1966 the 1st Cavalry Division, plus US Marine, South Vietnamese and South Korean troops made their combined, and complicated attack into this densely populated area to seek and destroy the NVA/VC force.[23] Sergeant Patrick Christopher "Christy" Nevin, from Balla, Co. Mayo, was serving with Bravo Company, 2nd Battalion, 12th Cavalry Regiment, as the Cav committed two brigades. His tour of duty began on 20 August 1965 when the 1st Cavalry Division arrived in Vietnam.[24] When the 1st Cavalry Regiment landed they ran into fierce opposition, including forty-five damaged choppers hit by ground fire.[25] The two regiments of NVA had joined a regiment of VC regulars nearly a year earlier and they had plenty of time to arrange their defences before the men of the Air Cav arrived. With the help of the peasantry every hamlet had been turned into a bastion. The approaches across the rice paddys and other open spaces were meticulously covered by interlocking fields of fire from automatic weapons housed in bunkers that had layers of packed earth for protection overhead. The camouflaged foxholes in the canal dikes had a little chamber hollowed out off to one side where a soldier could wait out a bombardment. There were also zigzag communication trenches for reinforcements, ammunition re-supply and the evacuation of wounded.[26]

The day after the landing Colonel Hal Moore flew in with reinforcements: two companies of the 2/12 Cavalry. This initial engagement peaked on 29/30 January, after which the communists faded away. By 2 February, the Cav felt they had completed taking over the plain around Bong Son. Moore's men returned to An Khe, while the 2/12 Cavalry stayed behind to rejoin its parent unit, the 1st Brigade, which continued operations to the east, on to Go Chai Mountain. In days of patrolling they found little sign of the enemy. On 19-21 February, one of the main actions occurred in an area known as the "Iron Triangle", an elaborate, well fortified defensive position twelve miles south of Bong Son. During the interrogation of a prisoner, he revealed the location of the NVA 22nd Regimental headquarters. Elements of the 2nd Brigade advanced into the area and were met by fierce resistance. Units from the NVA 22nd Regiment attempted to reinforce their headquarters, but they were cut down in the crossfire by the 1st Battalion, 12th Cavalry. For the next three days the area was saturated with artillery fire and B-52 strikes. On 22 February, there was contact with an estimated company-sized unit, probably from the North Vietnamese 12th Regiment, but the adversary again faded away. Irishman Christy Nevin was killed in a firefight the next day, Ash Wednesday, at Ankhe, one of 224 combat deaths for the 1st Cavalry in the operation.[27] He was the first Irishman to die in Vietnam.

## CHAPTER 6

# FIRST BLOOD

The strange and faraway war in Southeast Asia was brought home to Ireland in Spring 1966 when Sergeant Christy Nevin became the first Irish born soldier to be killed in action in Vietnam. Few people in Ireland had heard of the country in Southeast Asia where Irishmen were fighting, and now dying. Christy Nevin was born in Balla, Co. Mayo, in 1937 and emigrated to Chicago in 1954 when he was seventeen. Christy worked in a local pub and came home one Christmas Eve and asked to be allowed to go to America. "Nothing," his mother, May, said, "was ever the same since the day Christy left." Christy worked for eight years as a machinist in Chicago before he received his call-up papers in 1960. When his family asked him to come home Christy told his mother: "No, Mam, I'll never be called a deserter." Like many emigrants before him, Christy Nevin, felt that if America was good enough to offer him a new life, it was his duty to serve when called upon. While working in Chicago he regularly sent home money to his large family struggling back home in Balla.[1] "He volunteered for further service because he loved the army," his father, Michael, told the *Evening Press*, "and intended making it his career."[2] A local doctor arrived at the Nevin home and said Christy had met with an accident. His mother said, "Tell me the truth, he's dead." She said, "I thought it was the end of the world." When Christy Nevin's parents, and brother Bennie, went to the US Embassy in Dublin to collect a posthumous Purple Heart, anti-war protesters set up pickets. Reporters who went to the US Embassy to interview Christy's parents were told by the military attaché they would have to take photographs outside because of a series of anonymous phone calls threatening Embassy staff.[3] Christy's death was such a big news event that showband singer Brian Coll recorded a poignant song *The Blazing Star of Athenry* dedicated to him. (When Christy's mother, May, died it was played at her funeral.) Tom Kelly was fighting with the 173rd Airborne at the same time. He said: "I never found out for thirty years that Christy Nevin died in a battle we were in. He was supporting us."[4]

*Deep in the jungle of Vietnam a U.S. soldier lay*
*A sniper's bullet from the brush his young life stole away*
*In dying breath and whispered tones I heard him proudly say*
*I am just an Irish soldier fighting for the USA*

*For the little while he remembered those so dear*
*An Irish girl so beautiful with eyes so blue and clear*
*He relived the tender moments of the day he said goodbye*
*To the sweetheart that he called the "Blazing Star of Athenry"*[5]

The war in Vietnam, however, was a strange one. In March the endemic corruption of Premier Ky's government led to an armed Buddhist uprising with Da Nang and Hue falling to rebel forces. Three months later Premier Ky released his full military might on Buddhist rebel forces reclaiming Da Nang and Quang Tri. Dubliner Canice Wolahan witnessed a Buddhist monk setting himself on fire. "I couldn't understand why somebody would inflict something like that on themselves," he said. "I didn't think the situation was that bad."[6] But it was and some Americans and Australians felt the same animosity towards the South Vietnamese government as did their earlier countrymen fighting in Korea in the 1950s when the UN supported the despot Syngman Rhee. Ed Somers witnessed South Vietnamese brutality at first hand. As a member of the Regimental Police, 1 RAR, he was passing through a restricted area when he came across five bullet-riddled poles in a market square in Saigon where the government got rid of its undesirables, anyone from black marketers to political dissidents. Curious, Ed took some slides of the poles. "There was sand on the ground to hide the blood and the poles were rough and chipped away by bullets."[7]

A month after Christy Nevin's death another Irishman, Paul Maher, was killed in Vietnam. Paul Maher, from Dublin, was a Lance Corporal serving with the 3rd Battalion, 3rd Marine Regt., 3rd Marine Division. Born in 1945 he had emigrated to the US and was living in Hauppauge, New York, when he enlisted in the US Marine Corps in 1963. After basic training Paul was assigned to the 3rd Marine Regiment.[8] The 3rd Marines continued to actively train in Hawaii and Japan to remain combat ready for any eventuality. The Regiment was quick to respond to the call for forces in Vietnam, providing security for the Da Nang Airbase in May/June 1965. Paul was serving with Lima Company, 3rd Battalion, based on Hill 22, south of Da Nang, Quang Nam province, when he died. According to his former company commander, Captain Bill Lee: "We patrolled the villages surrounding the hill. The ones along the river Yen were particularly nasty. The VC roamed these villages of Bo Ban, La Chau, and Duong Lam. Our patrols in the daytime and ambushes at night were daily/nightly." Paul Maher died on one of these patrols, on 5 March 1966, when a mine was detonated. Paul was mortally wounded and two other Marines injured. "Technically the explosive device was called a mine," Bill Lee said. "We saw them as booby traps. Most were trip wire activated; many were home-made types made by the VC."[9]

The I Corps region assigned to the US Marines consisted of the five northernmost provinces of the Central Coast from Quang Ngai up to Quang Tri at the Demilitarised Zone. With a population of 2.6 million people, more than ninety-eight per cent of them lived within twenty-five miles of the sea (most considerably closer) and on less than a quarter of the land, on the coastal littoral of small rice deltas pressed between the Annamites and the South China Sea

The remaining three-quarters of the territory provided formidable rainforest and mountain redoubts for the Main Force Viet Cong and the NVA troops who had infiltrated into the South. However, there was barely enough rice to feed the sparse number of tribal people who normally inhabited the area. The Marines had established three base zones: around Chu Lai on the border of Quang Ngai and Quang Tin provinces, in and around the port and airbase at Da Nang, and north across the Hai Van Pass around the airfield at Phu Bai just below the ancient city of Hue. The idea was to reach out in both directions from the three base zones, slowly bringing more and more of the population under control until the whole of the littoral was joined in one pacified zone. It would not matter than how many thousands of enemy troops were out in the mountains. Their battalions would wither without the sustaining flow of food, recruits, and intelligence from the peasantry, and Hanoi would have to truck down food for every soldier who marched into I Corps.[10]

Major-General Lew Walt, a decorated WWII veteran, was the commander of the III Marine Amphibious Force, and was in theory one of Westmoreland's corps commanders. But the Marines never really take the Army or its commanders seriously. They are Marines first. (I Corps was also known as "Marineland.") Gen. Walt devoted about a third of his effort to fighting the Main Force VC and the NVA in order to chase them out of the populated deltas and to punish them by joining battle in the hinterland whenever the intelligence indicated he could do so on advantageous terms. Walt's principal effort, fully half the time of the Marine battalions, was invested in a painstaking campaign to rid the hamlets of the guerrillas and the political cadres, and not merely by killing and capturing them. To acquire armed Vietnamese manpower and expand control at the village and hamlet levels, Walt began integrating Marine rifle squads into Popular Force platoons. The Marine sergeant commanding the squad became the militia platoon leader, and the Vietnamese platoon leader became his deputy. The pattern of a Marine in charge and a Vietnamese deputy was repeated in the squads of the platoon. Several of these Combined Action Platoons would then be pulled together into a Combined Action Company under a Marine officer and a Vietnamese deputy. The plan was to gradually integrate Marines into virtually every militia platoon in the five provinces. The regular Marine battalions combined their thousands of day and night patrols and ambushes (they were conducting 7,000 platoon- and squad-size patrols and 5,000 night ambushes a month by April 1966) with a full-scale civic action programme among the peasantry. (Of all the US forces in Vietnam it was the Marines more than anyone that approached the "Civic Action" programme with zest. From their barrage of handouts in the month of January 1967 alone Marines gave away to the Vietnamese 101,536 lbs of food, 4,810 lbs of soap, 14,662 books and magazines, 106 lbs of candy, 1,215 toys and one midwifery kit. They also gave the Vietnamese 530 free haircuts.) While there was great progress in the I Corps TZ this was not good enough for Robert McNamara who claimed the Marine strategy was too slow and that it would take too many men too long to win the war.[11]

Rory O'Connell arrived in Vietnam in December 1965 as the Marine build-up continued in I Corps. He was assigned to A Company, 1st Battalion, 4th Marines. The 4th Marines had arrived in Vietnam in May 1965 and were stationed at Chu Lai. Rory had emigrated from Lahinch, Co. Clare, in 1964 to join the USAF. He wanted to join the Royal Air Force, like his brother Michael, but his brother told him there would be more opportunity in the United States and he should try and join the American air force. Rory stayed with an uncle in Flushing, New York, then moved to Norfolk, Virginia, where his sister lived. Instead of the USAF Rory enlisted in the USMC and was shipped to Parris Island for basic training. "I came to the States in January 1964 and joined the Marines in July 64 so I got a crash course in Americanisation. It was like shock treatment. It was a great experience, even though it was a rough life, but after that life has been a piece of cake and no problems are too difficult. I spent three months in Guantanamo Bay in Cuba before going to Nam, and then four-and-a-half months there after I got back."[12]

After completing basic training Rory volunteered for Vietnam, and was sent to Camp Pendleton, California, to await shipment overseas. He had an uncle in Santa Monica who he could visit before shipping out to Vietnam. The troopship, with 800 Marines and 1,400 Army troops onboard, was sixteen days at sea. "When we pulled into Okinawa the army guys were into their uniforms and off to see the sights. We were ordered up on deck for one hour of PT. That's the difference of the two services. We were ordered down below deck as the ship sailed away, not even allowed to get a last glimpse of land."[13] Rory joined his unit at the huge Marine base in Chu Lai. Located in Dung Quat Bay, the base was roughly fifty-six miles southeast of Da Nang. It consisted of a base with an airfield to help as support facilities to the major base at Da Nang. In mid-1966 there were 55,000 men in the III Marine Amphibious Force. They were formed into two reinforced divisions, the 1st Marines with a command post at Chu Lai and the 3rd Marines operating out of Da Nang. (The Marines also had an air wing in support.)[14] Rory O'Connell said: "I started out in Chu Lai and was there for a couple of months. Chu Lai was not a bad area. We set up ambushes; did perimeter duty; ran patrols. Then we moved up to Phu Bai." One night while Rory was on patrol around Chu Lai "the guy in front of me tripped a wire. These were grenades tied to the bushes on each side of the trail and we were lucky to be on the right side as it was a dud (a miracle). I wrote and told my Mom I have a new birthday and she had a Mass said for me in Lahinch the same day."[15]

"On St Patrick's Day, in 1966, we were up in the Phu Bai area and were sent out on a patrol and ambush. We left early in the day and cut our way through very heavy brush for hours where our arms were covered in blood from the scratches. After we got to the area we needed, our point went over the top of a hill only to spot a platoon of North Vietnamese troops. When he gave us the word we got in line and came over the hill and opened up on them. We had seven automatic rifles out of nine of us so it was like target practice. They would drop and another would take off running. We kept shooting all the way down the hill to where they were and there were trails of blood everywhere. We set in for the night in case they came back for the bodies but we didn't see them again. The choppers picked us up the next day and flew us back to the base. Our platoon commander who was a lieutenant from Chicago was waiting to greet us and as I approached him, he said: 'Ay! It's a grand lad that gets blood on St Paddy's Day.'"[16]

On 20 March Alpha Company took part in Operation Oregon, helicoptering into LZ Robin. As A Company expanded its perimeter they encountered two armed VC, signalling the start of "one of the Battalion's fiercest and hardest fought battles during the past six months". The target area was under continuous bombardment by mortars, artillery, and air during the entire engagement. A brief evaluation of the situation indicated that a village located in the tree line was heavily fortified with prepared positions and trench line. Bunkers and fighting holes completely covered the perimeter of the woods. Company A, in support of Company B, was temporarily halted due to interlocking bands of automatic weapons fire and requested an air strike. Four A-4 aircraft bombed and strafed the village and Coy A moved forward only to be halted again by heavy fire. By now the company had four dead and twenty-four wounded. The destroyer USS Anderson fired over ninety rounds into the target area. That didn't stop the VC either and the company endured another two-dozen casualties. As the Marines set up defensive perimeters for the night all the wounded, including Rory O'Connell, who was hit twice, were medevaced, before darkness fell.[17] "On March 20 1966 on Operation Oregon we were dropped in by choppers and after a platoon got pinned down and ran out of ammo they sent me and my buddy to get the ammo through to them. He went on one side of the trail and I went on the other. He got shot in the stomach and was medevaced and after I got the ammo through I was wounded twice on the way back to my platoon so I got my first Purple Heart. I was back in the field five days later and went on some more operations."[18]

"We moved up to Cam Lo just below the DMZ in August," Rory recalled. "It was different here. You could see it in the people's faces. They stared through us. Either they hated us or were scared of the people behind them. It even felt peculiar. I was also a tunnel rat for our platoon. Every time I heard word coming back 'O'Connell up!' I knew they found one and I had to go up and check it out.

"When our tanks got ambushed at the DMZ I was on the forward tank and while we were stopped to check out a village someone spotted a tunnel so I got in to check it out. I found documents and pictures of North Vietnamese. After the middle of the convoy got ambushed they were ready to pull out with me still down there. I heard someone yell they are pulling out and by the time I got out and got my gear on they were all on the tank ready to roll and helped pull me on the tank which was already moving so I almost got left there. Another time they called me and I had to squeeze into a hole where I had to wiggle just to get through but when I dropped down inside I started choking because before they called me the had dropped a smoke grenade down as they did sometimes looking for other entrances, but I had a rough time climbing back out through such a small hole. I found a guy another time who was crouched back in a corner who was very muscular compared to the regular VC so I took him out and turned him over to the interpretors. He started talking a mile a minute when they got him.[19]

"We were on a patrol along the DMZ on seventeen tanks and four 'ontos' (an armoured tracked vehicle with four mounted 106mm recoilless cannons) when the middle of the convoy got ambushed killing my company commander and a few others. His name was Lt Hartley and he was a great Marine having come up through the ranks. I took a picture of him four days before, saluting me."[20] On 23 August, Company A, with Company C, 3rd

Tank Battalion in direct support, conducted a tank infantry sweep north into the Con Thien area. This daylong operation resulted in three contacts; two mortar attacks and one ambush. Swift reaction by the tank/infantry team resulted in nine probable VC killed, while Marine losses were three dead, including 1st Lieutenant William Lee Hartley, and seventeen wounded. The tanks encountered mines on four occasions, with no personnel casualties. However, evacuation of the disabled tanks was not effected for another two days.[21]

"Four days later our position was overrun and I almost had my head blown off by a grenade and was taken out by chopper to Da Nang." The night before Rory O'Connell had volunteered to lead a ten-man squad outside the perimeter to intercept an expected enemy attack, but nothing happened that night. "I volunteered to take that squad out to set up security for two artillery pieces that they had moved the furthest north that the ever had to try to reach places that the planes couldn't. Everyone knew that the NVA would try to knock them out as soon as possible, that is why it was an all-volunteer squad and I said I would take it. We didn't expect to come back so everyone lined up to tell us goodbye not expecting to see us again. We dug in all day and strung concertina wire and filled sand bags around our positions. I got each position a case of grenades and all the ammo they needed. We had seven M-60 machine guns (not bad for a squad, ha!ha!) and a claymore mine in front of each position. Before we left Sergeant John Joys, of California, volunteered to go with me to help. But even though he outranked me it was my squad and he said he would come along to help me. Nothing happened but we were all ready for a wild night and we would have taken a bunch of them with us. The following night we got hammered and Sgt Joys got killed and received the Navy Cross, which is the next medal to the Medal of Honour, for his bravery. He was a great Marine and I think of him all the time." [22]

On the night, 25-26 August, Company A, located at the artillery positions at Cam Lo, began receiving heavy incoming mortar and S/A rounds. During the next hour and a half, Company A's lines were penetrated by an estimated two companies of VC and NVA. The official report read: "By virtue of a determined resistance, quick and immediate unit response, and many cases of individual courage and initiative, the attack was repulsed, and the enemy was driven from the position. Final results were seventy-five VC KIA (confirmed); USMC three KIA and thirteen WIA."[23]

"They were all over the place," Rory said, "climbing up on tanks with satchel charges. I was crawling out of a bunker to get ammunition when a concussion grenade blasted me in the face. Both ears were perforated and my left eye really badly injured." Rory was medevaced to a hospital in Da

Nang, then out to a hospital ship, before going to Japan "and finally back to a hospital in the States – the Navy hospital in Portsmouth, Virginia".[24]

Wallace Beene, *Stars and Stripes* Bureau Chief wrote of the battle: "A savage pre-dawn attack Friday by several hundred north Vietnamese troops was beaten back by U.S. Marines at this outpost (Cam Lo) only six miles below the DMZ. The enemy troops estimated at 300 to 400 men, hit the outpost from all sides with automatic weapons fire as Red soldiers armed with grenades and satchel charges cut through the wire and charged through the tent area. 'The fighting got up to within a few yards of my command post,' said 2d Lt. Gerard T. Galvin. 'One of my sergeants was killed throwing grenades outside the bunkers and one of the men inside was hit. If it hadn't been for the others I would be dead.' Galvin had assumed command of A Co., 1st Bn., 4th Marine Regt., 3d Marine Div., only two days before, after the previous commander was killed.

"At dawn, some 63 enemy bodies were found within the perimeter and many others were left on the wire and in the brush surrounding the area. Only one prisoner was taken. Marine casualties were described as light ... 'when the fighting was over it looked like a bowling alley with bodies stacked up where the bullets had cut away the brush,' Galvin said. At times, the enemy troops were shot off the tops of tanks where they were attempting to place satchel charges. The assault was apparently directed at wiping out the tanks and artillery supporting the Marine battalion dug in at a key valley located eight miles to the west. The Marines had been in the area only 10 days and moved the outpost to higher ground only two days before the assault. One tank retriever was destroyed during the attack and a number of vehicles had their tires shot off."[25]

"After I got released from the hospital," Rory O'Connell said, "I went back to Ireland for forty-five days and then back to Camp Lejeune and back to Guantanamo Bay for four and a half months. From there I started writing to a girl in Tennessee and after meeting her in January we got married in August. When I got back from Nam and I was sent back to Camp Lejeune – before we were sent back to Guantanamo – we did a lot of training of troops getting ready to go to Nam. As sergeants we were assigned to give classes on all subjects from tactics to weapons, etc., but I was always assigned to teach hand-to-hand combat because I was into that big time. Before I went to Nam my best friend and I, who was from Italy, joined a karate school on the base and when everyone else would go to town on liberty we would hit the gym and work out. His name was Michele Basso and he got killed in Nam. Also very bravely, volunteering to go to the rescue of Marines in deep trouble. When they found them they were in a circle but didn't stand a chance as they were overrun by a large NVA outfit. We were like brothers and always together. (Sgt Michele Basso was killed in action, in Vietnam, on 8 February 1968.) So when I went back to Guantanamo they assigned me about seventy-five sailors from ships that were in port, and some Seabees, to instruct in hand to hand and they really liked it and had me meet them in the gym after we were off duty."[26] Rory O'Connell has two children and lives in Greenwood, Indiana. He regularly visits his home town of Lahinch.

Back in Ireland the *Clare Champion* reported: "A young Lahinch man has been awarded the Purple Heart decoration after being wounded in action against the enemy in strife-stricken Vietnam. He is Lance Corporal Roderick D. (Rory) O'Connell, son of Mr. and Mrs. John O'Connell, Marine Parade, Lahinch. Cpl. O'Connell, now five months with the US Marine Corps in Vietnam, was severely injured in a military encounter with the Viet Cong. He was wounded in the right arm, shoulder and back, but is now well again and back in action. He is attached to the 1st Battalion, 4th Marines, 'A' Company, San Francisco home-based."

In a later issue the *Clare Champion* ran a story on Rory O'Connell and a school friend, Gus O'Loughlin, "Two Claremen back from different wars: Two young soldiers who have been serving with the fighting forces of two different countries in two very diverse parts of the world met for the first time in five years when they arrived home on leave to their homes in North Clare recently. Rory O'Connell (22), Lahinch, and Gus O'Loughlin (21), of Ennistymon, were buddies together in their younger days. They could hardly have realised that both would fight in their not so much later years in two of the most turbulent trouble spots in the world to-day – Vietnam and Aden.

"Rory left for the USA in December 1965, joined the Fourth Marines and served for eight and-a-half months in Vietnam, during which time he won two Purple Heart medals for being wounded in action. He was first wounded in Operation Oregon on a search and destroy mission in the rice paddys near Hue. His wounds in the shoulder, arm and back earned him his first Purple Heart. He was evacuated from the theatre of war by helicopter but was back in action soon after, when he was wounded for the second time at Cam-Lo by a concussion grenade. This time Rory was brought back to hospital in the United States. He leaves Ireland soon, but this time not for Vietnam but for the Second Marine Division in North Carolina, far away from the horrors of war. He told our reporter that he was '100 per cent behind the US stand in Vietnam.'

"Gus O'Loughlin has been serving with the Royal Signal Corps for two years with the Trem Slouman Scouts, which is a desert patrol in the British Protectorate of Aden. The fighting terrain there of desert and barren mountain, is in strong contrast to the jungle, swamps and paddy fields of Vietnam where his schoolboy friend Rory has been fighting ... He said that during his time in Aden he met quite a number of Irishmen, including, strangely enough, Michael O'Connell, serving with the RAF, who is a brother of his other friend, Rory O'Connell, who at the time was with the US forces in Vietnam."[27]

John Barrett, another school friend of Rory O'Connell, arrived in Vietnam in 1966. Like Rory, he was also born in Lahinch, Co. Clare, and also took the emigrant plane to America. He was drafted in May 1965, while working in a bank in Manhattan, and went to Fort Dix for basic training, and then chemical warfare training at Fort McCllelan, Alabama. John Barrett arrived on 8 August 1966, as a Specialist 4, to Headquarters Company, 1st Battalion, 1st Infantry Division.[28] The Big Red One Division was already in-country since the previous year. John "reported to Long Binh. I flew from Fort Dix to San Francisco; flew by Alaska where we stopped for re-fuelling and then landed in Tan Son Nhut. It all happened so quickly". Within a day John Barrett was in a combat zone. He was based at Phu Vinh, where the 1st Infantry Division had a supply base. "Initially, I was on supply convoys to ships collecting supplies of food and ammunition. It was a dangerous mission. You had roadside bombs and we came under fire, but luckily, none of our trucks were hit or blown up. We had a large perimeter around our compound and had to take turns patrolling that. We had a great captain and he made sure we were well taking care of, in every aspect."

"Sometime after someone went through my records and noticed I had worked in a bank, so I got an office job. I had a bit of stature as a sergeant (John was promoted to sergeant E5 in November 1966) but I was in a war zone, so it was not a nine to five job. We still came under attack from mortars and small arms and an odd time I still had to go out on convoys. I didn't mind. I felt it was fair. One of the most harrowing things I had to do was go out and identify men killed by roadside bombs. A lot of these guys had re-upped and stayed on when their tours were over and re-enlisted to get a bonus. A lot of these guys never made it. My job was to go out and identify them. Then I would have to write a letter home to their parents and of course I never told the truth. I always said they died quickly, not the way I saw them – blown to pieces. That was the worst part of Vietnam for me. Guys I knew quite well. I saw too many who didn't make it. It still affects me. It pains me a lot to think of it, even now."

After six months in Vietnam John Barrett was given five days R and R. He had seen enough of Vietnam and decided to go to Hong Kong for a break. Here he bought the best of suits and silk shirts and spent so much money he ran out and had to wire his aunt to send out more. John did not see any drug abuse by American servicemen, but there was plenty of drinking, including a severe bender in Saigon, which left him severely hung-over. "There were no Irishmen in my company," John said, "but there were a few Germans. I was still not a citizen and Vietnam was never a declared war. The government was worried that an alien might be killed and they wanted no more bad publicity. One day an officer came to me and said they were going to fly me to Guam to swear me in, but I said I didn't want to be a citizen, hoping they'd send me home. I was being a wiseass, but it didn't work."

Sgt John Barrett's two-year term in the US Army was up before he completed a year in Vietnam so he left Vietnam on 21 June 1967 after an eleven-month tour. He was discharged the next day. "We flew back to Maguire Air Force Base in New Jersey. A whole lot of guys got off at Tan Son Nhut from one doorway, while we were going up the other entrance. The planes couldn't stay too long on the ground, in case of coming under fire. I was the happiest man in the world, though I felt sorry for the other poor bastards. There were three aliens on our plane – me and two guys from Germany, who I didn't know. We were told we could not be mustered out. We were to be detained overnight. I was livid. I knew a lot more by now, so I requested to see the Inspector General, which was my right. I was in full uniform, saluted, and said, 'I have served America with distinction and expect to be treated as an equal. Why are we to be detained?' The Inspector General said, 'I agree. You will be taken care of immediately.' We were ushered out, even before the others."

John Barrett left the US Army the day he arrived home. A week later he was back at work in the bank in Manhattan. The bank had to guarantee his job while he was away. It was part of the agreement. John had saved $1,000 while he was in Vietnam and wanted to "blow it on a holiday", but the bank wanted him to start immediately and offered him a better job in stocks. He maintains it was probably the best thing that happened to him, as he didn't get time to dwell on his experiences. However, he had a lot of nightmares and found the roar of the subway trains affected him a lot and reminded him of incoming and outgoing artillery and mortars. John was awarded a Bronze Star for "meritorious achievement in ground operations against hostile forces". John Barrett received an honourable discharge in 1971 after his five years on the reserve list was over. He returned to Ireland in 1981.[29]

1966 was the year of the "big build-up" of US forces in Vietnam. On 31 December 1965 there were 184,300 US servicemen in-country; twelve months later that figure had risen to 385,300, with little sign of a reduction in flow. As new units arrived they were sent to areas throughout South Vietnam, thereby spreading the areas of conflict. The country was blocked off in four military areas – I Corps, the north up to the DMZ; II Corps Tactical Zone, Central Highlands; III CTZ, Saigon; and IV CTZ, the Mekong Delta.[30] General Westmoreland had started his preparing-to-win phase of 1966 by going over to the offensive "in high priority areas" with search-and-destroy operations against Main Force VC units and NVA regulars who were joining them. Westmoreland implied that he could finish this campaign by the end of the year or in the first half of 1967. If the Viet Cong and Hanoi had not acquired wisdom and given up the struggle by then, he said, he would launch a full-scale, nationwide offensive to complete "the defeat and destruction of the remaining enemy forces and base areas". This victory phase would take "a year to a year and a half", that is until mid-1968 or the end of the year.[31]

However, by the summer of 1966 the war was growing increasingly into a major conflict that was threatening to engulf the world. Vietnam's neutral neighbours, Laos and Cambodia, found themselves in the firing line as the NVA and VC used its border areas for supply and staging posts. Both the Soviet Union and China were thrown into a closer kinship with Ho Chi Minh, while Britain, a supporter of President Johnson's policy under Harold Wilson's premiership, nervously disassociated itself from this latest escalation of the war. Throughout the summer Secretary of Defence Robert McNamara grew more and more disenchanted with the progress of the war. In August, a secret seminar of experts had confirmed his impression that Operation Rolling Thunder, the bombing of North Vietnam, was not working. By November, he was questioning the very basis of Westmoreland's strategy. (Westmoreland was not interested in pacification. He wanted to win the war.) Although he was a prime architect of the Vietnam war and repeatedly overruled the Joint Chiefs of Staff (JCS) on strategic matters, McNamara would eventually become sceptical about whether the war could be won by deploying more troops to South Vietnam and intensifying the bombing of North Vietnam.*[32]

---

\* The failure of the air war against the North first opened McNamara's eyes The following year McNamara's recommendation to freeze troop levels, stop bombing North Vietnam and for America to hand over ground fighting to South Vietnam was rejected outright by President Johnson. McNamara's recommendations amounted to him saying that all the policies he had been promoting for years were wrong, and that his strategy for winning the war was a failure. Given that he had been forcing decisions with regard to the war on the JCS, he was left discredited and without any remaining support. Lyndon Johnson was dismayed that the man who had created the strategy for the war and supported it at every step had almost overnight changed his mind. McNamara seemed blind to the political and practical consequences of reversing policy. Largely as a result, on 29 November of that year, McNamara announced his resignation and that he would become President of the World Bank in the following year.

On the ground America's search and destroy campaign pressed ahead with some success, but the North Vietnamese Army was appearing in combat with more regularity. The US Marines had clashed with the NVA in Operation Utah in March and had inflicted serious casualties on them. An NVA force had then overrun a Special Forces camp in the A Shau valley on the Laotian border. In July an NVA division moved across the DMZ to challenge the ARVN defenders of Quong Tri province, putting I Corps into a panic. III MAF sent 3rd Marine Division headquarters, and two full regiments northwards to Quong Tri and Thua Thien provinces and an obscure crossroads along Route 9 named Khe Sanh. The Americans did not need another "front" or another type of Vietnam war, but by the end of 1966, it found both along the DMZ.[33] Worse, the human cost of the war continued to spiral upwards. Over 5,000 US servicemen had been killed and 37,738 wounded in 1966. More worrying, however, was the enormous number of civilian deaths.[34] About 25,000 civilians had been killed and another 50,000 seriously wounded, while refugees had swollen to more than two million.[35]

## CHAPTER 7

# JOURNAL OF A PLAGUE YEAR

All was not well in America in 1967. Race riots broke out in several cities and "Black Power" became more vocal and violent. The summer of 1967 was known as the "Summer of Love" and was typified by the slogan "make love not war" as protests against America's policies in Vietnam escalated. "Hell no, we won't go," and "Hey, hey, LBJ, how many kids did you kill today?" became the chant of left-wing students and draft-dodgers, many of who publicly burned their draft cards. Fifty thousand demonstrators marched on the Pentagon as young people began seriously questioning their country's role in Vietnam and the anti-war debate became increasingly bitter. Robert Kennedy's anti-war stand was winning him growing support. An opinion poll in October showed him ahead of President Johnson by twenty points. Another opinion poll in the same month revealed that forty-six percent of the public thought the war to be a mistake; only forty-four percent continued to back it. In the Haight-Ashbury district of San Francisco, the hippie movement came to public awareness as thousands of young people from across America flocked to the city to join in a popularised version of the hippie experience. In South Vietnam it made little difference as the war escalated, and inevitably, casualties rose. The US began to lose local civilian support as it declared open warfare on anything that moved during its search and destroy missions throughout areas deemed in enemy hands.

The war in Vietnam in early 1967 was still vastly different than what it was to become at year's end. There was still a sense of patriotism and serving Americans, while not wildly optimistic, still felt that they would eventually win the war. By the end of the year America had 449,000 troops in South Vietnam, while 9,378 men were killed in action. (There were an additional 1,680 non-hostile deaths for a total of 11,058.)[1] 1967 was also the most dangerous year for the Irish in Vietnam when eight Irish-born soldiers died. March 1967 was the worst month for the Irish in Vietnam. Four men from Ireland died in combat: L/Cpl Bernard Freyne, Ballaghderreen, Roscommon, killed in action 10 March; SP4 Michael Smith, Ballyconnell,

Co. Cavan, killed in action on 18 March; SP4 John Coyle, Birmingham (Cavan) killed in action on 29 March; Cpl Patrick Gallagher, Ballyhaunis, Co. Mayo, killed in action on 30 March. All of them were in their early twenties and in the prime of life. For the Irish in Vietnam 1967 was a plague year.

In early January 1967 the US 4th Infantry Division moved into the western area of the Central Highlands, determined to engage the NVA 1st and 10th Divisions. The 4th Infantry Division had deployed from Fort Lewis, Washington, via Tacoma, to Camp Holloway, Pleiku, Vietnam, in September 1966. However, its brigades were deployed to different locations, with the 1st Brigade near the South China Sea, 2nd Brigade in the Central Highlands, and the 3rd Brigade in the Mekong Delta. Since the beginning of the war the 4th Infantry Division's ranks had been depleted by men dispatched to replenish other units, and it had to be rebuilt for service overseas. Around 8,000 men, mostly draftees were sent to Fort Lewis and assigned to units to begin intensive training.[2] Dozens of Irishmen, drafted and recruited throughout early 1966, went with the division to Vietnam. Over the coming months of action in the Central Highlands and War Zone C five native-born Irishmen would die while serving with the 4th Infantry Division. Specialist 4 Timothy Daly, from Knockainey, Hospital, Co. Limerick, was twenty-two when he was killed on 3 February 1967. Born in 1945 he had only been in the US a short time, living in Edgewater, New Jersey, before he joined the Army. A quiet and serious young man who took his duties to his adopted country seriously. Tim arrived in country with the 4th Infantry Division in October 1966. The married man was killed by "non-hostile, ground casualty accidental self-destruction", a poignant reminder that, in a war with no front lines, there was no safe rear area either – as 10,798 deaths in Vietnam due to accidents, disease and other non-hostile causes attest.[3]

Operation Sam Houston began on 1 January 1967, with American units clearing the plains of Pleiku and Kontum Provinces, preparatory to more sustained campaigns west of the Nam Sathay river. The 2nd Brigade of the 4th Division crossed the Nam Sathay river in mid-February, entering some of the most difficult terrain imaginable. Mist-shrouded valleys, covered in dense jungle, were overshadowed by rugged mountains; daylight temperatures soared above 105 degrees and water was scarce; air and artillery support was virtually impossible to organise. Joined by the 1st Brigade, helicoptered into Plei Djereng, the division pushed slowly westwards, hoping to trap the NVA close to the Cambodian border. Instead, they suffered constant ambush in ideal guerrilla terrain. On 4 March Company C left the battalion firebase on a search and destroy mission. Sgt Edward Howell was serving with Company C, 1st Battalion, 22nd Regiment, 4th Infantry

Division, when he was mortally wounded in action. Howell was a regular army soldier and had been in the army since 1961. He was twenty-nine and a married man living in Cleveland, Ohio. Sergeant First Class Howell was wounded in action by small arms fire/grenade when the company ran into a minefield, on 11 March. One other soldier was killed outright, while Ed Howell died of his wounds on April 17. By mid-March, both brigades of the 4th Division had been forced to pull back east of the Se Sanh river. Another Irishman, John Coyle, was killed in action by small arms fire on 29 March. Born in Birmingham to Irish parents from Cavan, John grew up in the Bronx, where his parents had moved in 1951. He, too, arrived with the 4th Infantry Division in October 1966.[4]

Sam Houston officially ended on 5 April as the NVA began to avoid combat and to pull back many of its forces over the border to avoid further destruction. The Americans listed a total of 733 enemy killed compared to 169 total combat deaths for the 4th Division. The border and the sanctuary it afforded were among the enemy's greatest assets. Because American troops were forbidden from crossing into and operating in Cambodia and Laos, NVA and VC troops could pull back across the border to regroup and re-supply virtually unmolested. This added to American frustration throughout the war. Operation Junction City began on February 22 when twenty-two US battalions and four ARVN battalions began search and destroy operations in Tay Ninh and bordering provinces. Their objective was to engage the VC 9th Division and destroy COSVN (Central Office of South Vietnam – the headquarters of the Viet Cong) and other bases. It was the largest operation of the war to date and lasted until 14 May resulting in 282 Americans killed and an estimated 2,728 VC killed. The Americans hailed Junction City as a great success, but the reality was the allies were too weak to hold the cleared areas, and communist troops soon returned to War Zone C.[5]

Specialist 4 (Corporal) Michael Smith was serving with the 3rd Brigade, 4th Infantry Division, and had set sail on board a troopship for Vietnam on 22 September, in scenes reminiscent of WWII. During the voyage the men were given a smattering of further training, including an introduction to Vietnamese language and customs. Mike Smith had emigrated from Ballyconnell, Co. Cavan, in 1962 when he was seventeen. He was the third eldest of a family of eight – four boys and four girls. His eldest sister, Mary, was the only one who remembered him leaving, as all his other siblings were too young. As a schoolboy Mike played with Templeport in the Cavan School Gaelic Football League. He was a member of the Ballyconnell School of Irish Dancers and was a keen competitor at feisanna in Cavan and adjoining counties. Michael was working and attending night school, where he was awarded a scholarship, when he was drafted in 1965.5 Assigned to Headquarters Company, 2nd Battalion (Mechanised), 22nd Infantry Regiment, he deployed with the 4th Infantry Division to Vietnam in September 1966. The 3rd Brigade's base camp was at Dau Tieng, about forty miles northwest of Saigon on Highway 14. Mike was looking forward to a visit home after his time in Vietnam – another six months – was over. As a Radar Operator he had participated with the battalion in five previous major operations: Brementon, Attleboro, Cedar Falls, Gadsden, and Junction City. (American search and destroy operations were usually named after American towns and cities, like Junction City, Attleboro, etc.)

However, Michael tried to play down the danger and his participation in combat to his family in Ireland. In a letter to his father, around Tet 1967, Michael wrote:

"A short note to say everything is going good round here at present. There isn't supposed to be any fighting because of a cease fire, but there is scattered outbreaks of fighting here & there … What teams are in the Railway Cup this year?"

To his mother he wrote: "I'm sitting around here bored to death doing nothing, you probably think that's impossible but lately all we've been doing is playing cards, eating, & sleeping. I'm sure you hear the reports, on the radio about Americans getting killed here, but they never say that there's about 410,000 American men here, about 1 out of every 41,000 gets killed every week, and they are the guys that's out actually fighting.

I know you dad and the rest of the family worry about me, but if I honestly thought I was in any real danger I'd be in England or some other place, so don't worry about me. Sure I carry a gun but all I do with it is clean it, and it rusts and I clean it again and so on. I haven't fired a shot since I've been here and I haven't seen a Viet Cong."[6]

Michael's parents received a letter from him on 14 March in which he told them he was now in the danger zone. Phase Two of Junction City began in early March. It involved the 3rd Brigade and other units moving east-wards in War Zone C, conducting search and destroy operations against COSVN, Viet Cong, and North Vietnamese forces and installations. The Saigon river was to be bridged at its intersection with Route 246 west of An Loc and at that site the Special Forces and Civilian Irregular Defense Group (CIDG) camp with an airstrip for C-130's was to be built. On 17 March the advance element of the 2nd Battalion, 22nd Infantry, including the Reconnaissance Platoon, of which Mike Smith was a member, departed the base camp and was followed the next day by the remainder of the battalion. When the two groups met the battalion began moving north in order to reach their objective, which was to secure a landing. The Recon Platoon was the lead element, providing front security for the battalion, when they came under heavy enemy fire. The lead APC hit a landmine, resulting in two men killed and three wounded. Mike Smith was riding in the cargo hatch of the APC and was killed instantly.

Mike Smith's body was evacuated to the 45th Surgical Hospital in Tay Ninh. His parents were informed of his death by local Gardai. The day after Michael's grief-stricken parents were told of his death, they received a letter from him, written some time before he was killed. Michael's commanding officer, Captain Michael J. Curran, wrote to his parents expressing his condolences, saying: "Michael was an excellent soldier, well liked, and respected by all of us in the company … On all missions Michael performed his duties as a Radar Operator in a truly outstanding manner and demonstrated exceptional skill in his job. His performance was indeed an inspiration to all who were associated with him." Michael's remains were flown to his native home by the USAF, accompanied by Lieutenant Charles Carpenter. After service in Kilnavart Catholic Church Michael Smith was buried in the nearby cemetery. Lt Carpenter presented the American flag, which draped the coffin, to Michael's father, Thomas Smith. President Lyndon Johnson sent his condolences on 29 March:

Dear Mr. And Mrs. Smith:
Words are inadequate to express my sorrow in the loss of your son, Specialist Four Michael F. Smith, who died so bravely in Vietnam. May you take heart in the knowledge that your son gave his life for the defense of freedom and peace. His sacrifice has inspired us all to new resolve in that great cause. Mrs. Johnson joins me in expressing to you our pride and heartfelt sympathy in your time of bereavement. [7]

Many more young Irishmen arrived in Vietnam as the war escalated and more units were sent to Southeast Asia. An Irish-born comrade of Michael Smith, Patrick Doyle, said, "I was with you when you went down. I knew it was over. I remember when I first met Mike on the plane coming over here from Ireland. We had been friends since 1963. It was ironic that we both wound up in the same place. I was there when (he) was hit, I recognised (him) by his Irish claddagh ring. I wish that things were different. I hope we made a difference."

Belfastman Anthony Conlon served two tours of Vietnam with the 9th Infantry Division. Activated on 1 February 1966 for service in Vietnam, and sent there in December 1966-January 1967, the division served in III and IV Corps Tactical Zone. Born in Short Strand, Belfast, in 1945, Anthony emigrated to the US in 1964, when he was nineteen. He was decorated for bravery and wounded during two tours of Vietnam, but never granted American citizenship and had to return to Ireland. Anthony Conlon died in 2005 and it was only then his contribution to the United States was officially recognised. A representative of the American government attended Anthony's funeral at St Matthew's Church in Short Strand. Liam Kane, of the American Legion in Dublin, and Michael Coyne, a decorated Vietnam veteran, draped the Stars and Stripes over the coffin on behalf of the US government. Anthony's sister Maureen Knocker said she was proud of the recognition given to her brother. "The family are proud that he has now got the recognition that he deserved," she said. "I was proud to see the flag. It gave him prestige."[8]

\* \* \*

At the beginning of 1967 III MAF faced a new war, which would throw the US Marines against the best of the North Vietnamese army for almost two years. The NVA had turned I Corps into a critical theatre. American policy prohibited ground and artillery strikes into the DMZ and limited air strikes in the same area. Sensing this policy the NVA moved ground divisions and heavy artillery and rockets south of Ben Hai river (which bisected the DMZ) and set up extensive air defences to protect them. Forced by the non-incursion policy to assume a posture of static defence and reaction the 3rd Marine Division established eight bases for artillery support, ground defence, and counterattacks. The bases became synonymous with frustration, discomfort and casualties: Khe Sanh, The Rockpile, Ba Long, Ca Lu, Camp Carroll, Cam Lo, Cua Viet, and Gio Linh. From the sea to Khe Sanh four NVA divisions pressed against the Marine positions along the DMZ and the war here was more like WWI's Western Front than counterinsurgency. The strongpoints sprouted wire, mines, bunkers and craters. The countryside turned into a moonscape as the Marines and NVA pounded each other. The Marines endured and fought, but as one PFC told a reporter, the grunts could hardly wait until 1968 to vote against Lyndon Johnson.[9]

Bernard "Brian Óg" Freyne was serving with the Marines in Quang Nam province. He was an outstanding sportsman at home in Ballaghdereen, Co. Roscommon, before he emigrated to America. He was also a champion Irish step-dancer. While living in Woodside, Queens, he joined the US Marines in March 1966, following in the footsteps of his cousin Rory O'Connell, from Lahinch, Co. Clare. He was posted to Mike Company, 3rd Battalion, 1st Marine Regiment, 1st Marine Division.[10] In January 1966, the entire 1st Division, known as "The Old Breed," was earmarked for deployment to

Vietnam. With headquarters at Chu Lai its zone of operation was the southern two provinces of I Corps – Quang Tin and Quang Ngai – and later Quang Nam. During 1966 and 1967, division operations consisted primarily of offensive sweeps. Although the communists could not disrupt another series of elections in 1967, they rocketed the airbase and the logistical facilities at Da Nang, which forced the Marines to patrol the "rocket belt" that extended 5,000 to 9,000 meters around Da Nang.[11] On 10 March 1967 Brian was on patrol when they came under attack. His friend, Richard Lazarek, was hit, badly wounded in the leg. He became separated from the rest of the patrol taking cover in a gulch at the bottom of a hill. With thought only for his injured friend Brian Freyne crawled down the hill and was carrying Richard Lazarek back up to safety when a grenade, or landmine, explosion killed him. Richard Lazarek's other leg was nearly severed in the explosion and he received more severe injuries. When Lazarek regained consciousness the next day he learned that his friend had died instantly.[12] Brian Óg Freyne was twenty-one. When Brian's remains were brought back to his native home the whole town was at a standstill. Brian's cousin, Rory O'Connell, said, "Bernard, Brian Óg, as we called him, joined the Marines a year and a half after I did and was with a friend of mine from Canada when he got killed. My company commander at Camp Lejeune called me in and told me, but then I got a letter from him a week later. He was a really nice guy and took me ice-skating in Central Park and showed me around New York just after I got here." Rory O'Connell recalled how Brian had arrived in Vietnam after he was wounded in August 1966 and evacuated back to the US. Although separated, the cousins kept in touch and Brian Óg's last letter reached his cousin a week after the news that he had been killed in action.[13]

Another Irish-born US Marine, Patrick Gallagher, was also killed that month. Patrick Gallagher was born in 1945 and was the second eldest of nine children. He lived at Derrintogher, near Ballyhaunis, Co. Mayo. He emigrated to Long Island, New York, in 1962 when he was eighteen and stayed with his aunts until he got a job in real estate and started at law school. In February 1966 Patrick Gallagher returned to his home in May for three weeks. He did not tell his family he had been drafted into the US Marines and would be off to Vietnam on his return to America. He didn't want to worry them. In April 1966 he was sent to Vietnam, following in the footsteps of an Irish-American cousin through marriage, Gerald Moylan.[14] He was posted to Hotel Company, 2nd Battalion, 4th Marine Regiment, 3rd Marine Division. By the end of 1966, the two Marine divisions of III MAF were fighting two separate wars. In the north, the 3rd Marine Division fought a more or less conventional campaign while the 1st Marine Division took over the counter-guerrilla operations in the populous south. Although by December 1966, III MAF numbered nearly 70,000 troops, one Marine general summed up the year's frustrations, "… too much real estate – do not have enough troops".[15]

On 18 July 1966 Patrick Gallagher was in a defence post at Cam Lo when two grenades were thrown in. He kicked the first grenade out and jumped on the second one. As his buddies escaped, two more grenades exploded, and with seconds to spare, Gallagher had managed to fling the one he had jumped on out into the river, where it exploded on impact. His citation for the Navy Cross said: "Through his extraordinary heroism and inspiring valour in the face of almost certain death, he saved his comrades from probable injury and possible loss of life." Gallagher was awarded the Marines' highest honour, the Navy Cross, and promoted to corporal. "It is a pleasure to pin this on your breast," said Gen. Westmoreland, commander of all US forces in Vietnam, at the awards ceremony there. His bravery meant Patrick had to tell his family he was in Vietnam. He waited until the very last minute. On 28 January 1967, the day he heard about the award, he wrote home "that you were likely to be notified. So I thought I would let you know before you read it in the press." He began the letter: "I hope you won't be too mad at me for the news I got for you. When I was at home last year I had my orders for Vietnam when I went back to the US. I have been in Vietnam since last April (1966) and I will be leaving here in 60 days. Now don't get worried. Everything is going just fine here and I am enjoying it very much … I was afraid you might worry too much so I made my aunt and sister in New York promise they would not tell you I was there. I had planned on not telling you until I got back to the US." He made light of his heroism. "It was not much but they made a big thing of it," he said.

News of this local hero caused great excitement in Ireland. It was all over radio and television. RTÉ sent Seán Duignan to interview the family, and in Ballyhaunis great plans were laid for Patrick's homecoming at the end of April. However, Patrick Gallagher was shot dead when his patrol was ambushed at Dai Loc, near Da Nang, on 30 March, and it was his funeral which was covered by the media back home in Ireland and not the hero's homecoming. Eight Marines from Patrick's company were killed in that action. The US Embassy in Dublin contacted Father Rushe, parish priest in Ballyhaunis, who told Patrick's parents the bad news following that Sunday's Mass. On the day he was to arrive there they buried him instead. His cousin, Staff Sergeant Gerald Moylan, USMC, escorted Patrick Gallagher's remains back to Ballyhaunis and presented the Gallagher family with Patrick's Navy Cross, the Marine Corps' highest award for battlefield bravery. The *Western People* reported on 22 April 1967: "The funeral to the new cemetery was one of the largest ever to pass through the town of Ballyhaunis ... There was a poignant scene as Staff Sergeant Moylan laid a wreath on the grave on behalf of the US forces and then presented the American flag which draped the coffin, the Navy Cross insignia and the citation to Mrs Gallagher, mother of the deceased." At the graveside were two other mothers who had lost sons in Vietnam "Mr and Mrs Michael Nevin, Brize, Balla, Co. Mayo, whose son, Christopher (29), was killed in Vietnam in February, 1966, and Mrs Mary Freyne, Church Street, Ballaghadereen, whose son Corporal Bernard (Brian Óg) Freyne (21) was killed in Vietnam about a month ago." The Gallagher family received a letter from Bobby Kennedy, dated 10 April. He wrote: "Winston Churchill said, 'Courage is rightly esteemed as the first of all human qualities because it is the one that guarantees all others'. This courage Corporal Gallagher gave to all of us. To him and to his family are due the thanks of a humbly grateful nation." A little over a year later Bobby Kennedy, too, would be shot dead.[16]

Back in Quang Nam province Patrick Gallagher's loss was felt by his fellow Marines. Frank Erwin, who was right beside the Mayoman when he was killed, later wrote from his home in Florida. "His death was a profound loss to our entire company, as everyone looked to Patrick for courage in battle." When he visits Washington and The Wall Frank Erwin always stops at "Panel 17 East is where they all are," referring to Patrick Gallagher and the eight other Marines who perished at Dai Loc, near Da Nang, that March morning. On a more personal level Frank Erwin named one of his sons Patrick in honour of his young Irish friend who never got the chance to have a family.[17]

On 21 April USMC Pfc Maurice O'Callaghan became another fatal casualty of the war. An only son O'Callaghan lived in Iselin Linden, New Jersey. He was killed by small arms fire on 21 April in the Que Son Valley while serving with Fox Company, 2nd Battalion, 1st Marine Regiment, 1st Marine Division.[18] The Que Son Valley is located along the border of Quang Nam and Quang Tin provinces. Populous and rice-rich, the valley was viewed as one of the keys to controlling South Vietnam's five northern provinces by the communists and by early 1967 at least two regiments of the NVA 2nd Division had been infiltrated into the area. Since mid-January 1967 Fox Company, a reinforced US Marine company of the 2nd Battalion, had manned an outpost atop Nui Loc Son (Loc Son Mountain), which dominated the southern Que Son Valley. Fox Company ran daily and nightly patrols to deny the valley below to the enemy. Although the communist forces operating in the valley did not initially take much notice of the Marines, on 15 April the Fox Company commander advised the OC of the 1st Marine Regiment, that enemy units appeared to be preparing for an all-out assault on the outpost. A plan was approved for a multi-battalion assault and sweep aimed at clearing the enemy from the vicinity of the mountain.

On 21 April 1967, after observing a large enemy force move into the village of Binh Son, most of the company set out on a daylight patrol towards the village. As the Marines approached across the rice paddy's they were suddenly hit by hand grenades, intense small arms, automatic weapons and mortar fire by a dug-in NVA battalion that enjoyed a clear line of fire across level land with little cover. Fourteen Marines were killed and eighteen others wounded, while the rest were pinned down behind a low paddy dike. Here Pfc Gary Martini rescued two of his wounded comrades before he was mortally wounded. He was posthumously awarded the Medal of Honour. Air strikes and artillery were called in, but Fox Company was stuck and had difficulty moving because of the heavy enemy fire. The fierce fighting continued until other elements of the 1st Marines and the 3rd Battalion, 5th Marines, arrived and flanked the NVA from their fortifications. This allowed Fox Company to attack into Binh Son as the 3rd Battalion, 1st Marines, arrived to support them in a helicopter assault. The main body of the 3rd Battalion fought into the village to join Fox Company in engaging the enemy while other elements of the battalion landed from helicopters east of the battlefield to block the enemy's most likely escape route. By the time Fox Company was relieved they had lost twenty-six men plus an artillery forward observer.[19] Maurice O'Callaghan was one of the dead. His body was brought back to New Jersey for burial and later re-buried in his birthplace of Dublin. Declan Hughes of the Irish Veterans Memorial Project, said, "I spent a couple of months wandering around cemeteries in Dublin until I found him. He was buried in New Jersey in 1967 and re-buried in Dublin in 1976 when the family moved back to Ireland."[20]

Fox Company Corpsman Jerry Woods was wounded in February 1967 in the same village and was in the US Naval Hospital in Guam recovering when he met many of the seriously wounded survivors from his company. "It seemed that half of my company was there … Seems that a week or so after I got hit, my company (Fox) went on a company manoeuvre to where I (and seven others) had gotten it, to drive the rascals out. Why the entire company? Well, military intelligence told Fox Company there was a 'large group' of North Vietnamese regulars there that a company of Marines with 81mm mortar backup could take care of. With all due respect to the United States Marine Corps, even a reinforced rifle company of Marines ain't no match for a battalion of regular soldiers. Fox Company was basically wiped out."[21] Fox Company RTO Dennis Grall said, "I was just an observer, fortunately, as the regimental radio operator had volunteered to take my place on what was supposed to be a routine patrol. He survived, but several good friends did not. Again I had to relay the messages, calling in air strikes and getting reinforcements. The jets arrived quickly, but it was almost an hour before the helicopters could ferry in help from Da Nang. When those eighteen choppers flew into sight, my heart took a leap, and a lump stuck in my throat. They were too late to help save everyone, but they eventually turned back the enemy and allowed my friends to return to safety."[22]

* * *

By the summer of 1967, racial unrest had spread to the armed forces in Vietnam, a reflection of the social discord back in America. There was also mounting frustration with tactics and leadership in the field. Troops would fight for a hill, taking many casualties, and then after winning the battle, move on, leaving the hill to the enemy, only to have to return weeks later to retake the hill again. This kind of strategy was lost on the ordinary infantrymen, who were bearing the burdens of battle and many began periodically questioning the merits of these orders and strategies. In *Tiger Force* Michael Sallah and Mitch Weiss wrote: "In the end, the strategy had a deep impact on the troops. Psychologically, soldiers risking their lives in firefights need to see some tangible form of victory, some evidence that what they are doing is making a difference in the war. Winning control of a village or a piece of land – and securing it. The Marines raising the flag on Iwo Jima became a powerful symbol of victory during World War II. The South Pacific island was won, boosting the morale of U.S. troops and Americans at home. But in South Vietnam, there were no such scenes."[23]

Further south the pacification war continued and the Irish death toll mounted. Corporal Terence Patrick Fitzgerald was killed in action in Pleiku province while serving with the 4th Infantry Division on 26 May 1967. Terence was born in Paddington, London, to parents from Kerry and Galway, and spent his formative teenage years living on the family farm near Derrynane, Co. Kerry. He returned to London when he was sixteen, but wanted to see the world and soon left for further parts. "It wasn't long," his eldest brother John said, "before he was off, firstly as a tunneller, living on site, working all round the clock – a very tough life which no doubt stood him well in later life. Then he went off around the world, as a tin miner in Bolivia, a demolition expert in Jakarta, a gold miner and sheep herder in Australia, a postman in Alaska." In 1965 Terry ended up in San Francisco where he was drafted. He could have returned to Ireland but he answered the call, according to his brother, John, "as he wished to stay in America and gain citizenship".[24] It was the surname and the Irish accent that first caught the attention of Nicholas Ryan, a Clonmel-born draftee, as he trained for

Vietnam at Fort Lewis, Washington. The two Irishmen became fast friends. They arrived in Vietnam with the 4th Infantry Division in October 1966. "My very good friend Terence Patrick Fitzgerald was KIA in Pleiku Vietnam on the 26th of May 67," Nicholas Ryan recalled. "Terry was a great friend. We first met in Fort Lewis in 66. We were both members of the 4th Infantry Division, C Coy. We went to Vietnam by ship. Sailed from Seattle in September of 1966. Terry had a strong Kerry accent even though he was born in London of Irish parents. I am from Clonmel, Co. Tipperary, Ireland, so we often talked a lot about Ireland. Terry did spend a lot of his time in Kerry." On board ship the two friends attended Mass together every morning. Before reaching Vietnam, the Irishmen made a pact that if one was killed the other would make sure his remains got safely home.[25]

In the Spring of 1967 the 4th Infantry Division was involved in Operation Francis Marion and while combat was light in April, by May it had become vicious. In what became known as "Nine Days in May," three battalions of the 4th Infantry Division, totalling more than 2,000 men, faced off against 1,500 NVA troops.[26] An infantryman in Terry's squad recalled that 26 May 1967 was a particularly bad day. "We were working our way up a ridgeline and it made a jog to the left. Fitzgerald took a team from our squad to find the best route to the top of the hill. Soon after he left we were hit. They came back to help and were caught in a crossfire. Fitzgerald and two others from the team were killed by small arms fire. We carried them out after the battle." The citation for the posthumously awarded Silver Star, America's third-highest decoration, describes how Terry Fitzgerald's timely and decisive actions, combined with his calmness and leadership under fire, prevented a NVA unit from overrunning his outnumbered comrades. The bad news quickly reached Nick Ryan, who had broken a leg and was recuperating at the division base camp. His commanding officer could understand Ryan's pact with his friend, but pointed out that decisions regarding burial were that of the next of kin. Ryan was confident then that his friend was laid to rest in Kerry. He completed his tour of Vietnam and returned to his wife in California. It was not until a quarter of a century later when Nick Ryan discovered that his friend was buried not in Kerry, but in London, the city of his birth. He never knew that the man with the strong Kerry accent was born there and that Terry had so closely identified himself with his ancestral Kerry home that he never even mentioned it. Thirty years after he met Terry Fitzgerald, Nick Ryan met his brother, John, and paid a visit to Terry's grave in Kensal Green Cemetery, London.[27]

Limerick man John Collopy was killed in action on 15 July 1967. John lived in Dorchester, Boston, when he was drafted into the US Army on 24 April 1966 and went through basic training at Fort Riley, Kansas, with the

9th Infantry Division. He was posted to the 4th Infantry Division on 13 December 1966 and served with the weapons squad, Company A, 2nd Battalion (Mechanised Infantry), 22nd Infantry Regiment.[28] Their base camp was at Dau Tieng in the Michelin Rubber Plantation. On the night of 15 July Pfc John Collopy was in an M113 armoured personnel carrier that was struck by an RPG (shoulder-fired antitank rocket) in Long Khanh. The vehicle quickly exploded and John was badly wounded. He was evacuated to a US Army hospital in Tay Ninh and died shortly afterwards, one of three fatalities for his unit that night. A comrade, Gary Hart, wrote: "I was in the same infantry company as John Collopy, who was killed the night of July 15, 1967. John was in the weapons squad (4th squad) of our 1st Platoon of Alpha Company, 2nd Battalion (Mechanized Infantry), 22nd Inf. Regt, 3rd Brigade, 4th Inf. Div. I recorded his death in my diary as I had for the other 26 men of my Alpha Coy killed during my tour, which ended Sept. 21, 1967. John Collopy and our other KIAs will never be forgotten by his combat brothers who survived and are always in our prayers."[29] James F. Gebhardt "was in the same squad and platoon with John Collopy, who was killed on the night of 15 July 1967. John was in an M113 armoured personnel carrier that was struck by an RPG. When I got to him he was on a stretcher waiting for Medevac. John died just a few hours later in a US Army evacuation hospital in Tay Ninh. He was a good and loyal soldier who joined the US Army in order to hasten the day when he could become a United States citizen. I will always remember John Collopy."[30]

In the fall of 1967 the communists, in anticipation of the upcoming Tet Offensive began an operation timed to draw US forces away from the lowlands and at the same time score a much-needed victory. In October, the NVA 1st Division began to concentrate some of its units in central Kontum province for a thrust at the Special Forces CIDG camp at Dak To. US intelligence detected this concentration and in Operation MacArthur, moved the 4th Infantry Division and the 173rd Airborne to meet the communist threat. On November 2, a NVA defector provided the US forces with detailed information on the disposition of the communist forces and their targets, both at Dak To and the new CIDG base at Ben Het. Three US battalions were then deployed around Dak To and on 4 November, elements of the 4/503rd (173rd Airborne), fanned out for a search and destroy mission in their area of operations west of Dak To. A landing zone was cut from the jungle on Hill 823 preliminary to the establishment of a new fire support base there. Early on 6 November the Airborne ran into the NVA. Fierce firefights raged all day as the Americans consolidated their positions into strong perimeter defences and turned back all NVA assaults. Artillery and air support helped to hold the communists at bay. By the next morning, the

NVA withdrew in defeat. From 7-12 November, contact was continuous as battalions were combat assaulted behind the lead elements and into the base areas of two NVA regiments. The NVA forces were stopped and forced to withdraw. To the west of Ben Het the NVA committed their reserves to cover the withdrawal to the southwest of their two hard hit regiments. 31 Specialist 4 Edward Scully died of multiple fragmentation wounds on 13 November in Kontum. He was twenty-two. Edward Scully was serving with the 4th Battalion, 173rd Airborne. From Cork, he was living at West Point, New York. His tour of duty began on 28 July 1967 as the newly formed 4th Battalion of the 503rd arrived from Fort Campbell, Kentucky.[32]

US firepower was so overwhelming that Dak To was a disaster for the NVA, with one NVA general referring to it as "a pointless waste of men and resources". The NVA lost 1,400 men, but US troops had also taken heavy casualties, with nearly 300 dead. When the battle of Dak To ended on 22 November the NVA had been forced back across the Cambodian border. By the end of the year the US had won every battle in Vietnam and President Johnson was pressing for military victory before the elections in 1968. The Green Machine had demanded and been given 841,264 bodies by Christmas 1967, and the call in January 1968 was for another 33,000 young men. In Vietnam American forces had reached 540,000, but casualties were mounting to hundreds a week; costs had reached $33 billion a year, and dissent within the US was increasing.* The college and university campuses were in turmoil. Prior to 1967 the sons of the middle class had largely avoided the war through the escape hatch of a college deferment, but troop commitments were now so high that the draft began to take significant numbers of them as they graduated. While the NVA and VC casualties were much higher than that of the US, they did not approach even half the annual birth rate. The point was being reached where the communists were imposing unacceptable costs on the United States. An army undefeated in the field was losing the war.[33]

---

* In Ireland opposition to the Vietnam war was much more evident towards the end of 1967, with the Irish protest movement calling for an unconditional cessation of the bombing, backing the similar call by U Thant, the Secretary General of the UN. The official view of the Irish Department of External Affairs was that the only hope of halting the war was for the nations of Southeast Asia, including Vietnam, to organise themselves into a neutral area of law and limited armaments. There were criticisms of such a policy; particularly as Ireland was a member of the UN, for its failure to back U Thant's initiative and support the Pope's call for such an initiative in solving the conflict.[34]

## CHAPTER 8

# TIGERLAND

When the North Korean People's Army invaded across the 38th Parallel in Korea in June 1950 the US Army was unprepared for conflict. Units were thrown into the Korean peninsula piecemeal and quickly chewed up by the NKPA. By the time the war ended three years later – and like its follow-up conflict in Vietnam, it was never declared a war by the United States – the US Army was a highly-trained and well-equipped fighting force. So when the US Army entered another Asian conflict in Vietnam its troops were well-prepared for combat. At the time the US Armed Forces was one of the best-trained armies in the world. The Joint Chiefs of Staff had learned the mistakes of Korea and were not about to be caught out again by sending in raw untrained units against battle-hardened communist forces. At the beginning of the 1960s the US Army had 500,000 men under arms, while the United States Marine Corps had 170,000. There were divisions in Germany; 50,000 men still in South Korea, and a Marine Expeditionary Force ready to hit any trouble-spots. The Cold War army retained much of its WWII organisational character with an active force that varied between 500,000 and 1.6 million officers and men formed into between ten and twenty divisions, reinforced with corps troops and separate brigades.[1]

Basic training in the US Armed Forces was from six to twelve weeks, but by the mid-1960s the level of training took on a sharper edge with the return of Vietnam combat veterans and the reduction in training time to maintain the level of manpower required to support the war in Southeast Asia. From 1962 to 1975 an estimated 500,000 United States Marines served in Vietnam. In 1968 the Commandant of the Marine Corps, General Leonard F. Chapman stated that there were three kinds of Marines: "those in Vietnam, those who had just come back from Vietnam, and those who are getting ready to go to Vietnam." The average Marine was an eighteen or nineteen-year old male with a high school education, from an urban working class or rural small town background, and of an economic and racial mix that was more varied than American society as a whole. Motivation for enlistment was patriotism, self-advancement, personal reasons and the looming prospect of being drafted.[2] Many Irish-born emigrants choose to join the USMC for a variety of reasons. Some joined before the Vietnam conflict erupted, while others joined during the war years.

Rory O'Connell, from Lahinch, Co. Clare, joined the United States Marine Corps in July 1964, six months after arriving in America. He is a proud man – proud of his service in the US Marines and proud of his service in Vietnam. Like all young Marines, Rory spent some "time in hell" – Parris Island. "Parris Island was a hellish place. It was nothing to get an ass-whipping there," he said. "Parris Island was just like it was portrayed in the movie *Full Metal Jacket*, only a lot longer. That movie is the most accurate you'll ever see. *Full Metal Jacket* is only one-and-a-half hours long and we did that for three months. Three months of hell. All good, though, because they were just getting us ready for a lot worse to come, which paid off in the end. When they got done with us no one could ever hurt us again."[3]

Like other historical élite forces the US Marines prided themselves on the severe training that took individuals from diverse backgrounds and circumstances and gave them a sense of common identity.[4] Basic training for US Marines is widely recognised as the most demanding recruit training in the world and Parris Island is renowned as one of the toughest training grounds on earth. Marine Corps Recruit Depot Parris Island is near Beaufort, South Carolina. Recruits living east of the Mississippi river had to report there to receive their initial thirteen weeks training. During training, recruits learn everything from personal hygiene and cleanliness, to Marine Corps history. Physical fitness is emphasised during training, and recruits must meet a minimum standard of fitness to graduate. Stress is constantly applied by drill instructors (DI) to teach recruits how to work under pressure. This may be pivotal later on in surviving combat situations. Recruits are yelled at constantly, and forced to do simple tasks over and over again, which is supposed to instil teamwork and leadership traits. Only by passing the rigours of boot camp can one earn the title "United States Marine." Officers endured their own version of this training at Quantico, Virginia.[5]

"Parris Island is an island surrounded by a swamp with one long bridge," Rory O'Connell said, "with one way on and one way off, so all you had to do was what you were told to, to get off there. My Drill Instructor (DI) Robert Starbuck was killed in Nam after I got back and died very bravely receiving the Silver Star for bravery. (He recommended me for outstanding man of the platoon but someone else got it.) We had seventy-five men in our platoon. You couldn't leave your bunk at night to even use the toilet because one person was assigned as fire watch and would report you if you got out of bed. So when reveille came before dawn in the morning with a

DI screaming and banging trash cans you would hear 'Port Side, (meaning left side) make a head call' (meaning use the toilet) and you would see thirty-seven men rush to use the toilet with sixty seconds to use it and get back to the end of their bunks before the other side was called. Then it was out the door for a three-mile run and an obstacle course before breakfast. We even slept at attention.

"In the Marines we spent countless hours training for all kinds of combat and spent two or three days a week in the field in all kinds of weather. I've been wading up to my neck in water, crossing rivers in January and February, and freezing to death, only to get back to camp to no fires. So you just got into your wet sleeping bag and shivered all night. The same thing in snow so by the time we went anywhere we were well prepared for the worst conditions. In 1965 they took 300 of us out to a forest and dropped us off for three weeks to cut trails and hide food and ammo in the woods. They had Vietnamese villages where we went into on patrols and had to determine who the good guys were and who the VC were. After the three weeks they gave us a weekend pass, so five of us went to New York to the World Fair with our beards and USMC sweat shirts. When we got back in the forest they sent 5,000 Marines out to capture us. It was our job to harass them and attack them every chance we got so we had a ball. There were only about twenty of us that weren't captured after the week was up. Some of my friends that were with me there had already seen combat in the Dominican Republic. Our company spent three months on Guantanamo Bay in Cuba on guard duty on the fence while they were fighting. Then I went to Camp Pendleton in California for accelerated training, which consisted of running all day, even while you were standing in the chow line. They have a lot of big hills there so we were really fit before we got to Nam." Rory O'Connell was shipped to Vietnam in November 1965 to begin his thirteen-month tour of duty.[6]

Mike Flood, from Athy, Co. Kildare, remembered his trip to Parris Island vividly. He was only married nine months when he went into the Marines. "I got up at four o'clock, kissed Anne goodbye and got the subway to boot camp. Anne came down three months later. I knew the choices when I signed up for the Selective Services Act. The choices were: go back to Ireland, and I did not want to do that, there was nothing there for me; I could go to Canada; or join the Service, which was really the only option. Training was tough in Parris Island. I remember once on the rifle range my friend, Jim Kirk, asking a stupid question. The DI told us all to turn around and called Jim up to him. We heard a bit of a scuffle. The DI told us to turn around again, and Jim rejoined us – minus his front tooth. In boot camp you never ask a dumb question and you never tell the DI where you're from. I was from the Bronx, and so was my friend. These guys were all Southerners and they didn't like New Yorkers."[7]

It was essential that boot camp be physically and emotionally stressful. Yet certain abuses were unnecessary and counterproductive. Up until the late 1950s Parris Island was notorious for abuse and mistreatment. However, after six recruits drowned while been subject to a disciplinary march through Ribbon Creek marsh in 1956 more officer supervision of the DIs was instigated. It was forbidden to strike recruits and even use profanity. While these new measures were designed to prevent abuse of recruits, nevertheless the tough training and occasional mistreatments continued. With the expansion of the Marine Corps and the added intake of more recruits and draftees the training system would be more strained and the likelihood of abuse more probable.[8] However, the tough training in the USMC paid off. By 1965, the year the first Marine ground forces landed in Vietnam, the Marine Corps was in "superb shape."[9] Historian Allan Millett contends that in 1965 the US Marine Corps was more capable of performing its missions than at any other peacetime juncture in the history of the United States.[10]

Basic training in the US Army was tough, too. John Barrett was drafted in May 1965. He left the seaside village of Lahinch, Co. Clare, when he was seventeen. "We were born for export. We had a few tourists six weeks in the summer, other than that there was nothing else." John left Lahinch on 25 May 1962 to live with an aunt in Washington Heights, in New York City "a very Irish and Jewish neighbourhood. I couldn't wait to get there." John got a job in a bank in Manhattan ten days after arriving in the US. "I got on very well, just grew into it. But, I got very homesick – I was overwhelmed by it all. I couldn't wait to go home." John returned to Lahinch, but after a few days realised his life was back in America and returned. Three years to the day he arrived in America John Barrett was drafted into the US Army. He reported to the Armed Forces Physical Examining Station at 39 Whitehall Street, in Lower Manhattan. "I decided then and there to go and get it over with. I didn't have much fear about it. By now I was grown into the American way of life. Communism was threatening the world and we were told it was our patriotic duty. So on 29 June 1965 I reported to Whitehall Street and was taken to Fort Dix. The first thing was they cut off every rib of my hair. Basic training was demoralising. We were just scum to the drill sergeants. In the mornings they would come in and throw your bed up in the air. We had to drop and do fifty push-ups; crawl under barbed wire. All the time they were screaming at you. I found this very difficult, to be treated like a two-year-old. It was all designed to break you and they do."

After John Barrett was finished basic training he was chosen for specialist training in chemical warfare at Fort McClellan, Alabama. "It was an eight-week course. It was tough, but not as tough as basic training. Afterwards someone saw my record of working in a bank and I got a nine to five office job. I enjoyed that, but then orders came through of my transfer. I thought I'd be sent to Germany, as a lot of guys were going there, but I was going to Vietnam." John Barrett served an eleven-month tour in Vietnam with the 1st Infantry Division.[11]

Martin Hennigar, from Limerick, had much the same experience. "I reported to 39 Whitehall Street in New York at 7.30 am for induction to the US Army on 5th of August 1959. After a day of medical, physical, written and oral tests, I along with approximately 200 others were on our way by bus that evening at 10.30 pm to Fort Dix, New Jersey. After a week of more processing and work detail, I was assigned to the 2nd infantry Division in Fort Benning, Georgia, for basic training. It was probably one of the roughest places for training. It's as hot as hell in August, too. Ranger school is there, airborne school, too. It was the first time the thought 'What the hell am I doing here. I should have stayed home in Ireland,' came into my head. You would be in bed late, up at four, fallout for five, runs for miles, pull-ups. The pull-up bar was outside the mess hall and you had to do pull-ups before going in. You'd be pretty fit when you finish. You feel you accomplished something. You feel a different person. Anyone who went through had the same experience. When we arrived the drill sergeant greeted us saying: 'Welcome, ladies. I want you to think of me as your mother and your commanding officer as your father. We are not married, so guess what that makes all of you!' They break you down in basic training. They take your dignity away, and then build it back up. They get rid of a lot of guys, because some are not suitable. After the first ten days in Fort Dix they have ways of weeding out the guys who are not suitable. All of sudden they are not in the barracks anymore. They wouldn't announce it – they would be just gone. On a run in the forest around Fort Benning, we had a saying, 'Take ten, expect five, and get three.' You just had your pack off for a break and then: 'Back on your feet!' If you threw a cigarette butt on the ground at Fort Benning and were caught, you would have to dig a foxhole to bury it, not during the day, but at night, when all your work was done. We also had a saying – if you have any doubts about an officer, about saluting – 'If it moves salute it, if it don't paint it!' They love saluting in the army and they love painting, too. I'll tell you, they couldn't have made it much tougher for us in Fort Benning.

"On completion of basic training I was then assigned for Engineer Training at the US Army Engineer Training Center in Fort Leonard Wood, Missouri. We had been told that the top graduates of our course would have a choice of assignments. I ended up the Honour Graduate. I requested to be assigned to Germany, but unfortunately ended up in Korea. I complained, but was told that assignments were where my MOS (Military Occupation Specialist) was most needed. I completed a thirteen-month tour in Korea and on returning to the US, I was stationed in a missile site in Fort Tilden, New York. I, and three others, decided to re-enlist for Germany. I completed a three-year tour there. On returning to the US, I was again assigned to Fort Leonard Wood, Missouri, where the process of getting the first engineer battalion to go to Vietnam was already proceeding. Of course this was a military secret. We left for Vietnam in August 1965." Martin Hennigar served two tours in Vietnam. No doubt his professionalism and quality of training were contributing factors in Martin not getting fatally injured and surviving his tours of duty.[12]

Pat Landers, from Lackaroe, Youghal, Co. Cork, joined the Australian Army in 1966, signing on for a three-year term. He served a year in Vietnam as an infantryman. "Taking a stroll down George Street, in Sydney, one day I stopped at the Army recruiting office to look at the photos in the window. Being a lover of guns since I was a kid, the photos of soldiers carrying guns and jumping out of APCs, really appealed to me. I entered the recruiting office to be greeted by the most polite officer I have ever met. He gave me the highlights of army life and what it was like to be a soldier. I believed every word and signed on for three years. I had already registered for national service, but signed anyway. I was sent to a camp in Sydney to wait for more recruits to arrive. It was like a holiday camp there. We were then sent to Wagga Wagga for our training, which would take three months. This was no holiday camp, I can assure you.

"On our arrival we were issued with uniforms and rifles. We were then told what was expected of us – totally different than what I was told at the recruiting office in Sydney! I immediately got the nickname Irish and for the next three months they gave us hell – spit and polish; twenty-mile marches and endless hours on the parade ground. We got through our three months and marched out of Wagga Wagga. Before we left we were sent to the corps of our choice. My choice was infantry. We were then transported to Ingleburns (School of Infantry) in New South Wales, about thirty miles from Sydney. Our training there was for another three months. We were trained as infantry soldiers. It was hard, but we enjoyed being trained to fight and survive as a front line soldier, and believe me the training we got there saved our lives. We survived our three months and then faced three weeks in Canungra, southern Queensland, to be trained in the jungle. It was very like the jungles of Vietnam. The only thing missing in Canungra were the enemy. Some American troops also trained there before going to Vietnam. After Canungra we were ready for action in Vietnam. We lost quite a few men killed and wounded, but our training saved a lot of lives. After we finished training at Canungra we got three weeks leave and then off to Vietnam for our twelve months tour of duty. I survived my tour to return and march through the City of Adelaide with the 3rd Battalion."[13]

Prior to departure to Vietnam Australian units spent at least twelve months on intensive training regimes. Constant exercises held under battle conditions were capped off by a four-week special training programme at the Jungle Training Centre (JTC), Canungra, in southern Queensland. Canungra had become one of the world's most respected jungle training establishments since it reactivation in 1955 (it was closed at the end of WWII) to prepare troops for service in Malaya. These periods of intensive activity meant members of a battalion trained together as a fighting unit, learning their strengths and weaknesses. By the time they departed for Vietnam each battalion formed a cohesive jungle-fighting unit. The Australian practice was to rotate whole battalions in and out of Vietnam, while the individual men in each battalion remained together.[14]

The American system was quite different. Originally, whole divisions and units went to Vietnam together, but as the war dragged on, in practice, units remained in combat situations for the duration of the conflict, while individual soldiers were rotated in and out for a twelve month (Army) or thirteen month (Marine) tour of duty. This system, known as the Pipeline, filled up depleted units with replacements – volunteers and draftees – from across the United States, which left little sense of identity and loyalty to fellow soldiers who they did not know and had no geographical ties with. The level and length of training saved many soldiers lives in combat in Vietnam, but as the war progressed the period of training was reduced and this would contribute greatly to the new guy in the unit getting killed, or wounded, before anyone even learned his name.

## CHAPTER 9

# CHOPPERS AND LZs

The enduring image of the Vietnam war was the helicopter. Hundreds of Irishmen went into battle courtesy of the helicopter, but only one, John O'Sullivan, actually flew helicopters during the war. Tralee-born John O'Sullivan arrived in Vietnam in June 1968 as John Barnicle, an Irish-American from Chicago, was leaving. Little did John O'Sullivan know that he would meet and work with John Barnicle in Ireland many years later. John Barnicle arrived as a helicopter pilot in the Central Highlands in the summer of 1967, when the war in South Vietnam had a taken a turn for the worst for the Americans. Casualties for the first half of the year rivalled that for all of 1966. In the Central Highlands it was no secret the US was losing ground. Thousands of NVA were entrenched in miles of underground tunnels and the vast mountainous region along the Laotian border was under enemy control.[1] John Barnicle grew up on Chicago's South Side. He came from a traditional Irish-American background. Both his paternal and maternal grandparents were from Ireland — Mayo, Galway and Cork — and John grew up with a sense of his Irishness which is no longer seen in a city which once had a huge Irish population. "My grandparents came from Connemara and would speak Irish when they did not want us to know what they were talking about," he recalled. John wanted to fly and joined the military to be a pilot. "I had a choice of flying jets in the Marines, which would take six years, or the army, which took four years to fly helicopters." After basic training John was sent for nine months to primary helicopter training at Fort Wolters, Texas.[2] Student pilots then went on to advanced flight training at Fort Rucker, Alabama, and later to Fort Stewart, Georgia. All flight trainees were known as "warrant-officer candidates." A warrant officer is appointed, not commissioned, and specialises in a particular skill, like electronic-technician warrants, supply warrants, and warrant-officer pilots. The warrant ranks — WO-1, CW-2, CW-3, and CW-4 — correspond to second lieutenant, first lieutenant, captain, and major, and warrant officers receive the same privileges and nearly the same pay as commissioned officers.[3]

John Barnicle had a brother in the army who was sent to Korea on occupation duties as the military would not send two brothers to the same combat zone at the same time. (This came about during WWII when the five Irish-American Sullivan brothers were lost at sea when their destroyer was sunk off Guadalacanal. Since then the US military has refused to let brothers serve together.) John Barnicle arrived in Vietnam on 14 June 1967, landing at Cam Rahn Bay. "I was twenty-two, but I left Seattle, Washington, on 12 June and my birthday was on 13 June. I flew for ten hours and because I passed the international dateline, landed on 14 June, thereby I missed my birthday. So the year in Vietnam didn't matter." He then went on to Nha Trang and Qui Nhon "all in two days," John said. "I liked the Vietnamese people. They very simple, but tough. The VC were the best guerrilla force in the world." John never met any Irishmen in Vietnam, but met plenty of Irish-Americans. "The military did not encourage ethnicity. You knew the men in your unit, but you did not hang around together because you were Irish, Italian, black, or whatever. You were just all there together."[4]

John Barnicle was posted to 129th Assault Helicopter Company, flying out of Lane Army Airfield, outside Qui Nhon. He flew a Bell HU-1 Iroquois, known as the Huey, operating in a triangle from Chu Lai on the east coast to Pleiku, in the Central Highlands, and down to Nha Trang on the coast. Because the Huey had no armament except the machine guns the crew chief and gunner used, they were called slicks. Barnicle's job was to carry troops into the landing zones. In a typical air assault mission, Huey helicopters inserted infantry deep in enemy territory while Huey gunships, equipped with machine guns, rockets, and grenade launchers, often escorted the transports. Within minutes, helicopters could insert entire battalions into the heart of enemy territory. The Huey became a symbol of US combat forces in Southeast Asia and at its peak in March 1970, the US military operated more than 3,900 helicopters in Vietnam, two thirds of them Hueys. Their impact was profound, not only in the new tactics and strategies of airmobile operations, but on the survival rate of battlefield casualties. US military patients made up 390,000 of the total number of people transported by medevac helicopters in Southeast Asia, and almost a third of this total, 120,000, were combat casualties. The Huey airlifted ninety percent of these casualties directly to medical facilities. Helicopter pilots, lurps and tunnel rats were the only US servicemen who brushed with mortal danger so consistently. Helicopter crewmen were sitting targets for ground fire as they flew in and out of landing zones delivering men and equipment.[5] "We were in the middle of the action all the time," John recalled. "Nothing to hide behind, only a sandbag under your ass."[6] Casualties for pilots and crew members were high. Of the 26,541 helicopter pilots who flew in Vietnam 2,195 were killed in action, or died of wounds, while a further 2,717 crew members were also killed.[7] The aviation units were the sole combat element of the US Army that did not come apart under the stress of the war in Vietnam. Despite the high casualties the Army airmen never cracked. According to Neil Sheehan in *A Bright Shining Lie*: "Whether it was the oneness of man and acrobatic flying machine, whether it was the equally shared risk of officer pilot and enlisted crew member, whatever the reason, the men of the helicopters kept their discipline and their spirit. As the French parachutists became the paladins of that earlier war, so the U.S. Army aviators became the dark knights of this one."[8]

"I never lost a crew member," John said. "I was shot down once. I went down in some trees, and was picked up by another helicopter ... had a few engine failures, a few mishaps, but never a scratch on any crewman." As a Huey pilot John flew one mission per day. He also had a two-week stint in a Huey gunship. "It was great fun to fly, but you were on twenty-four hour duty." John preferred the lax privileges of a Huey slick pilot. "They made the rank of warrant officer for pilots. It was the best rank in the military. You had all the officers' privileges. Do your mission come back to base have a few beers in the officers mess and just conk out." His hardest time was a month of night flying. "Pitch black, no lights, any mishaps – good luck. At least in the day you can see the ground."[9]

In September 1967 John was assigned to the 9th Aviation Battalion, 9th Infantry Division, for the remaining eight months of his tour flying in the Mekong Delta area from Camp Bearcat. Slightly southeast of Saigon Camp Bearcat was like a great military city, the home of the 9th Infantry Division. "I was in two big actions, the Tet Offensive and the Cholon suburb battle. During Tet I once flew for seventeen hours without shutting the engine off. Bringing in ammunition and taking out dead and wounded. After Tet the VC was so defeated, if the political will was there, we could have won the war. While it was such a political victory it was a military disaster. The VC was so demoralised you could have took a taxi all the way to Hanoi."[10] Militarily, the Tet Offensive had been a tactical disaster for the communist forces. By the end of March, they had achieved none of their objectives. More than 40,000 VC and NVA troops died in the process, as opposed to just under 4,000 American and 5,000 ARVN deaths. By attacking everywhere at once, Giap had superior strength nowhere. He achieved great surprise, but he was unable to exploit it. Giap had been wrong in two key assumptions. The people of the South did not rally to the communist cause. The General Uprising never took place. Nor did the ARVN collapse. It may have buckled in a few areas, but by and large it fought, and fought amazingly well. The single biggest loser in the Tet Offensive was the Viet Cong. The guerrillas of the South led the main attacks and they suffered the heaviest casualties. The guerrilla infrastructure, so carefully developed over many years, had been destroyed with a single throw of the dice. From that point on, the war was entirely run by the North. The VC were never again a significant force on the battlefield.[11]

"Cholon was a Chinese suburb of Saigon and the VC infiltrated from below. That was a slaughter."[12] The second battle for Saigon began on 5 May with a "mini Tet Offensive" against 119 cities, towns and barracks. Fighting spread to Cholon – Saigon's densely populated Chinese district – Tan Son Nhut airbase and Phu Tho race track. The key to Cholon was the Phu Tho Racetrack. It was at the hub of most of the key streets in the area and, by holding it the VC could deny its use as a landing zone. The battle climaxed on 12 May with American jets dropping napalm and high explosives on VC positions. Two weeks later the third battle for Saigon began, with more heavy fighting in the Cholon suburb.[13]

Originally arriving in Vietnam John Barnicle bought a hand held film camera and was able to do some amateur filming. "For the first three months I was a co-pilot so my hands were free …" After transfer down south to the Mekong Delta John "flew into a Special Forces camp near the Cambodian border two days after the VC had tried to overrun it. They had overrun the outer perimeter. There were bodies everywhere. There were these red ants and they cleaned the bodies to the bone. You could see all these white bones coming in. Bodies everywhere, hanging on the wire, lying in holes. There were Cambodian mercenaries there, too. All told they killed about 500 VC. It was a slaughterhouse."[14] Tra Cu was a Green Beret "A" Team Base located on the Vam Co Dong river west of Cu Chi near the Parrot's Beak of Cambodia and Vietnam. It was occupied by Green Berets, South Vietnamese Special Forces and Cambodian mercenaries. It was called two names, "Hell on Earth," or the "The Asshole of the World." Casualties ran above one-hundred per cent including killed and wounded.[15] But John Barnicle's days in Southeast Asia were numbered. He left Vietnam on 9 June 1968, after flying "a lot of hours – 1,187 combat hours in my tour". John left the army in January 1970.[16]

Irish-born helicopter pilots in Vietnam were few and far between. Of the hundreds of Irishmen who served with the American armed forces in Southeast Asia, only one, John O'Sullivan, flew choppers in Vietnam. John O'Sullivan, from Tralee, Co. Kerry, served with the 174th Helicopter Assault Company. (Another Irishman, Mick Keneally, from Cork, served as a door gunner in Vietnam. On his return to the US he went back to flight school and qualified as a pilot.)[17] John O'Sullivan joined the 174th Assault

Helicopter Company as a pilot in June 1968. The 174th Assault Helicopter Company (AHC) was formed at Fort Benning, Georgia, in 1965, and deployed to Vietnam the following year. In 1968 the 174th was based in Duc Pho in Quang Ngai Province, in the southern I Corps theatre.[18] John O'Sullivan flew Dolphins (lift ships) for his first eight months and Sharks (gunships) for most of the rest of his extended tour. (Flying Tiger founder, Claire Chennault, gave his blessing to the 174th to paint the famous WWII Flying Tiger shark's teeth emblem on the front of their choppers.)

John O'Sullivan grew up in Tralee, Co. Kerry and emigrated with the rest of his family to New York in 1960 when he was sixteen. After graduating from high school in Brooklyn John went to work as a proof-reader in a company on Wall Street and then in October 1962 enlisted in the US Army. "You could wait to be conscripted and serve for two years or join up for three years, but have a choice where you wanted to go," John said. He cited a maternal grandfather, who was in the Munster Fusiliers during WWI and spent a number of years as a POW, as a big influence on his life. (John also had an uncle in the RAF and another uncle as an officer in the IRA.) He went to jump school and won his parachutist's wings with the 101st Airborne Division at Fort Campbell, Kentucky. He served three years in Germany – two-and-half years with the Berlin Brigade and another six months with the 8th Infantry Division. John "left as a sergeant on orders for Vietnam, but wasn't allowed to go as I wasn't an American citizen". He then applied for flight school in Fort Rucker, Alabama, and graduated nine months later in June 1968 as a helicopter pilot and Warrant Officer. "I was given security clearance to go to Vietnam as I was still not an American citizen." Within a month of graduating John was assigned to the 174th Helicopter Assault Company in South Vietnam. On O'Sullivan's first day in Vietnam his helicopter was shot down. Undeterred, John went off and got another chopper and resumed his mission.[19]

From 1 August to 31 October the 174th were involved in the defence of Ha Than and Task Force Galloway. Operation Vernon Lake II (1 November-31 December) followed in which John O'Sullivan won three of his eventual sixty-one awards. He was awarded the Distinguished Flying Cross for heroism on 19 November and another DFC and a Purple Heart on 29 December. The concept for Operation Vernon Lake II was to combat assault two infantry battalions into the Da Vach mountains, establish two fire support bases from which extensive recon in force and multiple combat assault operations could be conducted in the surrounding mountains and valleys to interdict the movement of the 3rd NVA Division and destroy their base camps. The 14th Combat Aviation Battalion provided helicopters for the operation with lift helicopters for air assault and command, and control helicopters for each battalion throughout the operation. On 3 November, while flying a command and control mission, John O'Sullivan spotted concrete reinforced bunkers, freshly dug trenches, and barbed wire, all part of an NVA base camp, which the 174th soon destroyed. In the following weeks, the 174th aided ground units in locating, re-conning, and destroying more than eighty enemy base camps, training sites, and headquarters. On 19 November, while re-conning an area where a USMC F-4 had been shot down and the pilots were still missing, Dolphin 428 came under enemy fire. John O'Sullivan was the aircraft commander. The ship took more than fifteen hits. Although critically wounded, the crew chief, Wayne Tice, returned fire until the aircraft was out of the area. Tice was medevaced to Chu Lai, but later died of wounds.[20]

On 1 December the 174th, along with the rest of the 14th Combat Aviation Battalion, was reassigned from the 1st Aviation Brigade and became part of the Americal Division. On 29 December John O'Sullivan's helicopter was badly damaged by enemy fire, and although he was wounded, he still managed to fly his chopper to a secure area. Only after he was assured all his passengers were safe did O'Sullivan reveal that he was wounded. John O'Sullivan's close calls, bravery, and "luck of the Irish" soon became legendary, as this newspaper reported: "For a Huey helicopter pilot named O'Sullivan, the 'luck of the Irish' is a reality, especially when he is flying the unfriendly skies of Vietnam ... O'Sullivan's 'luck' began to show itself on his first day in Vietnam when his helicopter received hostile fire west of LZ Liz and crashed. 'We were hit with small arms fire and grenade frags,' he said. 'When we tried to fly out of the area we lost power and went down.' O'Sullivan has been recommended on three different occasions for the Distinguished Flying Cross and once for the Soldier's Medal, proving his willingness to take necessary risks. St. Patrick would have been proud." Another newspaper report stated: "Weaving his helicopter through dense fog and heavy fire, a Brooklyn pilot demonstrated the luck of the Irish once again. WO1 John O'Sullivan was serving as pilot of the command and control helicopter of the 4th Bn., 21st Inf., 11th Inf. Bde. when the unit came under attack. As the battle progressed, one soldier was felled by an extreme case of battle fatigue, and a dustoff was called. Because of the inclement weather and hostile fire the three attempts to evacuate the casualty by chopper were unsuccessful. Disregarding all danger, O'Sullivan volunteered to attempt the evacuation. With a thorough knowledge of the area and skilful manoeuvring of his craft he dropped onto a hastily prepared landing zone and picked up the man. For his action O'Sullivan, assigned to the 174th Avn. Co., 14th CAB, received the Distinguished Flying Cross."[21]

As John O'Sullivan's first tour came to a close he re-extended to stay with his company for another year. (Almost all career aviators served two tours in Vietnam.) "I was single at the time," he told the Trenton *Evening Times,* "and I thought that if I stayed on, that would make one less married man, perhaps, who had to come over."[22] He left Vietnam in May 1969 and as one newspaper reported: "Before departing Vietnam for a 30-day state-side leave, WO1 John O'Sullivan, Brooklyn, New York, received 21 going away presents: the Silver Star Medal, Distinguished Flying Cross first, and Second Oak Leaf Clusters, Bronze Star Medal, Air Medal first through fif-teenth Oak Leaf Clusters, and the Purple Heart first and second Oak Leaf Clusters … The 'luck of the Irish' is no idle phrase to Mr. O'Sullivan. He was born in Ireland and is still a citizen of that legendary land. His 'Irish luck' was with him on January 30th. On that day Warrant Officer O'Sullivan was serving as aircraft commander of the 3rd Battalion, 1st Infantry, 11th LIB command and control helicopter." In this action John was again wounded and his chopper severely damaged. It took him five attempts to rescue several stranded men. Undeterred by his wounds John made two further passes over the enemy position to mark it for the gunships before flying his crippled helicopter to nearby Quang Ngai airfield.[23]

On his return to Vietnam John was assigned to Headquarters Company, but soon talked his way back to the sharks of 174th, saying, "I can't wait to get back and start flying again."[24] He flew gunships for the remainder of his time in Vietnam. The following is an edited version of an article titled 'The Sharks use modern equipment in grand old style,' by SP4 Peter R. Sorenson, 11th Inf Bde, FSB Bronco.

"Five miles east of Quang Ngai City, two Shark heavy fire teams alter-nated flying security for a combat assault of the 4th ARVN Regiment. The waves of men are ferried into the LZs by a dozen Dolphin utility ships. Two gunships patiently covered the sky train of utility ships. The two gunship pilots were in constant communication. 'The smoke-ship did alright this time; right between the treeline and LZ,' commented Captain Stephen Riddle. 'Darn wind makes it hard not to smoke the flight. That lead ship is too low,' replied Lieutenant John O'Sullivan. 'She'll get there before us if she doesn't pull up.' For three hours the gunship made the flight back and forth between staging areas and landing zones. The teams alternate stops at Quang Ngai City for fuel, re-armament and a short C-ration picnic. Returning to station, the gunships cruised the site of the last combat assault of the day. They gained altitude to over-see the put-down of utility ships and ARVN infantry. The Air Mission Control ships came on the horn: 'CA com-plete, LZ hot. I repeat hot.' 'Let's go get them,' called Capt. Riddle as he banked and descended to the left. 'I've got four or five on the run in uni-forms with weapons,' announced Lt O'Sullivan as he dove into a hedgerow saddle. Rockets, mini-guns and M-60 machine guns poured fire into the area. O'Sullivan pulled out to the sound of exploding rockets and the sight of black bellowing smoke. 'We've covered a couple with mini-gun. We've taken hits.' Riddle followed in by descending quickly with the down-ward motion of a Ferris wheel. An NVA frantically ran for a hedgerow and dived into it. The Shark abruptly swung back and forth as the ship was lined up for a rocket run. Riddle fired two rockets as the door gunners opened up with a steady stream of M-60 fire for flank security at the critical moment. The rockets hit right on target. Two more sets of two rockets are sent on their way before the Shark jerked upward out of its dive. It circled to the right to continue the deadly two Shark pinwheel. Riddle came on the intercom, 'Where did we take hits?' They took two or three rounds in the left rocket pod, with one tube damaged. During the next half hour, the gunships alternated angles of attack, destroyed a bunker and caused a secondary explosion and laid suppressive fire for the advancing ground troops. The two gunships reconned a large area surrounding the scene of contact. Wearily heading home above Highway 1, the two ships bantered back and forth about the day's action. 'We took a couple of rounds in the chin bubble. Guess who got his third Purple Heart?' said O'Sullivan. 'You?' came back the answer from Riddle. 'Yea, took a little shrapnel in the leg.' In a few minutes the city like lights of the perimeter of Fire Support Base Bronco were on the horizon and the day's mission was over."[25]

On 1 April 1970 John O'Sullivan gained his highest award, the Distinguished Service Cross, second only to the Medal of Honour, for extraordinary heroism. His citation said: "Second Lieutenant O'Sullivan distinguished himself while serving as fire team leader of a helicopter gunship team flying in support of allied operations near Quang Ngai. Although under a continuous hail of enemy automatic weapons fire, Lieutenant O'Sullivan led an aggressive attack on three companies of enemy soldiers that were entrenched in a Vietnamese village. Repeatedly exposing his aircraft to the intense enemy automatic weapons fire, he eliminated four enemy soldiers and destroyed two enemy bunkers.

His aircraft was then shot down by intense enemy fire as he descended to a low altitude to provide cover fire for another downed friendly helicopter. After surveying the damage to his downed ship, Lieutenant O'Sullivan returned to the cockpit and flew the crippled craft to a nearby airstrip. He then obtained another gunship and returned to the area to take command of the fire team. While covering the recovery of the downed helicopter, he eliminated five more of the enemy. Responding to an urgent appeal for assistance from another allied unit, he again braved intense fire as he assaulted three enemy machine gun positions. During this encounter, his gunship was damaged by enemy fire. Undaunted, he continued his aggressive assault, destroyed the enemy machine gun positions, and completely routed the enemy force."[26]

The following month the 174th broke up a regimental size NVA attack on Nghia Hanh, a CIDG camp. In heavy ground fighting the NVA were forced to assume a defensive stance. NVA elements attempted to flee south to their sanctuary in Song Ve River Valley, but were destroyed by the Sharks of the 174th and ARVN infantrymen delivered by the Dolphins. John O'Sullivan described the action: "The gunship pilots are familiar with the western and eastern mountain chains which rise up from the Song Ve. A 'Shark' gunship passed over the western ridge and noticed that it wasn't as 'bald' or as open as usual. From the base at the southern side – to the top – to the base at the northern side was a row of bushes that weren't there normally. A second pass of the area revealed an AK-47 attached to one of the limbs. What the pilot identified was a camouflaged, 800 yard, relief column of enemy soldiers headed for Nghia Hanh." The Sharks were turned loose on the trail. Thirty-eight, of the total 135 NVA dead, were credited to the 174th. A grim postscript to the action occurred a day and a half later when an American force in the Song Ve River Valley detained an NVA who identified himself as a regimental cook. He reported that he was ordered to wait in the valley for the element's return from the Nghia Hanh mission. Up until his capture none had returned.[27]

In August 1970 John O'Sullivan left Vietnam for the US. "I would have stayed longer," he said, "only they wouldn't let me." He was going home to be presented with the Army Aviator of the Year award. Sponsored by the Sikorsky Aircraft Division, the Army Aviator Award was for an airman who made an outstanding individual contribution to Army Aviation during the previous calendar year. "There were 25,000 pilots at the time; 10,000 helicopter pilots," John said. "Each unit selected one guy and put him forward. That's why I went back to the US. I wouldn't have went home only for it. I preferred to be doing something useful, like flying."[28] Before he finally got back to the States John O'Sullivan had won the Distinguished Service Cross, six Distinguished Flying Crosses, three Silver Stars, three Bronze Stars for valour, five Purple Hearts for wounds, the Army Commendation Medal for valour, and forty-two Air Medals. Those awards made him one of the most decorated men to serve in the Vietnam War. He had piled up 1,700 combat hours on 1,900 combat missions, during which he was shot out of the air nineteen times. John figured each helicopter in which he was downed cost the US government $500,000 – or close to $10 million in total. "I just hope," he said with a grin, "They don't make me pay it all back."[29]

In October 1970 General Bruce Palmer, Jr, Army Vice Chief of Staff, presented John O'Sullivan with the "Army Aviator of the Year" award during ceremonies held at the Shoreham Hotel, Washington, DC. His citation said: "A truly professional soldier, Lieutenant O'Sullivan has served honourably and courageously through the enlisted and warrant officer ranks to a battlefield commission. He has demonstrated great bravery and heroic distinction in the Republic of Vietnam on numerous occasions while serving as Fire Team Leader of an Armed Helicopter Gunship Team of the 174th Aviation Company, Americal Division." Gen. Palmer in congratulating John said: "This man served two straight years in Vietnam: he extended twice to stay with his beloved gunships. He was wounded five times — he has five Purple Hearts. He is soon to receive the Distinguished Service Cross, the second highest award this country gives for heroism, second only to the Medal of Honour. The fight in which he earned that DSC went on for eight hours, and he told me a little about it. For example, the first time he was shot down, he actually had to make an emergency landing to get rid of his rockets which were burning. The automatic jettison mechanism wouldn't work and he had to take them off manually, and all of this under fire. He made numerous trips back with his second gunship and while that was also shot up pretty badly, he managed to make it back to his base. I think you know that men, not machines, are the final arbiters of combat. This young man typifies the Army Aviator that we find throughout the United States."[30]

In December John married Carlow-born Siobhán Moore, whom he met in New York. The following February, he finally became a US citizen. John was one of the first aviators qualified to fly the UH-60A Blackhawk Helicopter and subsequently was certified as an instructor pilot for the machine. He also served as a military test pilot with the Avionics Research and Development Activity. John O'Sullivan retired with the rank of major after twenty years service with the US Army. He returned to Ireland in 1989 and is a senior partner with Premier Helicopters.[31]

## CHAPTER 10

# TOUR OF DUTY

Not all the Irish in Vietnam were serving in the military. Some were missionaries, priests or nuns. French Catholic missions had been active in Vietnam since the early seventeenth century and with considerable success. *Stars and Stripes* reporter Russ Anderson visited the Vinh Long Convent not long after the Tet Offensive in April 1968 and met Wexford-born Sister Mary. He filed this report from the Vinh Long Convent. "She was frightened and not ashamed of it. 'They'll be back. They'll come back to our convent,' she said. 'I know it and … my girls know it. And we don't know what to do about it.' Sister Mary isn't the type who scares easily. She has been in Vietnam for ten years and has heard bullets flying above her more than once. But it's never been like this for her, her sister nuns or the 100-plus occupants of her school of rehabilitation for girls. The school buildings, once neat and stately, are now pockmarked with bullet holes or shattered from rockets and mortars. The girls, once smiling and busy, are now shocked and idle. Many have left. Sister Mary is head of the school administered by eight nuns – five Irish, two Vietnamese and one Malay. There are more than 100 girls aged nine to sixteen. The school sits on a few hundred square yards of property bordering on the U.S. Army's Vinh Long AB. 'Several of our girls had to live with the Viet Cong before they came here,' Sister Mary said. 'They know how vicious and determined they are.' Then the Irish nun told the story that has her worried about the future:

'We have a new girl here. She told me that just before she arrived she had talked to a Viet Cong official who wore three stars on his uniform. He told her that the Viet Cong would liberate Vinh Long from the Americans. This was after Tet. Their major target was the airbase and our convent would be in the way, he told her. The girl told him that we were good people and shouldn't be harmed. But he said our school would be the Viet Cong jumping off place for the attack on the base.' This is what happened during the Tet Offensive and Sister Mary is afraid it will happen again. 'We have so little security here,' she says. 'The Vietnamese government is responsible for our protection but they only provide three soldiers. They are very brave soldiers. But only three.' It was an American helicopter pilot and crew who rescued the girls during the last Viet Cong attack on the convent. 'Captain (Robin) Miller and his men were just fantastic,' Sister Mary recalls. 'But now that he's gone ... well, we just don't know.' (Miller has since been wounded and hospitalised with a shattered hand.) Meanwhile, the convent's population has dwindled from 200 to a little over 100. Sister Mary said many of the girls were sent away for their own protection. 'But they're starting to come back on their own,' she says. Asked if she feared: for the safety of herself and the other nuns, Sister Mary replied: 'We have only to look at Hue.' The nuns are trying to get the school back to normal. Small repairs are being made so the girls can get back to their dormitories. They are now crowded into one small room."[1]

James Pringle was in Vietnam working for Associated Press as a combat photographer. Born in Galway City in 1919 James A. (Jim) Pringle started his career as a compositor at *The Connaught Tribune,* where his father also worked. He served as a war correspondent for Associated Press covering the Blitz, the Allies advance across Europe and took some of the first pictures of Dachau concentration camp. Pringle became Associated Press' star photographer and covered the Korean War, the Hungarian Revolt of 1956, the Algerian Revolution, the Arab-Israeli wars and the conflict in Vietnam, winning his colleagues' esteem for his craftsmanship and their awe for his Irish fearlessness in the face of fire. "Why, they can't hit me," he once said as bullets buzzed overhead. "After all, I carry an Irish passport." James Pringle died of cancer, aged fifty-one, in Rome, in 1970.[2]

While Irish men and women arrived in Southeast Asia in several capacities it was mainly as an infantryman that the majority of the Irish found their way to Vietnam. Galway-born Michael Coyne arrived in Vietnam in April 1967. He served a year and three months, was wounded five times and was awarded two Bronze Stars for valour. Michael Coyne was born in 1945 and spent his first years in tiny Cornamona in the Connemara region. His family moved to the Meath Gaeltacht when he was eight as part of the Land Commission relocation programme which moved people from congested Gaeltacht areas to the less populous regions in the east of the country. He left school at thirteen, stole £10 from his father and ran off to England, where he found work in the cotton mills of Rochdale. He was discovered to be underage and sent back to home "where there was hell to pay". When Michael was sixteen his mother was diagnosed with cancer and one of his uncles, John Casey, who lived in Chicago, offered to bring the young boy over to America. He worked first as landscape gardener, and later for an Irish furrier, Jerome C. McCarthy, until his draft notice came in October

1966. "I was able to avoid the draft a few times but in the end I decided to volunteer because there was a mood of patriotism and idealism." Michael had his misgivings, though: "Going into military life was a serious shock to me. Like most of the rest of the guys who were drafted I would have got out the next day if I could." After two weeks at Fort Campbell, in Kentucky, Mick began his basic training at Fort Stewart, Georgia. "I initially trained as an engineer but wound up as a projectionist. It was a handy number. I travelled around showing films. The others were all going to Germany, but I volunteered for Vietnam. There was a big push on everywhere to try to get people to volunteer for Vietnam. And I had met other people who had been in Vietnam and told me it was a piece of cake."

In April 1967 Michael Coyne got his wish. His first impression of Vietnam was the heat. "It was stifling," he said. "My first morning there I could hardly get up out of bed ... I was a jeep driver for a colonel, which again was a handy number, but then I was caught smoking a bit of pot and I was thrown into a tank. I didn't show up back at the base and I was sent to the tanks. I had never seen a tank in my life, but I lived in one for a year. Vacancies would come up – vacancies you didn't want."[3] Michael was transferred as a scout to 1st Platoon, Company D, 1st Squadron, 11th Armoured Cavalry Regiment. "The 11th Armoured was an independent unit, but we would be assigned to work with the 9th Infantry Division, 1st Infantry Division, the 196th Light Infantry and the Airborne. We would go out on the roads, set up guard as trucks came through. We were in action in the Hobo Woods, the Iron Triangle, Highway 1 and Highway 13. We were the best-armed, up-to-date regiment in the world with our own tanks, helicopters, artillery – you name it we had it." Michael did not meet any other Irishmen in Vietnam, but "most of the men in my squadron were Scots Irish from the southern states." A neighbour and school friend of his, Sean Munnelly, emigrated to New York when he was sixteen and was drafted and sent to Vietnam. "What are the odds of two neighbours from the same area, who went to the same school and emigrated at the same time, and end up in Vietnam around the same time," Michael marvels.[4]

The 11th Armoured Cavalry Regiment had arrived in the III Corps Tactical Zone in September 1966 and was stationed first at Long Binh, northeast of Saigon, and then further south near Xuan Loc. The main operational area was the provinces around Saigon and up to the Cambodian border. Known as The Blackhorse Regiment, the 11th Cavalry's motto "Allon", means "Let's Go" and equipped with M48 tanks and M113 APCs they quickly engaged the enemy. Their success in battle prompted the army to convert personnel carriers in other units in a similar fashion. By the time Michael Coyne arrived the Blackhorse were veterans of Operation Attleboro, and the Iron Triangle battles of 1966, and Junction City (February 1967). The unit clearly demonstrated its rapid mobility when Saigon came under siege in the Tet Offensive. The Blackhorse raced over 100 kilometres in eight hours to the defence of the city and fought street by street in Bien Hoa to overcome the attacking Viet Cong.[5] "I was on that race. We left tanks burning everywhere ... Patton arrived a week before I left," Mick Coyne remembered.[6] In July 1968 Colonel George S. Patton, the son of the great WWII commander, assumed command and soon applied his expertise in armoured combat and moved the armour off the roads and into the jungles in search of the enemy. So successful was the Blackhorse's search and destroy missions within the enemy's main supply routes between Cambodia and Saigon, that the enemy could no longer move freely and were forced to find sanctuary inside neutral Cambodia. Patton coined the phrase, "Find the Bastards, then pile on."[7]

"I first experienced combat in December 1967 but I was in combat virtually every day from then until I left. I took part in every major battle," Coyne said, "including the Tet Offensive and the Mini-Tet." He spent most of his tour of duty as a back deck machine gunner on an M48 tank. "I was a scout, but I did everything there was to do on a tank. I was even a tank commander when Sergeant (Danny) Cline was shot in the head. I pulled him out in the middle of a battle and took over." With his first pay cheque, Michael had bought an 8mm Bell and Howell film camera and began filming the war from his tank. "It was a diary really. I wanted to have some sort of record of what was going on. I lost all my film, though, except for one. I posted my last remaining film near the Cambodian border in a small local post office, which somehow reached a friend in Indiana." Michael Coyne still has this remaining film and it bears testament to his war in Vietnam.[8]

The job of the 11th Armoured was to keep the highways clear, but they were also ordered to the aid of other troops when a firefight broke out. "Any kind of major battle at all, we'd be called in," he said. "The tank I was on was always the first tank into action. Tank number 13 or 12 was always up front. M48 tank, 90mm main gun, mounted .50 calibre, plus 30 calibre machine gun. Most times I was a back deck gunner and manned a .50. The engine was the most vulnerable. The crew were able to change the engine in an hour. One day the track was blown off and we were putting on the track and there was bullets hitting all over and we had to just keep going. You couldn't stop." Michael was wounded five times. "I was wounded a few times and, after three injuries, you are usually taken out. I knew I had been hit so I was starting to ask 'When am I getting out?' but they didn't seem interested." In total he received five Purple Hearts and two Bronze stars for valour. Four of Coyne's Purple Hearts were awarded because of shrapnel wounds incurred whenever his tank was hit. Much of the shrapnel is still in his body – one piece worked its way out recently. He was wounded on 13 May 1968 suffering second-degree burns and shrapnel to the forearms. Just over two weeks later, on 30 May, he was again wounded by an AK47 round while dragging wounded comrades to the rear. Company D was engaged in an assault across rice paddy's near Duc Hoa when tanks and other vehicles became mired in mud. When the assault was halted for reorganisation purposes, four other vehicles carrying nine wounded crewmen were unable to withdraw. Coyne moved with a voluntary retrieving team through soaked rice paddy's under a constant hail of enemy fire to assist in treating and moving the wounded men to the cover of another vehicle. Coyne and two companions mounted the vehicle, freed it from the mud and drove it through a volley of enemy fire to the rear area from which the men could be medically evacuated.

For this action he was awarded another Purple Heart and a Bronze Star for valour. His citation for the Bronze Star reads: "At Duc Hoa when tanks and several armoured cavalry assault vehicles became mired in the combat zone and nine crewmen were wounded, Private Coyne immediately volunteered to join a team to retrieve the wounded. He moved through soaked rice paddy's under a constant sheering hail of enemy fire. Private Coyne moved from man to man and assisted in treating and moving the wounded men. Private Coyne's unwavering devotion to duty and great personal courage in the face of enemy fire belong with the highest traditions of military service and bring great credit upon himself, his unit and the United States Army."

Seven of the men Mick Coyne served with died in battle. "I saw plenty of people killed. I saw people killed every day and some days I saw five, six people getting killed, all young men. No matter where you went to, there was always a lot of bodies along the way. A lot of young men died. Nearly everybody I soldiered with was either killed or wounded. Three of the tanks I was in were hit by rockets. You would just have to leave half the crew dead and move on to another. There was a big turnover of men. Some lasted two days, some six months; others were killed a few days before they were due to go home. Some were killed on the last day." Mick was not aware of feeling frightened until the end of his tour of duty. "I suddenly felt I might get out of this alive and then I worried that I wouldn't. For ten months I didn't think I'd survive but near the end I started to believe I just might make it."[9] The sights he saw in Vietnam will never leave him. "This particular day I was sitting up on the tank. Smithy was on the ground. He had just got off the tank behind us. The lieutenant got off and came up to us and said 'We need another man to carry a radio to check out this fork in the trail.' That was me. I was pulling down the antenna on the radio and Smithy jumped up spontaneously, 'I'll check it.' It was so sudden. He took the full force of an RPG rocket. I looked at my arm. There was his rib cage sticking out of my arm. I pulled it out. What I couldn't believe … his legs stood there after the top of his body was blown off for maybe three seconds. I'll never forget that incident." Another time an officer was blown to pieces by a mine, leaving only the heel of a boot intact. (Smithy was Sergeant Donald Smith, from Kansas City. He was killed on 16 April 1968 in Phuoc Long province.)[10]

Surrounded by casual violence and death Michael Coyne kept the demons at bay by smoking dope. "I began smoking as everyone else was. You wouldn't survive in that company being different."[11] He maintains drugs were part of a grander plan to keep soldiers malleable: "They gave you all kinds of stuff to keep you going. Speed, poppers. They even gave you these things called 'jolly green giants', which I only took once. They had me jumping over the tank and unable to sleep for three days. But they sure made you gung ho for battle. We were all extensions of a gun really. We weren't there because we had no brains. You don't need brains for that (war). Every army in the world gets high as kites. Marijuana is a field combat drug. That's why it was there. That's why we were smoking it."[12] In rear areas some men smoked marijuana and others drank alcohol to relax. Some men did both and some men did neither. Very few smoked in the field and some who did wound up dead or wounded, because to survive in the field you had to have your full wits about you.

For Mick the war was politicising. "When the shooting starts you forget the idealism that brought you here. Ideology is out the window. Full stop. Then it's buddy help buddy. That's what it's all about. Nobody gives a shit. You become less than human in certain ways. It's very hard to say that about myself, but that is a part of the human condition. We're all able for that. Everything that humankind can conceive, we can do." Growing up in Galway he learned about the struggles of the Irish to be free from British oppression and began to draw parallels with what he was doing in Vietnam. (His uncle had been an IRA Volunteer during the early Irish Troubles.) A sobering experience happened on a red dirt road near An Loc on the Cambodian border when he was asked to search a frightened Vietnamese man who had emerged from the jungle. "I remember one day I was sitting on the tank and this guy emerged from the jungle. Someone was to go and check him out. Search him. I realised that I was no better than a Black and Tan. I felt uncomfortable with the war after that. I grew up with stories of the Black and Tans in Ireland. I just seen the relationship with what I was doing myself. Suddenly I realised I was no better than a Black and Tan that terrorised my country in the past. I don't think I would have thought about that side of it if I hadn't been Irish." Mick Coyne began to admire and respect his enemies who withstood everything the Americans threw at them and to hate the war and everything it stood for. "The Vietnamese were heroes. They stood and they fought and they won ...[13] Towards the end of my tour some of the younger guys coming out to Vietnam were fairly conscientious and political. I knew all the new thinking on politics because of these guys. Radical thinking was seeping in. Revolution was in the air, but there was no racial unrest in our unit. "[14]

Towards the end of Mick Coyne's tour he contacted malaria and was hospitalised. By this time he had become increasingly politicised, disillusioned with the war and critical of American policy. "There was a sense that we were fighting the wrong war, a war we couldn't win. By the end I hated the whole business. I was counting the days to get out. At the time I was delighted to get malaria. Lads were getting killed on their last day." He was admitted to the 93rd Evacuation Hospital suffering from falciparum malaria. According to his clinical record: "He had been in good health until 1 Jul 68 when he developed chills, fever of 104, headaches, nausea, vomiting and generalised aches." Coyne was shipped back to the US and returned to Chicago as the Windy City was caught up in the riots at the Democratic National Convention. On his first day back in Chicago anti-war protesters beat up Michael, "swanning around in my uniform. I got a right battering," he said. "Punched on the ground and everything, which made me wonder what it was all for." The furrier's business in Chicago gave Mick his old job back when he was discharged in August 1968 but he was restless and soon headed south to Miami where he worked at the airport as an electrician. He never took out US citizenship and in 1970 Mick returned to Ireland, where he became involved in left-wing politics, civil rights, and trade union issues. In 1972 he was in Dublin protesting outside the British Embassy over the killings of thirteen civil rights demonstrators in Derry. A year later he moved to London and was soon protesting over the wrongful jailing of the Guildford Four and the Birmingham Six. He joined the Workers Revolutionary Party, a small Trotskyist political party and campaigned on social issues. Later Mick served a year in the Merchant Navy, and worked for a time in Saudi Arabia before finally returning to Jenkinsontown, Co. Meath, in 1979. He is a committed trade unionist and socialist and admits, "I would never have become a communist if I hadn't been in Vietnam."[15]

Seán Levins was living in Richmond Hill, Queens, when he was drafted in 1966. From Termonfeckin, Co. Louth, Seán had emigrated in July 1965 to New York. After his basic training he was assigned to the HQ Battery, 7th Battalion, 15th Artillery, who were based at Fort Bragg, North Carolina. Seán was assigned straight into the artillery survey section as a forward observer. As the war in Vietnam rapidly escalated that Autumn, and the requirement for additional troop strength was exercised, the 7th Battalion, 15th Artillery, was alerted to begin preparations for overseas deployment. After an intensive period of unit training and equipment maintenance, the 7th Battalion deployed to Vietnam, onboard the USNS *Walker*, in early June 1967. "We sailed from San Francisco, in June 1967, and it took us thirty-one days to get to Vietnam," Seán recalled. Landing at Qui Nhon, on 1 July, the Battalion was assigned to the 41st Artillery Group, 1st Field Force. They were assigned to a base camp about two kilometres south of Phu Cat Airbase, in the Central Highlands area, to provide Heavy Artillery support to the 1st Air Cavalry Division. "I was the only Irishman in HQ Battery, but there were quite a few Irishmen in the rest of the unit. Danny O'Shea, a Kerryman, was in the gun battery. I was assigned as a radio liaison operator with the Koreans, Vietnamese Marines, and later the ARVN. It was a quite enough tour, but I did have some friends killed." Sean was based at LZ English located just north of the Bong Son river; LZ Uplift, on Highway One, south of the Bong Son river; and LZ Salem. Here he liased with the Republic of Korea (ROK) 1st Capital Division, and the ARVN 22nd Infantry Division. A friend and neighbour "John Hardy sent me out a Christmas pudding and a bottle of poteen for my birthday. I didn't take any R and R, as I was just counting the days to go home. Quite suddenly, in July 1968, an officer said to me, 'Get your shit together, you're going home,' which came as a surprise to me as I thought I had seventeen days left." However, because Seán hadn't taken any leave he was due to go home early. "The army owed me seventeen days, so I got to go home early, and I got paid for them, too." Seán Levins returned to New York where he married his Mayo-born wife, Sally Mulkeen. He returned to Ireland in 1975.[16]

Mike Flood, from Ardscull, Kilmeade, Athy, Co. Kildare, arrived in Vietnam on 24 September 1968 to the 1st Marine Division area. He had emigrated in 1964 going to live in New York City with his older sister. He was working locally in Kilrush Engineering when he decided to emigrate and settle in the Bronx, NYC. His childhood sweetheart, Anne, from nearby Narraghmore, joined Mike in New York in 1965 and they returned to Kildare in 1967 to marry. Mike was drafted in the Spring of 1968 and chose to enlist in the US Marines because he wanted a choice of which unit he served with. He picked the Marines because of their good reputation.[17] "When I got to Vietnam in September of 68, I was feeling pretty strange, confused, out-of-place and basically scared shitless. I spent the first few days in Da Nang filling sandbags." Here he met "another Irish guy, a middle-aged, high-ranking NCO, who was always nice to me. He was constantly playing the Clancy Brothers music and it was blaring all the time from his compound. He used to shout at me, 'C'mon, Irish, give 'em hell' ... After that I was put on a truck and sent to the 2nd Battalion, 1st Marines area at Tu Cau Road and the MSR. There I combed the faces of the crowd looking for familiarity – but found none. I was assigned to Hotel Company and finally issued an M-16, which I had felt naked without, but I still felt like a boot – with my combat fatigues straight out of the cleaners. On my way to the PX a familiar face from boot camp appeared on the horizon. It was James Kirk, my buddy from the Bronx, NYC, whom I had gone through boot camp with at Parris Island. After PI we had gone to ITR and BST at Camp Lejeune together, but we were separated at Camp Pendleton; I was sent to .50-caliber school at Twenty Nine Palms and Kirk went to Vietnam. Now, here he was thirty days later, with a fearful look on his face and leaning on crutches. I rushed over to him and said, 'What the fuck happened to you?' He replied, 'I got hit! We've got to get the fuck out of here – we're all going to be killed! My mother's gonna write to my congressman to get me out of here!' Then I said to myself: Holy shit, if he's only here a month and wounded already, I'm going to be killed. Welcome to Vietnam, Mike!"

James Kirk said, "From that day on, we found God and went to mass and communion on the few occasions when we could. Leaving the compound on PPB's (platoon patrol base) with a rifle in one hand and a rosary in the other, I knew why there are no atheists in foxholes! It's now twenty-four years later," Jim wrote in 1992, "and Mike and I, together with our families, are still the best of buddies – and godparents to each other's children. We visit regularly and we always remember that day in Nam when we had our Bronx reunion – only now we can laugh about it! And Mom is still writing to my congressman!"[18] Mike and Jim have remained firm friends and visited Ireland together. Jim Kirk was also of Irish extraction; his maternal grandparents were from Kerry and Galway while his father had roots in Ireland and Scotland.[19] Jim Kirk arrived in Vietnam in August 1968 and left in September 1969. He was discharged from the USMC on 1st October 1969. "They gave me an early out, as so many Marines were coming home from Vietnam and if they had a short time left they let them out."[20] Mike Flood agreed: "We were crazy when we came back from Vietnam. They just let us out early. It was too much trouble to try and discipline us. As Jim used to say: 'What are they going to do with us, send us to Vietnam!'"[21]

In 1967 the 1st Marine Division had handed over Quang Tin and Quang Ngai provinces to the ARVN, a Korean marine brigade and the US Americal (23rd Infantry) Division. Despite this the Old Breed still had a tough war to fight in some of the most inhospitable areas, like Go Noi Island, the "Arizona Territory," and the Que Son Mountains.[22] "In October of 1968," Mike wrote, "I experienced my first combat in Vietnam. I remember that it was near the end of October, because I had been in Nam about four weeks then. My first month had been quiet, but that was all to change on a dreary and wet fall day. By October 1968 my company, Hotel 2/1, was preparing to move out of our battalion area to a place called the 'Riveria,' at least that's what I think it was called. The morning started out with all kinds of activity and the usual rumours about where the area was, etc. All I know was that there was a shitload of stuff to carry. By the time I saddle up I was like a walking ammo dump. I remember I had so much stuff to load on my back that two Marines had to help put my pack on, and I had all I could do to stand up when they let go of the pack.

"I remember my squad leader, Mark 'Dusty' Hathaway, put me in front of this big Marine named Robert Pahcheka. I had become good friends with Pahchecka since being assigned to Charlie Squad, 1st Platoon, Hotel Company, 2/1. He was more or less keeping an eye on me, showing me the ropes. We left battalion and crossed the sand dunes going east from our area. After we crossed the dunes single file we entered a large body of water, shoulder deep. About half way across, my good friend Pahcheka came in handy when I stepped into a hole, went under and my helmet started to float away. He grabbed me, got me back on my feet and put my helmet back on my head. When we got to the other side, just before getting out of the water all hell broke loose. The point man and the Marines up front got ambushed. It was a short firefight. I was pretty amazed by all of this – my first combat and all. Two or three Marines were wounded and medevaced out. Little did I know then that in the next 24 hours, so many painful things would happen to change my life forever – at least the way I looked at life, after that day and long night.

"The rest of the day was pretty quiet. We all got busy getting used to the new terrain, what was later to become known as 'Hand Grenade Hill.' I remember that as darkness fell we moved back up the hill from where we had been just before nightfall. It wasn't much of a hill, kind of small. As we settled in for the night, we dug foxholes in the soft sand, and I prepared a spot behind our hole so I could get some sleep when I was not on watch. Dusty set us up – there were five of us – and he put Dennis Cain, Robert Garrett and my friend (the big Marine) Robert Pahcheka in one of the holes. If you were looking at the hill from our side, they would be at five o'clock, and Dusty and myself were in the next hole at about seven o'clock. What happened next is a blank to me until sometime in the middle of the night. Dusty was in the hole on watch. I was sleeping outside of it in the sand, when all hell broke loose, lots of shooting and loud explosions. I landed in the foxhole head first, my mouth and nose full of sand. I got turned right side up in a hurry and let fly as many grenades as I could.

"After a bit of a lull Dusty left to check out the others while I stayed in the hole tossing grenades out from time to time. I was doing this when I thought I heard or saw something. Dusty came back later and said that Cain and Garret were dead and Pacheka was in bad shape. That really shook me up; we had become so close. I think I shed a few tears and then got angry. It was weird the next morning – you know, the squad was gone. Things were never the same after that. We got some replacements, but it was different. I didn't get close to anybody after that and I stayed angry for years, probably at least 20, until I learned to deal with it and let the healing happen."

The Riviera was according to Marines who served there, the most hostile area in Vietnam, the most booby-trapped and mined area in the country. While based at Hand Grenade Hill Mike Flood was "on patrol over by No Name Island, Doug Bastyre and I came across a VC tunnel on a very tiny island. (It was more like a mound of dirt in the middle of some shoulder-deep stinking and filthy water.) We noticed a small entrance. The area was too small to toss in a grenade – we figured if there was ammo down there it would blow us to hell. And we didn't have any smoke grenades or whatever else we could have used. So we took turns covering one another while we dug the cover off. We smoked a pack of cigarettes one after another while we were doing this. Later on, after it was all over and we got one VC kill, Doug told me he had never smoked before." Doug Bastyre was killed in action on 25 February 1969, the day after Mike Flood was seriously injured.[23]

When Mike was wounded another Marine he became close to, James Burks, took over as squad leader. He was killed in action on 3 March 1969. "I'll never forget that date because it was four days before I was to meet my wife, Anne, in Hawaii for R&R." On 24 February 1969 Mike Flood was seriously injured by a booby trap bomb. "Being wounded changes everything," he said. "My main artery in my right arm was severed. I got shrapnel in my lung and leg. I thought I lost my leg. The choppers saved my life." Mike spent over two months in hospital in Da Nang and returned to his unit on 1 May. "I thought I was going home, but they sent me back." Mike was wounded again, this time by friendly fire. Mike, as company barber, was cutting hair in Hotel Company's base camp when he was wounded. "It hurt like hell. I was accidentally shot by a Marine, who picked up his loaded rifle and discharged it. I had got a job as the company barber and I was cutting this guy's hair – we had a load of new replacements. Was I such a bad barber? It was about nine or ten at night. We were in tents and the bullet went through the wood of the tent, splintered, and the shrapnel went into me. (Squad tents were used as living quarters in the base camp and had plywood flooring and wooden hardback frames.) I was shot in the neck and upper right arm. I was in terrible pain. It felt like my body blew up. It seemed like I was looking at my body from outside." Mike was back in hospital again for another few weeks. He left Vietnam on 1 September 1969 for treatment in Japan and then stateside arriving in October.[24]

Mike Flood's wife, Anne, was twenty-one, living in a foreign country, with no one to turn to. Nine months after their marriage Mike had left for boot camp. She had seen him only fleetingly before he left for overseas duty. Anne got the bad news about Mike from Vietnam via telegram, twice within a few weeks. The first time two Marines arrived at her door in the Bronx. "Is he dead or alive?" she screamed.[25] The first telegram read: "This is to confirm that your husband Corporal Michael P. Flood USMC was injured on 24 February 1969 in Unang Province, Republic of Vietnam. He sustained fragmentation wounds to right arms, both legs, and back with laceration of the right radical artery and nerve from hostile explosive device while on patrol. He is presently receiving treatment at the station hospital, Da Nang. His condition and prognosis were good. Your anxiety is realised and you are assured that he is receiving the best of care. It is that he will communicate with you soon informing you of his welfare. His mailing address remains the same. His parents have been notified."[26]

Mike was moved to the USAF Hospital at Clark Airbase, in the Philippines, and then to the US Naval Hospital in Guam, for further treatment, and when he was well enough he was returned to duty. On 15 October Anne received another telegram telling her that Mike had again been seriously wounded, had arrived back stateside and was in St Albans Naval Hospital, New York: "Your husband Sgt Michael Flood USMC admitted this hospital 14 October 1969 from overseas. Diagnosis fragment wounds to right neck and right upper knee. Present condition good. Your presence is not medically indicated. You are assured he is receiving the best medical care. You will be notified promptly of any significant change in his condition."[27]

Anne Flood said: "We were a young married couple when Mike was drafted into the Marine Corps. When we applied for a visa to enter the US in 1965, one of the requirements was that a male would sign up for the Selective Service. Therefore, it came as no big surprise that he was drafted. We were disappointed, but accepted because we knew that was the way it was – even though many of our friends never signed up and got away with it. Our last happy day before he went was on St Patrick's Day 1968. The next day was a rainy day and at 6am Mike left. I felt so lonely as I was only twenty-one and had no family in the US and was all-alone.

"When I went to boot camp for his graduation I felt so alone as Mike and I were not allowed to spend any time alone. (Not good for a newly married couple and for married life.) But, that is the Marine Corps. I did not know at this time that he was scheduled to be shipped to Vietnam. When Mike finally told me I was devastated, but was unable to express this to Mike after all this was his profession now – one I had to accept, like it or not. I spent our first anniversary separated from him. (What a way to start a marriage!) I went to visit Mike in California the week before he left. When I was leaving California to return alone to New York at midnight, the day before he left, the airlines held the plane up for us as we said our goodbyes on the tarmac. When I got on the plane I realised so many people were crying. I was updated to first class.

"I went back to work and Vietnam was a scary topic to talk about. Nobody knew what to say, so they said nothing. That was worst. I worked for the telephone company – split hours: 7am-10am, 6pm-10pm. On February 24 1969, four days before Mike's twenty-fourth birthday, I came home from work at 10.30pm to find two US Navy officers waiting for me – I was unaware they waited several hours for me to get home – to notify me Mike had been wounded in combat. I was all-alone, and they had a list of his wounds. It was double Dutch to me as the medical terminology was confusing. They told me I would get a telegram the next day confirming their notification. Sure enough, I did. I did not know for more than a week where Mike was, or what condition he was in. It was impossible to get any information as the casualties were very high and communication was very poor during these times.

"I stayed home from work for two days before returning to work. I remember telling a co-worker about Mike being wounded and she told me no one wanted to hear me. I was hurt, as I felt so alone. I was friendly with a family from Fermanagh and they were very good to me. My family were calling from Ireland but I had no information for them. That was the worst. After a week I made up a story and told them he had contacted me just to relieve their worries. It was a while before Mike was strong enough to call me on a Ham radio. All either of us could do was cry. He was trying to be brave – a true Marine – but the sound of a voice can say a lot. Later, I found out someone was holding him up and holding a microphone to his mouth. Mike was evacuated to Clarke Air Force Base, in the Philippines. He was supposed to go to Guam, but due to a high fever was removed to a hospital in the Philippines. His records went to Guam and that is why I was unable to get any info. This was a terrible time of not knowing what was happening and having to be brave, for his parents did not help.

"Mike spent several months recuperating in Guam. I was not encouraged to visit and did not force the issue. The Marines were sticklers on doing the right thing. One did not cross them or question their decisions especially an

Irish immigrant and especially with no one to advise, or guide her. (Both of us were Irish citizens.) Time went on but I held on to my faith and took one day at a time. Mike healed. He got strong after several months and then was sent back to the war zone. What a worry. No communication, but several letters from Mike telling me what he thought I should hear as his letters were read before they were sent home. I used to buy the daily paper to see if his name was on the casualty list. I was looking forward to his return home. However, again, the Navy officers appeared at an un-Godly hour to notify me he had been shot in the neck and had other injuries. This time, as he had only a few months of duty left, he would be shipped back to a hospital close to home. After several weeks with little or no communication I discovered, after a co-worker called all the hospitals in the New York/ New Jersey area, that he had arrived at St Albans in Jamaica, Queens. I went to see Mike during a split shift. What a sight! A skeleton 112 pounds; eyes dead; walking hunched in a pyjamas. It was awkward meeting as he was unaware I knew where he was. To this day I don't know why he did not call me when he was back in New York. Maybe he wanted to put on some weight before I saw him. He was not in a good physical, or emotional state, and it was obvious even to me then that the road to recovery would be hard and painful for him and for me to watch. Sure enough getting back into civilian life was hard and has its consequences to this day. The nightmares were hard and painful for many years for both of us, one we are still dealing with every day."[28]

But Mike and Anne Flood were survivors. They had left an impoverished Ireland to make a new life for themselves in America, so they persevered and survived. It took a long time and Mike maintained he was angry a lot. He was angry at the disrespect shown to returning veterans; angry that so many of his friends and comrades had died, or were maimed; angry that no one cared. Mike was angry for twenty years, until he quit drinking, quit being angry and saw that the war was not of his doing. He was only doing his duty. He had done nothing wrong. America had asked him to go and fight in Vietnam and that was what he did. And then after awhile Americans realised that the veterans were not to blame, they had did what was asked of them and it no longer became an embarrassment to say you had served your country. It was then Mike Flood, and many other veterans, quit been angry.

For many returning veterans, and their families, Vietnam made its mark on their subsequent lives. The Vietnam War for Gerry Duignan became a tremendous soul-searching experience of life and loss. Patrick Gerard Duignan was born in Rinn, Carrick-on-Shannon, County Roscommon, in 1945. His father fought in the War of Independence and this was a big influence on Gerry Duignan's military outlook. Gerry finished school with an honours leaving in June 1964, hoping to become a teacher of history and Irish, but he also wanted to see the world and after working for six months on the buildings got a visa and headed to America. Gerry settled in Long Island in January 1965 going to work as a bank clerk in J. P. Morgan's, on Wall Street. After a year in the bank he was bored and on the advice of a service veteran, who worked in J. P. Morgan's, Gerry joined the United States Air Force on 25 July 1965. Before he joined the service Gerry was told he would have to take out US citizenship and had to swear an oath in front of a judge that he intended to become a US citizen. On joining the USAF Gerry Duignan was immediately shipped out to San Antonio, Texas, for basic training. Because of the escalating conflict in Southeast Asia and the need for personnel basic training was reduced from sixteen weeks to eight weeks. After basic training Gerry was sent to Perso School, Amarillo, Texas, known as "Little West Point." The entire class except Gerry and another recruit were then shipped to Germany, but because Gerry Duignan was not an American citizen he had no security clearance and remained in the US. "I wanted to go to Vietnam because that's where all the action was, where all the excitement was going on, where all the fellows were going, so I volunteered for Vietnam." Unlike most of his friends, who were keen to avoid the draft, he had sought out Vietnam veterans to find out what it was really like. However, after he volunteered for duty in Vietnam Gerry was investigated by the FBI and ended up having as much trouble getting to Vietnam as others had trying to avoid going.

"I arrived home to Ireland in July 1967 with the knowledge that I could be in Vietnam by Christmas. I had completed two years with the USAF and was a member of a Command Inspection Team that tours bases in America on a regular basis. When I returned to duty after my holidays in Rinn, Carrick-on-Shannon, Ireland, I had orders to report for Special Training in California and Seattle, Washington, prior to a Christmas departure to Vietnam." Financial reasons was another factor in many servicemen volunteering for duty in Vietnam. As a staff sergeant Gerry Duignan received his basic pay and tax-free allowances for being in a hostile zone, plus combat pay and flight pay. (Married men received more allowances.) His money was deposited in a designated bank, which gave him ten per cent interest on his money. Dollars were illegal in Vietnam and troops were paid in military script, to prevent their use on the black market. They could only get dollars when they were going on R and R. Gerry also learned Vietnamese before he shipped out.[29] "I arrived in Vietnam on New Year's Day 1968 and was assigned to Base X in the Central Highlands, later known as Phu Cat. As I travelled the Highway 1 from Qui Nhon to Phu Cat on a glorious evening

Capt. Edmond Landers.
Killed in action 1968.

173rd Airborne drop on
an LZ 1965.

The last photo sent home by Capt. Ed Landers, 2nd from the right.
Taken less than two weeks before he was killed in action.

Religious service at 1st Infantry Division base camp, 1968.

Martin Doherty
killed in action 5 December 1969.

Dan Danaher
1st RAR, Bien Hoa area, 1965.

Pat O'Leary, 101st Airborne, Ashau Valley, 1969.

Ed Somers, 1st RAR, in the bush, Bien Hoa area, 1965.

Kevin Deegan and Mick Cahill, in the Persian Gulf, 1964.

Jim Kirk and Mike Flood, Bronx buddies in Vietnam, 1969.

Capt. Ed Landers, base camp, 1968.

Ed Somers on left, just back from Vietnam, while Tony O'Reilly, 2nd from right,
and friends are on their way to Vietnam, 1966.

4th Infantry Division troops on board transport bound for Vietnam.

Danny O'Shea and Sean Levins, 1968.

Tom Klein and Peter Nee, 1968.

Funeral of Michael Smith (21) to Kilnavart Cemetery, Ballyconnell, Co. Cavan.
Michael was killed in action 18 March 1967.

Lt. John Driver,
101st Airborne,
killed in action, April 1969.

Martin Henniger at Vun Ro, 1968.

The family man, Ed Landers with his wife
Theresa and baby Chantelle.

Mrs. Theresa Landers being presented
with her husbands medals from U.S.
Ambassador to Ireland.
Nephew Walter O'Shea is on the right.

Lt. Wayne Knight refuels C63 rescue chopper on the Thai-Burma border,
on his way to pick up Joe Hennessy.

American bunkers at Vun Ro, 1968.

Dan Danaher, 1st RAR, on left.

Rory O'Connell, back left, and fellow Marine sergeants, Camp Lejeune, NC.

Lt. John O'Sullivan with his Shark gunship, on Duc Pho base.

Peter Nee, on left, having a beer with an Air Force colleague.

Pat Landers, on right, in the bush with 3rd RAR.

Pat Nee, on the day he graduated from
Parris Island 1964.

Sgt. John Barrett, 1st Infantry Division,
Vietnam 1967.

Australians preparing Bien Hoa base camp, 1965.

John Dobbin, British Merchant Navy, heading up river to Saigon, 1967.

Joe Hennessy, in his Air America office, Udorn, Thailand.

John Dullahan and ARVN ally, in the bush, 1972.

Gerry Duignan, at the
Binh Dinh Orphanage.

174th AHC Sharks patrol the skies.

Pat Landers, on right,
on his last day in Vietnam.

Christmas Day 1965. The Australians and Americans enjoy a bicycle race.
Dan Danaher, standing fourth on the left. Tom Kelly, front second from the left.

Gerry Duignan, US Air Force, Vietnam.

Michael Coyne, returned to Vietnam in 2000.
Outside the War Museum beside an M48 tank.

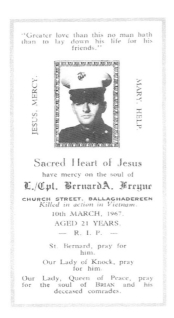

"Greater love than this no man hath than to lay down his life for his friends."

JESUS, MERCY.    MARY, HELP.

Sacred Heart of Jesus
have mercy on the soul of
L./Cpl. Bernard A. Freyne
CHURCH STREET, BALLAGHADEREEN
Killed in action in Vietnam.
10th MARCH, 1967.
AGED 21 YEARS.
— R. I. P. —

St. Bernard, pray for him.
Our Lady of Knock, pray for him.
Our Lady, Queen of Peace, pray for the soul of BRIAN and his deceased comrades.

Christmas Day celebrations 1969.
Mike Flood, second from left.

Mass Card for Brian Óg Freyne.

in 1968, little did I think that this would become my home for the next four and a half years, and make a forever mark on my life."[30]

"Phu Cat was located twenty miles north of the city of Qui Nnhon, off Highway 1 in the Binh Dinh province, II Corps. Binh Dinh was fiercely anti-government and was never under the thumb of Central Government in Saigon. Phu Cat lay in a ten-mile wide lowland area between the South China Sea and the Central Highlands. This was primarily an agricultural and rice growing area. It was bordered by dense underbrush and trees. It lay between the Song Dap Da river and the Song La Vi river. When I arrived I was assigned to the 37th Combat Support and they flew F100s on secret missions over North Vietnam without the approval of US Congress. This operation was known as 'Misty.' During Tet and its aftermath, the base and surrounding area was subject to fierce assault and the little town of Dap Da was destroyed. A US General later coined the phrase 'We had to destroy the town in order to save it.' We were give a citation for bravery and valour by the then President L. B. Johnson. Many years later we were to receive the Cross of Gallantry from the Vietnamese Government. But we were also famous for other reasons. We had a unit called 'Ranch Hand' and they became famous for their use of Agent Orange. I had first-hand knowledge of their work. We also had a unit called 'Spooky Gunships AC47s.' These were later replaced by 'Shadow AC119G' and then later by 'Stinger AC119K.' These were used in support of army units and the firebases along the trail."[31]

Gerry Duignan's primary job at Phu Cat was in personnel. He talked to every person who came to the base; told them what to expect, what to do. When they were leaving it was the same. And while there Gerry looked after their records, their well being. "We called it 'manpower' – shifting people here and there. There was a continuous movement of people in and out. We all had a specific job. Even if there was an attack on the base we had units to go to. Despite the violence and mayhem Gerry became more involved with the local people. "In January 1968 whilst on a mission with a fellow airman, I came across an orphanage in a remote area of the Binh Dinh province. Here was home to about 100-120 children from infants to early teens, mostly girls. There were five nuns and lots of community help. They existed mostly on charity and on the wits of the nuns. In those early days after Tet, they adopted me and I became a part of that little group." Gerry spent any free time he had teaching English at the orphanage with a colleague, Sergeant di Pepe. Their classes were popular and packed out every evening. On the base no one in authority was told about these classes.[32] The Viet Cong cracked down heavily on fraternizing with the enemy – except on a commercial basis. Once a Vietnamese girl who worked in the Cu Chi base PX was known to be seeking permission to marry an American soldier. One morning her head was found on a post outside the main gate, with a note that said, "This is what happens to Vietnamese people who go around with the enemy." A special mobile punishment unit of Viet Cong was responsible for such executions.[33] "The way I felt about the Vietnamese as a people I thought they were lovely. In the beginning I had chance to get out into the villages. I got to mix with them. I really played almost a deadly situation. I worked for the Americans and socialised with the Vietnamese. I used to teach school in a village. I knew that it was an unauthorised zone. The VC had to know about me, but I felt safer with the people I worked with." Only Gerry's close friends knew of his Irish background. The Mother Superior thought he was French. "I told her I was Irish. She had studied in Paris, and was quite familiar with Ireland and 'the Troubles.' She knew it was a Catholic country. I explained I had emigrated to America. The headmaster of the school knew everything about France so it was easy to explain the whereabouts of Ireland."[34]

A normal tour of duty in Vietnam was twelve months – thirteen for Marine and Navy personnel – but Gerry Duignan served the equivalent of four tours. To counteract the bad press Vietnam was getting the US armed forces offered a month-long holiday trip to anywhere in the world if a serviceman extended his tour. After Gerry's twelve-month tour was up he extended his tour every six months, travelling to Ireland four times, and also visiting Australia, New Zealand and Africa, where his sister lived. Travel to your destination was not included in the thirty days holiday, so if it took you several days to reach, and return, from your destination, this was also included in your time off. Every time he re-enlisted Gerry jetted off for a month's holidays before completing the further six months. He felt it was a great way to see the world.[35]

"In 1970 the mission changed and the 37th went to Thailand. It was replaced by the 12th from Cam Rhan Bay and were now code-named 'Cobra,'" Gerry wrote. "I became a part of all this. They flew in support of the invasions in Laos and Cambodia as well as backing the US forces in close support in I and II Corps. They flew F4D's with 12 Mk 82 LD bombs. At the end of 1971, the base was turned over to the South Vietnamese Air Force and they were flying A37B's. They flew in support of their own units in II Corps. During the 1972 Easter Offensive, the VNAF units out of Phu Cat were effective in halting attacks down Highway 19 from Kontum to Pleiku. In 1973, when the NVA drove an offensive into Binh Dinh province, the units from Phu Cat aggressively and effectively halted the attacks and allowed the ARVN to counter attack successfully.

"In 1975, the final thrust began by the NVA after Tet, and its forces swept down from the North. By 6 March Highway 19 was cut in several places and Highway 1 was under pressure as the ARVN was in disarray. The roads were clogged by refugees and retreating soldiers. The air force units at Phu Cat did not panic but dropped supplies and provided fire support to slow the NVA advance. Pleiku fell on 14 March but the Phu Cat units flying fire support, took out all-available personnel before it was overran. These VNAF A37B's at Phu Cat now flew an all out effort against the advancing NVA. They put up the greatest fight of the war. Pilots in some cases had to load their own aircraft and also fight to protect the airfield. As the NVA advance continued, the area became untenable and Qui Nhon fell on 31 March 1975."[36]

Gerry Duignan remained in Vietnam until June 1972. He met quite a few more Irishmen in his four-year stint. He remembered a Protestant Belfast-born former professional footballer, Sergeant Reed, and a Belfast Catholic named Evans, also a good footballer, trading republican and loyalist songs in a rare victory celebration after a match against a Vietnamese unit. He even has a photograph from the *Roscommon Herald* taken in Tan Son Nhut airbase of three Roscommon men in uniform, sitting on a bench reading a copy of the *Roscommon Herald*. The other two men, both from Boyle, were Chaplain (Captain) Patrick Feely, who was based at Ton Son Nhut, and Sergeant Mike Noone, who was stationed at Binh Thuy.[37] On return to the United States Gerry was stationed at the USAF base in Minot, North Dakota. Minot was a Strategic Air Command base, which housed heavy bombers and Minuteman nuclear missiles. Gerry had become disillusioned with the military and served out the remaining nine months of his enlistment at Minot. After his discharge he went to Canada, where he had an aunt, and stayed for three months, returning to Ireland in 1976.[38]

## CHAPTER 11

# SAND IN THE WIND

A merica 1968 – a year of riots, protests and the assassinations of Robert
F. Kennedy and Martin Luther King. Political unrest also spread to
Ireland that year when Northern Catholics, taking their cue from the
American civil rights campaign began marching in protest against the injus-
tices of the Northern Ireland state. Their peaceful protests were met by
State violence, which soon spiralled into another round of Ireland's "troubles." The Troubles in Northern Ireland would make sure that many Irish
would continue to emigrate to other parts of the world. In South Vietnam
1968 was the turning point of the conflict when the communists launched
an all-out bid to win the war. At the beginning of the year it appeared that
the US had the upper hand in Vietnam, but the Tet Offensive at the end of
January shattered this illusion. The American public saw a supposedly beat-
en enemy waging war in the very heart of Saigon – even in the US Embassy
itself. Television pictures beamed into US homes told a story of American
failure and communist success. The offensive was largely crushed by 10
February with heavy losses for the communists, but the military victory for
the US was a political disaster. While the US military was now more confident and powerful, the war had been lost in the minds of the American people. After three years of war the majority of the American people wanted
out of Vietnam.

By mid-1967, the war had reached a turning point and officers at MACV
began to "proclaim light at the end of the tunnel". US attrition objectives
were being achieved: VC and NVA units were apparently losing more forces
in South Vietnam than could be replaced through recruitment and infiltration. Policy makers in Hanoi also came to the conclusion that the war was
stalemated and that battlefield trends were not in their favour. In response,
they called for a "General Offensive, General Uprising." Known in America
as the "Tet Offensive," because it occurred during the celebration of the
Chinese lunar New Year, the countrywide attacks were intended to spark an
insurrection among South Vietnamese civilians and military forces, destroy-

ing the Saigon regime. The North Vietnamese hoped to leave US forces isolated along the South Vietnamese border, forcing the Johnson administration to negotiate an end to the war. Hanoi even planned to re-enact the siege of Dien Bien Phu at Khe Sanh firebase. Towards the end of 1967 American and ARVN intelligence found signs of increased communist activity, but the enemy's specific intentions remained unclear. In late January 1968 two NVA divisions began a siege of the undermanned US Marine base at Khe Sanh near the DMZ. The siege lasted from 21 January to 30 March and ended in an overwhelming American victory. Although the NVA pounded the base with as many as a thousand shells and rockets a day, its infantry attacks on the hill posts and the perimeter itself did no lasting damage to the position. American air power pulverised NVA positions with 100,000 tons of bombs, while artillery and mortar expenditures may have gone as high as 200,000 rounds. On the ground, Marines and ARVN rangers beat back all assaults on the perimeter and outposts despite some sharp night fighting. The relative casualties spoke volumes: 205 defenders dead and about 800 seriously wounded, as against probably 10,000 NVA killed in action.[1]

During the war it had become the practice for both sides to declare a truce to celebrate the beginning of the lunar New Year – the greatest celebration and holiday in the Vietnamese calendar – and the Tet of 1968 was no exception. A thirty-six-hour truce began at 6pm on Tet Eve, 29 January. But this year the communists had planned a major surprise offensive for Tet, with complete victory the goal. With unanticipated fury the communists threw some 80,000 NVA and VC regulars against the garrisons of 105 South Vietnamese cities and towns on 29-31 January in Giap's great Tet Offensive.[2] In Saigon the VC attacked the middle-class districts, which were duly destroyed by US firepower, thus creating more animosity towards the Americans.[3]

During the first hours of Tet the US Embassy in Saigon, the symbol of America, was attacked by a group of twenty VC sappers. Most of them were killed and TV cameras were there to record the siege and battle around the grounds of the Embassy. The two major VC errors were their failure to attack and eliminate both the Provost Marshall Compound and the 716th Military Police Battalion Headquarters. Much to the Americans surprise they attacked neither. The elimination of the Provost Marshal Compound with its military police control would have neutralised, or severely hampered, control of the command's eyes and ears, while an attack on the 716th MP Btn HQ would have severely hampered them from forming and dispatching the military police reaction forces that were vital to the defence of Saigon. The 716th MP Battalion, with approximately 1,000 men, was responsible for the security of the 130 American installations in the greater Saigon area. Only one-third were on duty, even though they were warned of trouble. Saigon had all the problems of a big city, plus the fact that it was in a combat zone. Coupled with thousands of Americans living and working there, passing through, or on leave, were diplomats, civilian workers and members of the media to help make policing Saigon a nightmare.[4]

When the battle for the US Embassy was over one crew of reporters interviewed some of the American defenders. One man interviewed on television gave his name as Captain Robert J. O'Brien. Though he spoke with an American accent, Capt O'Brien said he was from southern Ireland. Thirty-six year old Robert O'Brien lived in Marshfield, Massachusetts. Like US embassies worldwide the Saigon building also had a US Marine Security Guard Battalion for protection of classified material and US government officials and property. In January 1968 the detachment consisted of one officer, Captain Robert O'Brien, and sixty-seven enlisted men.

Until the Tet Offensive the war had mostly bypassed the Marines assigned to the Saigon embassy. On the afternoon of 30 January, however, a State Department security officer met with Capt. O'Brien and informed him of the possibility of a VC attack that evening or some time during the Tet holiday in the Saigon area. Capt O'Brien immediately increased the alert status and put a second man on all one-man posts. He also placed a rooftop watch on the Embassy's chancery building and assigned two men to the Norodom compound next to the Embassy compound. That night accompanied by a sergeant O'Brien visited all of the posts and finding nothing out of the ordinary returned to Marine House, which doubled as the headquarters and barracks for the guard. He then stretched out on a sofa and gave orders to wake him in time so he could make another tour at 0300.

However, at 0245 a group of about twenty VC sappers, armed with satchel charges, automatic weapons, grenades and B-40 rockets, blew a hole in the wall surrounding the Embassy compound near the northeast gate. They quickly killed four MPs as they tried to raise the alarm.[5] As the attack was beginning, Corporal Dennis L. Ryan, who was on duty at the Marine House, as the duty non-commissioned officer, heard several explosions coming from the direction of the Embassy. Ryan rushed immediately to the movie room to awaken Capt. O'Brien and briefed him on what he had heard. Upon completing this briefing, he went through the house insuring that all the personnel were awake. Then he proceeded to the front gate of Marine House where he received the incoming telephone call from Lance Corporal Wilson at Post 1112. Upon being awakened and briefed by Corporal Ryan, Capt O'Brien could hear additional explosions and automatic weapons fire coming from the Embassy. O'Brien with Sgt Richard

Frattarelli, his driver, jumped into their radio-equipped sedan and followed by a jeep with three more Marines, raced to the Embassy, some five blocks away.

At 3.20am O'Brien, arrived at the east side of the Embassy wall. As they arrived at the Vietnamese police checkpoint, which was on the corner of Mac Dinh Chi and Hung Trap Tu, the Vietnamese police were yelling, "VC," and pointing at the Embassy. Capt. O'Brien then had his team dismount and move toward the vehicle gate on foot. While a military police team was dispersing on the front side of the Embassy, O'Brien's team proceeded toward the side gate on foot utilising the cover and concealment offered by the trees on both sides of the street. As the sappers in the front compound fired rockets at several of the upper floors of the Embassy, O'Brien neared the vehicle gate and began calling to the military policemen. He did not receive any response as the two American policemen stationed there had been killed minutes earlier. Upon reaching the gate, O'Brien observed six Viet Cong near the flowerpots and pillars, which were located close to the chancery building. Approaching the sappers who had their backs toward the team, Captain O'Brien remembered being, "momentarily stunned by the abrupt … confrontation with the VC." He quickly recovered and yelled for Sergeant Reed to begin firing with the team's only Beretta submachine gun. At the same time, Capt O'Brien, Sergeant Frattarelli and Sergeant Patulio began firing their .38 calibre pistols. Sergeant Reed's burst of automatic weapons fire killed one Viet Cong and possibly wounded another. The sappers quickly recovered and began returning a large volume of automatic weapons fire. An intense fire-fight ensued for the next few minutes, forcing O'Brien to withdraw his team back across the street where Corporal Inemer was providing cover fire.

At the vehicle gate, O'Brien decided to send Sgt Frattarelli back to the sedan in order to contact Gunnery Sergeant Morrison and request more men and ammunition. Arriving at the sedan, Fratterelli contacted Morrison and was briefed on the activities along the front side of the Embassy. Morrison had already communicated with the US Ambassador. The Ambassador was safe and had moved from his residence to the house of one of the Embassy security officers. While this conversation was taking place, two more Marines arrived at Capt O'Brien's location. Soon after Mr Champsey and Robert Furey, State Department Security Adviser, arrived and were taken to Capt O'Brien. It was then decided to attempt to shoot the lock off the vehicle gate. The intense sniper fire then forced Furey and O'Brien to withdraw where they learned that another patrol of military policemen had just arrived. Two men then went on the roof of a building ,across the street and began firing into the compound. A few minutes later,

O'Brien and Crampsey decided to move behind the compound to the top of the building across from the mission co-ordinator's office in order to cover any further attempts to enter the compound through the vehicle gate.

With MPs and Marines surrounding the Embassy and the continuing harassing fire, the VC had little chance to escape and no prospect of reaching the Chancery itself. Additional reinforcements arrived at daylight and the Marines and MPs forced their way into the compound from both the northeast wall and through the Norodom compound gate. The VC only offered a desultory resistance and took what refuge they could. More reinforcements arrived, but all that was left was the mopping up. At 0900, Captain O'Brien grouped his Marines together and made a floor-to-floor sweep of the Chancery to make sure none of the attackers had somehow taken refuge there. It would be another two hours before the building would be clear. From this one action four Vietnamese and five American MPs were killed, while seventeen VC were killed and two captured.

O'Brien estimated that there were about 200 people swarming around the Embassy grounds and the building itself, including "reporters, writers, cameramen, MPs, 101st Airborne troops and civilians." People were "taking pictures, asking questions, and picking up anything in sight, everything was up for grabs." Finally by late morning, the crowd had thinned out and the Marines had effected some "semblance of order." While being one of the most dramatic events of the Tet Offensive, especially considering the play it received upon American television, the attack on the Embassy was in reality a sideshow. The attack had failed miserably. The VC never reached the Chancery building, but largely milled about the compound until finally being killed or taken prisoner. However, despite its futility, the assault on the Embassy compound provided a huge propaganda coup for the Viet Cong.[6]

In the I Corps area the main communist effort was aimed at the area's two biggest cities, Da Nang and Hue. In I Corps the offensive found the Americans and ARVN in great strength and decent alertness, but not deployed for heavy fighting along the coast. In addition, US command arrangements were in the process of rearrangement as MACV moved the 101st Airborne Division and the 1st Cavalry Division into Quang Tri province to enter the DMZ war. The communist attacks in Quang Nam province lasted about a week and failed dramatically. Da Nang escaped occupation, but Hue, the ancient imperial capital, was seized in less than a day. Seven communist battalions, supported by at least four others, seized virtually all of Hue and raised their flag over the walls of the city's ancient Citadel. Some 5,000 inhabitants died, or disappeared in a subsequent orgy of terrorism. Thousands of civilians believed to be potentially hostile to communist control, including government officials, religious figures, and expatriate residents, were executed. Dozens of graves were uncovered with the bodies of at least 2,800 victims. In some of the graves victims were found bound together; some appeared tortured; others were even reported to have been apparently buried alive. Among the dead were Stephen Miller of the US Information Service, three German doctors and two French missionaries. Terror was a common feature of Hanoi's strategy of intimidation, but that which was practised routinely in the countryside generally went unreported. The atrocities in Hue were different, both in terms of sheer scale and the publicity accorded it. Many Americans pointed to Hue saying it was a prelude of what would happen in South Vietnam if the communists ever took power. The US Marines were sent in to retake the Imperial City. It took a month to recapture Hue as the Marines and ARVN fought for the city street by street. Having barely become familiar with fighting in the paddy fields, the Marines now found themselves engaged in the highly specialised business of street fighting. Seventy per cent of homes were destroyed in the battle for Hue and when the fighting finally ended 4,601 communists had died, along with 216 American and 384 South Vietnamese troops.[7]

Irish-American Father (Major) Aloysius P. McGonigal was an Army chaplain serving with the US Marines during the Tet Offensive. He had a comfortable desk job at the USARV compound in Saigon, but seldom was there because of his devotion to the men in the field. McGonigal was killed on 17 February during the Battle of Hue. Though told that he was to remain in the rear, he knew his place was with those in harm's way. He entered the city when no one else seemed to be able to get across the Perfume river. He administered the last rites to dying soldiers and comforted the wounded through three days of intense fighting near Hue Citadel before being fatally wounded. Aloysius P. McGonigal grew up in Philadelphia, the sixth of twelve children. He enjoyed studying foreign languages and loved music and sports, especially tennis, baseball and basketball. He graduated from Northeast Catholic High School and received degrees from Woodstock (MD) College and Fordham University in New York City. He was attending Georgetown University in Washington, DC, when he was called into the Army Chaplain Corps. The major was assigned to units in Korea in 1962-63, and shipped out to Vietnam in December 1966 where he was first assigned to the 1st Infantry Brigade of the 9th Infantry Division, and later to Headquarters, US Army Vietnam. He was working toward a Doctorate degree at the time of his death. He was dedicated to "his troops" and regularly ended his letters home with the simple request: "Pray for the troops."[8]

Associated Press reporter George McArthur, wrote this report from

Hue, which was published in the *Seattle Times*, on 20 February 1968. "The slight priest with owlish eyeglasses really had no business being there. But the infantrymen he loved were being killed before the battlements of Hue's Imperial Citadel, and the Rev. Aloysius P. McGonigal, 46, wanted to go. The chaplain died, a bullet wound in his forehead, with a unit that was not his own in a battle he could have missed. He virtually had fought his way to the battlefield. Most soldiers die almost anonymously, known only to their close comrades, to the sergeants and to the company officers. Father McGonigal was known all over the I Corps area and elsewhere in South Vietnam. He roamed with a fierce devotion to 'the men in the field.' His 5-feet-6 frame almost disappeared inside a flak jacket. An Army major, his last assignment was to the United States Army Compound in Hue. He travelled all over the northern provinces and had extended his year-long tour in Vietnam. He took his extension leave in his ancestral homeland of Ireland, which was virtually written on his smiling face. They were expecting him to leave his post at Hue and take a desk job in Da Nang. His replacement actually was on the way up the day Father McGonigal headed for the north side of the Perfume River, where the battle for the Citadel was raging.

"'There was no Catholic priest with the 1st Battalion of the 5th Marines, which was assaulting the walls and the father wanted to go,' said Dr. Stephen Bernie, an Army doctor from Dayton, Ohio, who had travelled frequently with the priest. Father McGonigal had been angrily walking the advisory compound for three days before he joined the battle, ordered by the compound commander to stay put. The priest finally wangled his way to join a unit with which he never before had served. 'He wanted to be in the field; that was all he wanted,' said a sergeant who knew him well. 'Saying Mass at headquarters wasn't his idea of his job.'"[9] Fr McGonigal died as he would have wanted, helping his men in their time of need.

The Tet Offensive did not turn out as Hanoi had hoped. Tet had failed to end the war and conditions would become much worse for the communists after the failed offensive. The overriding purpose had been to give the impression of their having overwhelming power and presence in South Vietnam. Hanoi thought it would weaken the Americans will to continue the fight, which might lead to a general uprising against the government by the people and military of South Vietnam. While Tet was crucial in turning the tide of opposition in America to the war, Hanoi was wrong on the other counts. In fact, the Americans and ARVN fought side by side with more efficiency than ever. The clandestine Viet Cong government could not replace the losses of Tet — communist losses were thought to be as high as 40,000 — from its shrunken recruiting base, and demoralisation was widespread within the guerrilla movement that remained. The VC fighters did not see the will-breaking effect their sacrifice had in the United States. They saw only the loss of their comrades on missions that had become so unrealistic in military terms by May that they were suicidal. From now on the onus would shift on the NVA who supplied most of the replacements for the VCs losses.[10]

However, while Tet was a military disaster for Hanoi it was a political disaster for America. The destruction involved in crushing the offensive and the unsavoury methods of the Saigon regime shocked US audiences and called into question the morality of the war. Public enthusiasm for the war waned and President Johnson, a strong advocate of pursuing the war to victory, responded to this new will of the American people by announcing on 31 March, on national television, that he would not be seeking re-election. He also said that he had instructed the Defence Department to place specified limitations on the bombing of targets in North Vietnam. On 2 April the 20th Parallel was identified as the line north of which no further bombings by the US would take place. On that same day it was announced from Washington and Hanoi that the two countries would soon commence talks aimed at bringing the war to an end. Paris was selected as the site for these discussions.[11] (In the *Irish Press* of 20 April 1968 it was even suggested that the Irish government could be potential hosts for peace talks.)[12] On 10 May W. Averell Harriman for the United States and Xuan Thuy for North Vietnam held their first meeting.[13]

The existence of the Paris Peace Talks, rather than diminishing the level of combat, actually intensified it, as each side aimed at establishing its strength on the battlefield as a leverage for establishing its strength in the negotiations. With the NVA replacing the VC in many areas the war took on a different phase. By the first week of April the two-month siege at Khe Sanh had been lifted and the US military congratulated itself on a job well done. Two months later, the Marine garrison at Khe Sanh was moved back to the now secure Route 9 line and the American base, for which so many had given their lives was abandoned and demolished. Coupled with the replacement of General Westmoreland as MACV commander in June, it all seemed to confirm the total disarray of US policy in Vietnam. While the communists were still full of fight in effect US disengagement from Vietnam began that April when Johnson's Secretary of Defence, Clark Clifford, had rejected demands from Westmoreland and the JCS for 206,000 men to be added to the armed forces world-wide.[14]

Tet-related battles continued for four more months, but with the large-scale defeat of the Tet Offensive MACV returned to its pacification operations. On 22 May 1968 Cork native Michael Murphy was killed in an ambush while leading a patrol for the South Vietnamese Police Field Forces about nineteen miles south of Saigon. Michael Murphy had taken a detachment from a fortified police compound to set up a night ambush against the Viet Cong. Instead, his patrol was ambushed and Murphy was fatally wounded. He was on leave from the Alaska State Troopers and was serving as a policeman with the Office of Public Safety (OPS) in South Vietnam at the time. The Agency for International Development's Public Safety Division sponsored a programme to support South Vietnam's local, regional and national police forces with advisers from American police forces. AID/PSD also provided equipment and training in tactics, techniques and procedures. The programmes success in helping Saigon secure the countryside was one reason given for Hanoi's initial phase of the 1968 Tet Offensive – to force combat units to return to previously secured rural areas.[15] Michael Murphy was on three years leave from the Alaska State Troopers when he died and was due to return to Alaska in August 1968.

Michael Murphy was born in Cork City in 1928, and enlisted in the Irish Navy when he was sixteen. After World War II, he joined the Royal Air Force Police and served three years in Malaya and the Far East before joining the Liverpool Police. In 1951, Michael Murphy returned to Malaya as a lieutenant in the Malayan Constabulary and served there until 1954 when he was invalided out of the service due to gunshot wounds. That same year – sponsored by a distant relative in Boston – Mike Murphy emigrated to the United States. He went to Alaska in 1961 and joined the Alaska State Troopers in July 1962. He was the resident trooper in the Seward area during the March 1964 earthquake in Alaska. Mike was on patrol on the Seward highway, which connects that port city with Anchorage. After the earthquake, which completely demolished the highway and stranded his patrol car, he received a radio message to proceed to Seward as rapidly as possible since the city had been devastated by the tidal wave which followed the earthquake. Leaving his car in the vicinity of a landslide, he proceeded on foot for the remaining nineteen miles; crossing over collapsed bridges and destroyed roadways until he finally reached the city nine hours later. For his devotion to duty Michael was the recipient of a commendation for special praise, which appeared in the *United States Senate Journal* on 2 May 1964.

Mike Murphy frequently mentioned the deep appreciation he felt toward the United States for his citizenship, and felt he had a debt to repay. It was this feeling which motivated him to submit an application for a leave of absence in 1966 and accept a position as a policeman with the Office of Public Safety in South Vietnam. Because of Murphy's previous experience in jungle campaigning against insurgents in Malaya, he was uniquely qualified for this assignment. Murphy corresponded regularly with many of his trooper friends in Alaska and in his last letter, which arrived two weeks before his death, he said, "I have always felt that dying is the only certainty in this life and therefore is of little consequence. What really matters is how a man dies and the reason or cause for which he dies." Under Alaska State regulations, Murphy would have been eligible for reinstatement as a trooper if he had returned before the expiration of the three-year leave period. Because of Michael Murphy's love for Alaska, his body was returned there from Vietnam and buried with full honours in Seward on 4 June 1968. The Police Medal of Valour was awarded posthumously to Michael Murphy and was presented to his widow, Alice, on 25 October 1968, by Commissioner of Public Safety Mel Personett and Chief Pat Wellington.[16]

Back home in Ireland *The Irish Times* of 27 May 1968 reported on Mike Murphy's death: "Killed in Vietnam. News has been received of the death while serving with the US Forces in Vietnam of Mr Michael Murphy, eldest son of the late Mr William Murphy, formerly of Military Police services, Collins Barracks, Cork. His mother is Mrs Esther Hacket, 16 Morton Street, Clonmel, Co. Tipperary. Mr Murphy who had resided in the US for some years, leaves a wife and three children."[17]

From 1-4 June, elements of the lst Brigade, 9th Infantry Division, led by the legendary Colonel "Gunfighter" Henry Emerson, relentlessly tracked two VC battalions through the treacherous Plain of Reeds and joined with artillery and air strikes to kill over 225 enemy soldiers.[18] Dong Thap Muoi (Plain of Reeds) is in Kien Tuong Province, near the Cambodian border. The forest is on the north bank of the Mekong river. First Lieutenant Anthony Paul O'Reilly, Galway, was one of the American casualties in the fierce fighting. Lieutenant O'Reilly tried to rescue a surrounded unit and in a lone sortie, he was killed by automatic fire from the Viet Cong. It was 3 June. He was just three days past his thirtieth birthday. He was posthumously awarded the Distinguished Service Cross, America's second highest award for bravery. A letter to his sister, Joan, arrived at her workplace, Holles Street Maternity Hospital, Dublin, on 4 June. Little did Nurse Joan O'Reilly know that as she read this letter, her beloved older brother was already dead.

Anthony O'Reilly was born at 4 Eyre Street, Galway, in 1938. His youngest sister, Joan, remembers his love for the Corrib and rowing. "If you ever wanted to find him, you could be sure he was down there rowing." After finishing school Anthony went to England to work. "He used to write to Mom every week and I would have the job of running to the Post Office on Fridays to post the letter from home to him," Joan said. When he returned from England, after two years, Anthony set his sights on America and went to Kettering, Ohio, where his sister, Irene, lived. He decided to join the Army in 1960 and get his mandatory military service finished with and then set about his other ambitions in America. But it turned out he loved the Army and stayed in the service. Anthony became a star soldier. He was sent to Germany as an instructor and made the unusual progress of rising through the ranks to officer level in his twenties.

"He used to come home twice a year when he was in Germany," Joan recalled. "He later returned to the U.S. Then in the Autumn of 1967, he told us he would not be contactable for awhile as he would be on special duties. That could have also happened in earlier years and I think he was actually on standby at the time of the Cuban crisis. But this was different. He left his apartment and he left his car and belongings with my sister and her husband in Dayton, Ohio." However, Anthony O'Reilly was on his way to Vietnam but he did not want to tell his family, so they would not worry. The only person to know was his brother-in-law in Ohio and he was sworn to secrecy. Eventually, Anthony's sister, Irene Lapsins, got her husband to admit the secret and contact was established between the O'Reilly's and Anthony, now in Vietnam. The correspondence continued until the fateful day when Anthony was killed in action. His tour of duty began on 28 November 1967 when he was posted to A Company, 2nd Battalion, 39th Regiment, 9th Infantry Division, at Camp Bearcat. He fought through the Tet and Mini-Tet Offensives, experiencing some of the division's heaviest fighting of the war. A local priest informed Pauline O'Reilly, of Anthony's death, while she was at work in the County Buildings, and then Pauline made the sad journey to see her widowed mother at 4 Eyre Street. Anthony O'Reilly's body was brought home for burial at Cemetery Cross, Galway, where his Distinguished Service Cross was presented to his grieving mother. A claddagh ring Mary had given her son before he went to America was also returned and was later buried with Anthony's mother when she died in 1985.[19]

The *Irish Times* of 13 September 1968 reported: "Mother receives son's posthumous bravery awards. A number of bravery awards, citations and decorations won by her son in Vietnam were presented to a Galway mother at a ceremony in Galway. Mrs Mary O'Reilly, Eyre Street, Galway, had the Bronze Star medal and Purple Heart presented to her by Col J. Connor, defence attaché, US Embassy, Dublin. Mrs O'Reilly also received two citations accompanying the bravery awards as well as medals for good conduct, national defence and veteran service."[20]

While there were many Irish males in the armed forces in Vietnam, Irish females also had their representatives. Almost 10,000 women served in Vietnam during the war. They are the war's forgotten heroines. Over 150,000 US troops were hospitalised during the war and it is to the credit of the medical staff that the majority survived. The army nurses worked eight-hour shifts in various units: intensive care, post-op and medical wards.

In their spare time some went to the outlying villages on the Medical Civilian Aid Programme (MEDCAP), assisting Vietnamese civilians with basic medical care.[21] Second-Lieutenant Pamela Donovan died of illness while serving with the 85th Evacuation Hospital in Gia Dinh. Born in 1942 in Wirral, Merseyside, Liverpool, to Irish parents Pamela and her family moved back to Dublin, where Pam was raised and educated, before the family moved to Brighton, Massachusetts, in 1956. Pamela graduated from St. Elizabeth's Hospital School of Nursing and became a registered nurse in 1965. Two years later she became an American citizen so she could join the US Army Nurse Corps, though it is thought she had to give up her Irish passport to volunteer for Vietnam. Pamela began her tour of duty in Vietnam on 10 April 1968 with the 85th Evacuation Hospital in Qui Nhon when she "expressed the desire to aid our servicemen wounded in combat. Since going to Vietnam, in letters to her parents, she praised the 'bravery and morale of the boys fighting at the front' on several occasions."[22] She became seriously ill with an unusual Southeast Asian variant of pneumonia and died on 8 July 1968. Pamela Donovan was buried in Mount Hope Cemetery, Boston.[23] The *Irish Times* of 13 July carried a death notice: "Pamela Donovan, beloved daughter of Mr and Mrs Edward A. Donovan, Brighton, Massachusetts, USA (and late of Rathgar, Dublin) prayers, please."[24]

A tribute to Pamela Donovan in a Special Commemorative issue of *The VVA Veteran* reads: "Pamela Donovan's journey to Vietnam was longer than most. She was born and raised in Ireland; her family moved to the U.S. when she was a teenager. Her strong Catholic background led her to try life in a religious community. Donovan later left, but a strong sense of mission stayed with her. She had begun the legal process for naturalisation to become a U.S. citizen, but it was accelerated when she enlisted. (Doreen) Spelts* has only now begun to research Donovan, but the nurse's parents, who have since moved back to England, wrote Spelts to explain why their daughter had joined our army, and our country. 'She was much affected by battlefield portrayals on the news, and she shared with us her distress that all the (American soldiers) were in such dreadful circumstances. She had

---

* Doreen Spelts worked for Congressman Peter Kostmayer's office in Doylestown, PA. In 1984, when Bucks County decided to build a monument to local residents who died in Vietnam, Spelts was assigned to liaison duties with the memorial committee. At one point she found herself wondering if any American women had died in Vietnam. A pamphlet from the National Archives gave her the answer as well as the names of the eight women, the dates of their deaths, and the fact that all were nurses (seven army nurses, and one air force nurse).

learned that all the nurses were volunteers, and she told us that she had decided she should volunteer.'"[25]

Another Irish native, Philip Seán Bancroft, arrived in Vietnam on 5 November 1967 shortly after completing his basic training. He enlisted in the Marines at eighteen, directly after leaving high school. He was assigned to the 1st Marine Division in Quang Nam. Philip was made a corporal at nineteen, a testament to his leadership qualities and bravery in action. Born in Belfast in 1949 Philip Bancroft and his family left the divided city for Pittsburgh in the early 1950s. He was mortally wounded by a rocket, or mortar round, on 30 September 1968, thirty-six days short of completing his year in Vietnam. Med-evaced for treatment Philip said to the doctor treating him, "Doc, will I make it?" "Of course you will," the doctor replied convincingly, even though he knew there was no chance the young Irishman would survive his wounds.[26] In a war where the average age of combat soldiers was nineteen, Phil Bancroft is the only teenage Irish casualty. More than three decades on, Robert Louis Park still grieves the death in Vietnam of his buddy Philip Seán Bancroft. "Not even time has healed the loss," wrote the former Marine from West Virginia in October 1999. In Vietnam, Park — a lanky West Virginian who claims Irish lineage through a grandfather named Pattison — made an unlikely partner for the shorter and slightly-built Irishman. Recalling their first meeting in Vietnam, Park, who had himself just turned twenty, remembers "thinking to myself that I was young — but this kid was just a baby," one tough baby "pound for pound". Bob Park said, "Phil was the best damn Marine I ever served with, and one of the few I trusted to watch my back. I walked a lot of point (lead man on patrols) and Phil was my cover man." They became firm friends, and had the same appreciation for wry humour and practical jokes, developed with Park playing the protective role of an older brother.

On the night of 30 September 1968 when Philip was mortally wounded in a mortar and rocket attack, Bob was stationed some distance away, out of earshot. His commanding officer, convinced that Park would likely die too as he tried to reach his buddy in darkness and under fire, gave orders that he not be informed till daylight. By then, Bancroft had been med-evaced for treatment. Later, Park's lieutenant took him aside and broke the news. "I'd seen a lot of men wounded, and a lot of men die. But I wasn't prepared for what happened to me next. I cried. I guess I knew that I had just lost the best friend I had — or ever will have."[27]

\* \* \*

Provincial Irish newspapers carried reports on the many local men who were serving or had served in Vietnam. Much of the reporting was from a local point of view. The *Leinster Leader* of June 1968 carried a report on Castleblaney native Neill Cullen, who had served over two years with the US Army, including a year "fighting in Vietnam," who had returned home the previous summer for a holiday and "met Patricia Brennan, of Enfield, a schoolteacher, and sister of Tony Brennan, All-Ireland Meath footballer". Neill Cullen and Patricia Brennan married in New York in June 1968. While the *Cork Examiner* of 19 December reported on the exploits of a County Cork native with the headline "Cork Doctor decorated for Valour. Dr (Capt) Michael A. McConnell, Battalion Surgeon, 1/12 Cavalry, 1st Air Cavalry Division, was awarded the Silver Star for actions on 28 May 1968 in Gia Dinh "exposing himself to hostile fire as he treated the wounded". Capt McConnell was earlier awarded a Bronze Star and Air Combat Medal for other operations.[28] From May until September 1968 the 1st Cavalry Division participated in local pacification and "MedCap" (Medical outreach programmes to offer medical support to the Vietnamese local population) missions in I Corps.[29]

In the fall the new MACV commander General Creighton Abrams began to shift US strategy from attrition to a greater emphasis on combined operations, pacification area security, and what was soon to be called "Vietnamisation." At this point the United States undoubtedly had its best and most experienced team in Saigon under Ambassador Ellsworth Bunker and General Abrams, the latter one of the best American generals of the twentieth century. For the first time annual plans co-ordinated with the South Vietnamese government were drawn up. But the writing was on the wall. Gen. Westmoreland had asked the President to mobilise the reserves and give him another 206,756 men to win the war. His "reward" was to be brought home to be chief of staff of the army. Johnson wanted to negotiate a mutual withdrawal of the NVA and US forces, while the Vietnamese communists were only interested in an American withdrawal. They sat down for the years of haggling they had known might ensue until the course of the war and the continued alienation of the American public could settle the issue. At the end of October they were to trade Johnson unwritten, indefinite assurances of de-escalation along the DMZ and around Saigon and the other major cities for an end to all bombing of the North and admission to the talks of a delegation from the National Liberation Front. This concession by the US put the Saigon regime and the Viet Cong on an equal footing.[30]

Overall 1968 had been a bad year for the Americans. Over 14,000 US troops were killed in Vietnam in 1968, the highest annual American death toll of the war. The worst American war crime of the conflict occurred on 16 March 1968 – although it was not revealed in the press until 6

November 1969 – when US infantrymen massacred some 400 unresisting and unarmed old men, women and children, including babies, in the village of My Lai.[31] On 31 March Lyndon Johnson made a televised address to the American people. He surprised everyone by stating that he would not run for president in 1968. Having served only one full term as president, Johnson's announcement came as a total shock. Johnson's decision not to seek re-election was based primarily on personal factors; he was exhausted by the toll the war had taken on him and believed that a new administration might be better placed to deal with the quagmire of Southeast Asia.[32] Johnson was not alone. America wanted to get out of Vietnam as soon as possible. Militarily they were winning, but psychologically they were losing.

## CHAPTER 12

# AIR AMERICA

The neighbouring countries of Laos, Cambodia and Thailand also became embroiled in the conflict in Vietnam. While Thailand would emerge virtually unscathed from the war, Laos and Cambodia would suffer direct consequences in that communist movements would replace their governments. Laos was dragged into the Vietnam War when the eastern parts of the country were invaded and occupied by the North Vietnamese Army, which used Laotian territory as a staging ground and supply route for its war against the South. In response, the United States initiated a bombing campaign against the North Vietnamese, supported regular and irregular anti-communist forces in Laos and supported a South Vietnamese invasion of Laos. The result of these actions was a series of coups and, ultimately, civil war between the Royal Laotian government and the communist Pathet Lao.

This conflict in Laos brought immense grief to the family of a young Irishman in December 1968. The *Irish Times* of 18 December reported that a young West Cork man, Factna McCarthy, Main Street, Dunmanway, an Air America employee, who saw service in Vietnam with the USMC, was one of three killed when a helicopter he was crewing blew up on the ground at Houei Ma, in Laos, on 7 December.[1]

Following Requiem Mass celebrated by Rev. Daniel Burns CC, in St Patrick's Church, Dunmanway, on 18 December, the remains of Factna McCarthy, were interred in the family plot in St Patrick's Cemetery, Dunmanway, in the presence of a large gathering. The remains were accompanied from Laos to Dunmanway by Captain Charles Weitz, of Air America, and his wife, both of whom were good friends of the deceased. Predeceased by his father the chief mourners were Kathleen McCarthy (mother) and Liam, Terence and Daniel McCarthy (brothers). Factna's name appears on the Air America Memorial plaque in the University of Dallas, Texas, as Patrick F. McCarthy. In Ireland he was known as Factna, to his American friends he was known as Pat.[2]

At that time the exploits of Air America who operated as the transport wing of the Central Intelligence Agency (CIA) were largely unknown, although they had been operating in Laos as early as 1954.

The Ho Chi Minh Trail was a logistical system that ran from North Vietnam to the South through the neighbouring kingdoms of Laos and Cambodia. It weaved its way down through the Hmong hill tribesmen lands in Laos.  Air America delivered ordnance, fuel and food to Laotian Government forces and in particular to General Vang Pao leader of the Hmong hill tribe in an effort to help these people stop the incursion into their lands, by using the delivered supplies to fight the intruders, the Pathet Lao guerrillas.[3] As the CIA operation in Laos grew, Air America, along with Continental Air Services, came to provide a fleet of about sixty unarmed workhorse aircraft, from single-engine planes to large C-123 and Caribou transports, together with a wide range of helicopters. It maintained a network of over 200 grass and dirt airstrips scattered across the Laotian Mountains. At its height the CIA operations in Laos tied down the bulk of two NVA divisions, which would otherwise have been available for deployment in Vietnam.[4] Air America employed both civilian and ex-servicemen and Factna McCarthy went to work with them not long after returning from duty in Vietnam. He felt at home on meeting Captain Steve Stevens and Captain Marius Burke, pilots he served with in the same Marine Corps Squadron during 1960/62 at MCAS, New River, North Carolina, and who were now also employed with Air America. Pat had been a crew chief/mechanic on the Sikorsky H-37s, which they flew when all three were in the Marine Corps. (Marius Burke, an Irish-American with descendents in Carrigholt, Co. Clare, was still flying choppers right up to the last days of the war during the fall of Saigon in 1975.) After attending secondary school (Carmelite College, Castlemartyr, Co. Cork) Factna McCarthy went to England seeking employment. In England he worked with an airline company in Bristol. He left for America in 1956 and initially stayed with an uncle in New York. A few years later Factna was conscripted, and served a tour with the USMC in Vietnam. He made only one trip home after going to America.[5]

Joe Hennessy worked as an Operations Manager for Air America in Thailand where he met Factna "Pat" McCarthy. Joe was born in New York, but was brought up in Ireland. His father came from Offaly and his mother from Limerick. In 1952 he started working in Operations for an Airline then called Seaboard & Western, before going to work with Transocean. The main traffic for both these carriers was MATS passengers (US service men). He finds it ironic that those are "the same passengers they are now protesting about going through there, fifty odd years later." He was instrumental in the formation of an Irish independent carrier called Shannon Air Ltd. This

Company had one DC-4 and two DC-7s and did ad-hoc charter work worldwide. Two of their many charters included moving the Irish equestrian team, including their horses, from Shannon to Japan for the Olympics in the 1960s, and moving Moslems from all over Africa to Jedda in Saudi Arabia for their annual pilgrimage to Mecca, which was called the Hadj. Impeded by the continued obstruction by the national carrier that company was forced out of business.

Joe returned to America and went to work for the Air Asia Corporation in Washington DC who seconded him to CAT in Taiwan. That company in turn seconded him to Air America, which was then the transport wing of the CIA. He was based in Udorn, Thailand. "It was no different to any other airline I worked with. They were moving passengers and cargo on the aircraft, " Joe said. In Thailand he met a fellow Irishman, Pat McCarthy, who was a crew chief with Air America. Pat's job was to insure the helicopter he crewed didn't break down. It was important to keep the choppers moving as some of the places they landed in Laos was known as "Indian country" to employees and enemy territory to all others. Joe wrote of his exploits in Thailand and Laos together with his meeting fellow Irishman, Pat McCarthy, in an article now being used as a reference by the University of Dallas.[6]

"Air America ... some may have heard the name, the more educated who have, for reasons best known to themselves, look over their shoulders before commenting. In the movie, *Air America*, Mel Gibson's portrayal of a flamboyant, Gung Ho, irresponsible pilot working with that Airline gave a very a distorted image of the civilian pilots working with Air America. They flew under extreme difficulties and at great risk to themselves, with a company designated to stem the tide of communist forces seeping down through Laos. Gibson's portrayal in no way depicted the proper image and credit due to those men and their actions, exercised in the course of duty.

"At the end of WW2 General Claire Chennault and Whiting Willauer were instrumental in the formation of the airline Civil Air Transport in China. This carrier was created to operate a commercial passenger and cargo service in South East Asia. In the 1950s the CIA secretly bought CAT, and under the guise of a commercial operator this company furnished 'aircraft and crews for secret intelligence operations'. During the Korean War they 'made more than 100 hazardous flights over Mainland China, air dropping agents and supplies'. Air America was what could be called a subsidiary of CAT and was the transport wing of the Central Intelligence Agency, better known as the CIA. Its job was to transport personnel and supplies when and where they were required.

"In 1954, according to the Geneva Conference, Laos got the status of an independent state and like every other state in the world there were groups for and against such a configuration. The Royal Lao Government was the designated governing authority. However, the Pathet Laos (PL) whose pro-communist characteristics during the Cold War, resulted in their endeavouring to take control of that country as they engaged in guerrilla type tactics to overthrow the appointed authority in Laos.

"The Ho Chi Min trail, the main communist supply line, wove its way down through Laos as did the communists and their supplies while they continued their rampage to take over that country. South and west of the Mekong River came Thailand, and though its border outposts suffered an occasional PL attack, their encroachment into Thailand was curtailed despite the fact of that being, no doubt, their next goal. From there the remainder of South East Asia was open to them. The Australians and New Zealanders were very aware of this and they had no intention of allowing communist infiltration into their respective countries.

"But, to reminisce for a moment. In November 1954, CAT pilots flying C-119s in French Air Force markings, flew over six-hundred air drop supply missions to the besieged French paratroops garrison at Dien Bien Phu. During these missions several of these aircraft suffered severe flak damage. During one sortie, an aircraft flown by John B. 'Earthquake Magoon' McGovern, and his co-pilot Wallace Bufford was shot down, resulting in the death of both these men. The kicker survived. McGovern and Bufford were amongst the first Americans killed in combat in the Vietnam War. The crash occurred just south of Dien Bien Phu, and while there has been a delay recovering the remains it is expected that this will eventually be accomplished. After the fall of Dien Bien Phu, CAT crews flying the same C-119s continued dropping supplies to isolated French outposts in Indochina. As a result of the Geneva Agreement signed in July 1954, between August and October of that same year CAT transported 19,808 men, women and children south of the 17th parallel in twelve C-46 aircraft.

"In 1955 the rice crop failed and famine threatened several provinces in Laos. Air America again came to the rescue, this time using three C-46s based out of Udorn in Thailand. They air dropped over a 1,000 tons of relief supplies. Rice was packed in eight stone bags. An eight stone bag would then be encased in a sixteen stone bag. The bags would then be allowed to free-fall from the aircraft. Normally the inside bag would burst on impact but would be contained by the outer bag, saving the rice. Such operations allowed drops into unconventional locations such as on to the sides of mountains and/or marked locations in the jungle.

"When the troubles started in Laos in 1959 there was concern for the Hmong tribesmen there, lest they suffer retaliation from the communists as a result of their association with the French. Vang Pao, a Hmong leader, was motivated by General Phoumi of the Royal Lao Army and assisted by the US Special Forces trained and turned the Hmong into a fighting force to be reckoned with. Vang Pao maintained they would fight the communists or leave the country while adding that he could raise an army of 10,000 men. These tribesmen were scattered over the mountains in Laos. The CIA realised the necessity of good communications as a result of which Air America entered the Rotary Wing business in earnest and supported the Hmong during their many battles but in particular with the one fought against the Pathet Lao, at Pa Dong. Charles Mateer and Walter Wizbowski were the first two Air America helicopter pilots killed as they attempted to land supplies to besieged Hmong in bad weather. Ousted from Pa Dong, Vang Pao moved his forces southeast to Pha Khao. The United States Special Forces had trained 9,000 Hmong tribesmen and furnished them with equipment to engage in guerrilla tactics. As their numbers grew, so did the Air America Rotary Wing Fleet who went on to become their lifeline. While the men were away fighting Air America kept the villages supplied with food while furnishing supplies and equipment to their fighting men. This hallmarked the beginning of the Air America operation out of Udorn in Thailand

"In the mid 1960s the company I worked with went out of business and I headed back to New York to try find another job. The day after I arrived, I saw an advertisement in the *New York Times* from an employment agency, who needed FAA licensed dispatchers. I had an interview with the Air Asia Company in Washington on the following day. I was told that the position was with CAT in Taiwan. When the gentlemen at the interview saw that the location was not a problem for me, all they asked was 'When can you start?' 'Immediately,' was my reply and so the Air Asia Company, on behalf of their subsidiary Civil Air Transport, in Taipei, hired me.

"The following week I left Shannon for Heathrow, picked up a JAL DC8 via Munich / Anchorage, before continuing on to Tokyo, where I overnighted. Next day, I continued on to Okinawa, to pick up a CAT Convair 880, which got me to Taipei several hours later. In Taipei I met Al Ozorio who introduced me to so many people over the next couple of days that I really came to the stage that I did not know who was who. One day Al called me into his office, and out of the blue told me that I was seconded to Air America and said, 'You will be going to Udorn, tomorrow.' 'Udorn,' I thought, 'where in God's name is that?' After my meeting, I headed to the operations office and asked the man behind the counter, 'Where is Udorn?' and he went on to show me on the map exactly where it was. The following day I met Hank Schultz, an A&P, also a new arrival to the Company and who was like myself heading for Udorn. We both boarded the CAT airplane for Hong Kong where I met Joe Kane, a former Transocean crewmember but who now was the CAT Station Manager there. The transit was brief and we were soon back in the air headed for Bangkok where we arrived late in the evening. The CAT people had arranged a hotel and all the trimmings that came to an abrupt halt on the following morning, when we boarded a train. Prior to leaving Bangkok we were told that bandits occasionally held up the train, and should that happen on this occasion we should just give them what we had, without creating hassle. For once I had reservations as to whether I had chosen the right career in the first instance. Dispatching airplanes was one thing however hearing that the James Gang has a subsidiary, which had no qualms about taking someone out, and operating in Thailand was something else.

"However, we eventually got to Udorn, and set up in the Siri Udorn Hotel. Arriving at the airport on the following day I met Dick Ford who was my immediate boss. He was a retired army Lt Colonel and he proved to be an exceptionally pleasant man.* The operations office was big, with an abnormally large movement board to facilitate the large number of aircraft that were operating there. A very efficient cordial staff of Thai personnel manned this office and they soon showed me the do's and don'ts of the operation. I immediately became aware my position in Air America was no different to the ones I had had with the other Airlines. My job for the most part was juggling aeroplanes and crew, which was a thing I had a lot of experience doing. I learned crews were type rated and those assigned to fixed wing aircraft such as C-130s, C-123s, DC-3s, and Porters did not jump into helicopters to start charging all over Laos buying guns as Mel Gibson's actions would seem to indicate.

"North of the Mekong was 'Indian Country,' Rotary wing aircraft operating there were required to call in with position reports every ten minutes. The C-123 fleet was on what one might call a charter basis. There were two Customers, AB1, which was run by Jack Deegan, later substituted by Jim Butler. This group was assigned one C-123. Roger Bartell ran AB2 and two C-123s were assigned to this 'customer.' (Captain Roger Bartell, 101st Airborne Division, was the US Army military liaison officer for Air America.) These 'customers' were located in different parts of the Airport and the aircraft assigned them shuttled back and forth carrying supplies

* Lt Col Richard George Ford (retired) was commissioned in 1938 and served during WWII in the Asia-Pacific theatre, then Europe and Taiwan after the war. He is the great grandson of Irish Famine emigrants and a relative served on the USS *Monitor* during the American Civil War.

from Udorn to various zones 'up country' all day. The aircraft were normally allocated in this manner. However, on occasions it would be necessary to give AB1 preference and so allocate them additional C-123s.

"As well there were DC-3s, Porters, Sikorsky UH-34s and who knows what else. The day came to life around 5am and as mechanics checked the aircraft, tankers pumped fuel aboard as forklifts shot up and down the ramp loading pallets, some which were rigged with parachutes for dropping. I often wondered why other Airlines did not adapt to this type of delivery; it saves lots of money in wear and tear, as well as landing charges. The Operations Office prepared the flight plans as crews had breakfast in the cafeteria better known as the Club Rendezvous. Finished they immediately headed for the office to be briefed on the weather, NVA activity, flight plans, fuel loads, and possible ultimate destinations.

"The C-123s and DC-3s usually carried a crew of two pilots and a kicker. The man known as 'the kicker' rigged the chutes for drops. Once the drag chute went flying through the rear door his next priority was to keep out of the way, as the pallets left the airplane, like a bat out of hell. Porters carried one pilot while helicopters, a pilot, a kicker or flight mechanic. The first morning I just stood and watched taking note of what went on. In WW2 movies I had seen flight crews getting prepared to fly but I never thought I would witness such an experience. They took careful note of what was said, commented on 'Charlie's' activities and as though they were going on a joy flight, picked up their chutes. Some carried them by the straps others threw them over their shoulders and with a smile the captain would quip 'See you.' With that they were on their way across the ramp to their respective aircraft. Once everything was moving the operations people went and had breakfast.

"And on one such morning I saw this low sized, red-headed, smiling character, with a chute hanging from his shoulder approach me. 'I'm from Cork,' said the smiling Pat McCarthy who flew as a crew chief on the Sikorskys 'I live in Limerick,' I replied, as we shook each other's hand. The Thais considered our accents to be the common denominator and made him aware of my presence, which resulted in Pat going out of his way to make himself known to me. We spoke for a few moments. 'I gotta go … Slán,' he smiled as he left the operations office. 'Slán,' I replied. From that day, every time we met, we got the greatest kick out of uttering the couple of words of Gaelic we could remember to each other. The Thais and Americans alike tried to figure out what this language was and no doubt wondered if we were in fact a possible threat to security.

"Some weeks later I received a letter from the personnel department in Taipei, with insurance papers, and a bunch of other stuff, which included my company ID number. I looked at it, nodded my head and thought 'James Bond 007 … how are you.' Here now was I '009', two pints ahead of him, in real life, but then Bond never worked with Air America.

"Not alone did Air America transport supplies but they were always on hand to go looking for those Air Force Wallies, who despite all the money that had been spent on their training, and all they had been told about the evasive action they should take in order to avoid getting themselves shot down But did they listen … did they listen … oh no … Some of them still went and managed to go and just do that. And who went looking for them … Air America crews, these were the fellows who had no training for such tactics, but they still went looking and found most of them. They were in fact so successful in this type operation that someone thought that there had to be something in it for the Air America crews and that was what gave them such incentive. A rumour quickly spread that for each Air Force crewmember they rescued they were paid a bonus of $1,500, which was completely untrue. The normal procedure in such instances would be for anyone in a plane going in was to start calling 'Mayday.' Immediately this was picked up his location was determined and whoever was nearest would charge in his direction. On coming near where ever the fellow went in they normally would be able to speak with him on the ground. They would stay far enough away to avoid fire and would ask the fellow on the ground to 'show smoke'. As soon as they saw the smoke they would whip in and depending on the location pick, or winch him up. (The rescue pilot would use the winch to prevent the rotors getting entangled in the trees.) They would then drop the fellow off at the nearest friendly place they could find and he could find his own way home from there. Sometimes the pilots wouldn't even know the people's names they had picked up. Most times they would just hover a couple of inches off the ground so that the fellow could get off and they were gone.

"From the mid to the late 1960s the police action in Laos had turned into a real war and there was I in the middle of it all. Security at the time did not allow me to write home and say what I was doing. In fact when Mary wrote the address I had was an APO Box in San Francisco. Anyway, if I had mentioned what I was involved in she would probably have thought, 'He should keep his head covered now he's having hallucinations.'

"From 1965 to 67 Air America lost a total of eleven crewmembers up in Laos, five of which were as a result of enemy action. In fact I could very easily been the twelfth. As I sat in the office on the morning of December 8 1966, word came through; one of the Sikorskys, Hotel 22, had crashed up country, very far up country. 'Joe you go up there … get some pictures of the aircraft,' said Dick Ford as he handed me a camera. 'You can get a ride withTom Richardson up to Luang Prabang. And I'll have a chopper pick you up and take you on up to the crash site.'

"With camera in hand I got a lift out to Tom Richardson's DC-3, and when it was loaded we headed north. A couple hours later we landed in LP. I was picked up in a jeep and shot across the ramp to a waiting Sikorsky UH34 whose called sign was Hotel 21. Aboard I saw Marius Burke was riding shotgun and without formality, we cranked and headed further north. Some hours later we came into land on the top of a hill. The wreckage of Hotel 22 was at the bottom of this. I made my way down the very steep incline and took all the pictures I could of what was left of the airplane. Fortunately the crew got out without injury. Finished, I made my way back up the hill and met Marius. 'It will be getting dark soon, so we'd better be getting out of here,' he said.

"Anything in the air after darkness in Laos was fair game not that they wouldn't have a crack at you during the daylight, but I am sure crews felt that in the daylight they could at least see where they were going. The crew got aboard. I got in, moved up the airplane and sat on the floor. There were two other passengers. One was the kicker from Hotel 22 and the other was a mechanic. I sat there, heard the crew going through the pre-flight, listened as the engine fired up, felt a slight vibration as the rotors were engaged and for a couple of moments we sat there, burning and turning. Then the chopper lifted off the ground and started to back quickly off the pad. In a matter of seconds I felt the airplane sinking. 'We've lost ground effect,' the kicker shouted and as he did the Captain pushed the nose down to gain forward speed and turn, but the aircraft continued forward and sinking. 'We're going in,' the kicker shouted, as he jumped through the opened door, seconds before we crashed into the side of the hill.

"I grabbed the stay above me, and held on as the fuselage continued to tumble and bounce its way down the hill. Anything that wasn't tied down was flying around, as the cabin bounced off the side of the hill on its way down. I got a belt of a toolbox in the ribs but I still held on until the wreckage finally came to rest at the bottom of the hill. Fortunately, for us the aircraft did not burst into flames. I started to crawl back inside the wreckage, and on coming to an opening Marius Burke and Tom Pitkin helped drag me from the shambled wreck. Shattered rotors mingled with tangled, twisted wreckage, as it lay strewn all over the bottom of the hill.

"Slowly we made our way back up the hill, and when at last back there I got on the emergency radio and called 'Mayday' a couple of times in the hope that someone might hear me, but no luck. We dared not continue using the radio or light a fire lest the PLs home in on our position. They no doubt had more artillery that we had, so we certainly were no match for them. The emergency equipment was broken out. The tent was set up; cans that looked like their sell by date had expired years before Dunnes (Stores) had thrown them out were broken out. Frankly I couldn't say what the stuff tasted like I just ate what I got. After darkness our position allowed us to overlook the jungle, and occasionally flashes of gunfire could be seen in the darkness. The captain organised sentry duty. We got into the tent kept close together to keep warm, and as I lay there for what seemed like hours got a gentle tug on the shoulder as it was my turn to play soldier. The man I relieved un-cocked the M16 before handing it to me. I immediately re-cocked it, nervously, sat, not knowing what to expect but I know had anything, anything what so ever in front of me had moved I would have pulled that trigger. All were awake at dawn on the following morning. We waited and we waited and eventually about 10am we saw a chopper far in the distance sweeping back and forth, looking for us, in a line parallel to our position. Marius fired a flare, but they did not see it. When the aircraft turned to sweep back he fired another one. All waited and hoped he would see it. Suddenly the chopper turned and started to head in our direction a cheer went up from the couple of us that was there, thrilled that he now knew out location. The lumbering big nosed Sikorsky H-34 would by no means qualify, if there were such a thing as a helicopter beauty competition, but to us on that particular day she looked like Marilyn Monroe."

At dawn the day after the crash the search for the downed helicopter began. The pilot of the first chopper to arrive on the scene was Captain Wayne Knight. He brought Joe and the rest of the stranded crew back to Luang Prabang, where they were put on a C-130 to Udorn. While Joe Hennessy was recovering in a Bangkok hospital he got an "unexpected visitor from Ireland. 'My name is Burrows, I'm from Enniskillen, I'm Church of Ireland, but whipped into see you when I heard you were Irish,' said the visitor as he stood over my bed some weeks later in the Bangkok Christian Hospital. Small in stature, he smiled and every day from then on he came to see me. 'Look at this!' he quipped many visits later as he held up the newspaper they called the *Bangkok Post*. IRISH GUN BOAT FIRES ON RUSSIAN TRAWLER read the headline. On reading the story I went on to find out that some Russian trawler had been caught fishing inside the twelve-mile limit in Irish waters. When the Russian Captain saw this Irish frigate approaching, he cut his nets and started to run for the high seas. He had no intention of waiting around for a boarding party. However the Captain on the Irish frigate fired a couple of shots across the Russian's bow, and that quickly put a stop to his gallop. Had the Russian known they fired the last two shells they had, he sure, as hell would not have waited for the boarding party.

"The 'Secret War' in Laos, as it became known, was for a time, what might be called seasonal. From October to May the PLs and their buddies the NVA went on the offensive, shooting anything that moved, in particular the Hmong and Government forces. However when the monsoon season came around these fellows had the advantage of having the mobility provided by Air America and kicked butt deep into enemy territory. The situation there was described as 'a mirror image of Vietnam'. The North Vietnamese, impatient with the progress of the Pathet Lao, introduced major new combat forces into Laos and took control of the year's dry season offensive, resulting in the Hmong loosing more than 1,000 men. In 1969 despite their decline in strength the Hmong discarded their guerrilla tactics, and using the increased air power available to them, launched a major offensive against the PL and NVA. As a result of which they reversed their position, and reclaimed all that was theirs as a result of which they captured 1,700 tons of food, 2,500 tons of ammunition, 640 heavy weapons and 25 Soviet tanks. Their success was short lived as the NVA brought in two divisions to reclaim all they had lost.

"It soon became obvious that Laos would become communist dominated State despite all the efforts to insure that this would not happen. Between 1972 and 1974, twenty-three Air America crew were killed in flight operations in Laos. On 27 January 1973 the Paris Agreement on Vietnam was resolved. American troops would move out of Vietnam. The following month, a cease-fire, resulted in the formation of a coalition government for Laos. On the 3 June 1974 Air America ceased operations in Laos and moved to Saigon, where they flew until 1975. The CIA then disbanded the Company but, Air America, like the West Clare Railway, will forever remain a myth and while people will speak and read about it, many will wonder if in fact the writings are a work of fiction.

"The crews, operations personnel, mechanics and all others employed with Air America, were employed by an airline. All other airlines in the world did the identical same work, moving passengers and cargo from one place to another with circumstances dictating policy as to places and loads. The people of Air America gave it there all, to the extent that one hundred of them in total gave their lives in the course of duty in Laos. 'Never in the history of the British Empire has so much been done by so few for so many,' complimented Winston Churchill on the actions of the Royal Air Force during WW2. Had Mr Churchill been around in the mid 1970s he could just as easily have said, 'Never in the history of Civilian Aviation, have employees shown loyalty as did the personnel of Air America. Some gave the ultimate, which did not deter the remainder from carrying on, despite knowing the possible consequences.'

"A total of 243 Air America personnel gave their lives and those missing presumed dead, in the course of duty, during Air America's tenure in South East Asia.[7] 12 February 1969 was no different to any other day. Most aircraft were in the air. Glancing at the large clock in the Operations Office I saw that it was 1200. It was about to go to lunch when the phone rang. It was Bob Crone, one of the Operations Managers from Vientiane, who due to their work load at that particular time had a requirement for an additional C-123 to help them with their workload. Our board showed we had a C-123, which was presently en-route from LP to Udorn, and I requested that he position Vientiane. At 1400 I called the Operations Office in Vientiane to inquire when this aircraft would be released by them to us. I asked to speak with Bob only to be told that he had been killed an hour previously. The story I heard was that soon after he had spoken to me, he and a pilot were flying a Piper Cub that was blown out of the air by PL fire. These two men from Vientiane, and Pat McCarthy from Udorn, Thailand, were only three of the one hundred Air America people, who had life snuffed from their grasp in the course of duty in Laos. They may be gone, but are not forgotten as their names are engraved for all to see, on the CAT/Air America Role of Honour Memorial on display at the McDermott Library, at the University of Texas, in Dallas, Texas."

> *'Slán' I murmured on reading the name,*
> *Of Pat McCarthy who from Cork came,*
> *For north of the Mekong, came a thunderous sound,*
> *As Pat in the chopper blew up on the ground.*
> *No more he'll reply, his spirit is free,*
> *But his mortal remains lay in Cork, by the Lee.* \*[8]

Joe Hennessy is now retired and living in Limerick. Captain William J. Fraser, Crew Chief Pat McCarthy and Bernardo L. Dychitan were killed when their helicopter blew up on 7 December 1968.[9] The helicopter, a Bell 205, blew up on the ground before take-off. It seems as a sack of grenades were thrown on board, a pin dislodged and exploded, triggering off the grenades.[10]

---

\* The River Lee rises in the Shehy Mountains on the western border of County Cork and flows eastwards through Cork city.

CHAPTER 13

# DARKNESS FALLS

O n Wednesday 15 May 1968 Captain Edmond Landers was killed in
action while engaging Viet Cong elements in Gia-Dinh Province. He
was thirty-one years old and a native of Oola, Co. Limerick. It was five days
after Ed Landers was killed before word reached his wife and family back
home in Ireland and another nine days before his remains returned home.
On 29 May his body arrived at Dublin Airport, escorted by Captain Terence
M. Barnes (Survivor Assistance Officer), United States Army and Sergeant
Harry Dewald, United States Air Force, his brother-in-law. His casket was
draped in the flag of the United States and was brought to the village church
in Oola the same day, where it lay overnight after a short religious ceremony. The following day, after Requiem Mass, Captain Edmond Landers was
buried in the local cemetery. There were poignant scenes as the flag was cer-
emoniously folded and presented to his young widow, Teresa, before the
casket was lowered into the ground. Later that year, in November 1968, a
US military headstone of white granite, bearing Captain Landers' name,
arrived from the United States, and was erected to mark his final resting
place.

Thirty-one years later, on 2 May 1999, a special dedication ceremony
was held at Adare Manor, County Limerick, at the conclusion of the Irish
tour of "The Wall That Heals". A memorial statue commissioned by the
owner, Thomas Kane, a Vietnam veteran, was dedicated to the memory of
the Irish US servicemen who died in Vietnam. It was also dedicated to the
members of the Irish Defence Forces who died on UN missions from the
Congo to the Lebanon. This memorial depicts the body of a dead serviceman, wrapped in his poncho, his face covered, nothing visible except for his
right arm and combat boots, with his helmet placed under his feet. Hosted
by Thomas Kane the dedication ceremony was attended by Irish Prime
Minister Bertie Ahearn; the US Ambassador to Ireland, Michael O'Sullivan;
Lieutenant-General David Stapleton, Chief of Staff of the Irish Defence
Forces; Major General Larry Lust of the US Army; Major-General Matthew

Caulfield US Marine Corps, and Brigadier-General David Taylor, GOC 1 Southern Brigade, Irish Army.

During the ceremony, Maj.-Gen. Larry Lust of the US Army presented Mrs. Theresa Landers and her daughter Chantelle with two outstanding gallantry decorations, which had been awarded posthumously to Capt. Landers over thirty years previously. The medals were the Republic of Vietnam Gallantry Cross with Palm and the National Order of Vietnam, Fifth Class. He explained to those present the significance of these awards and also stated that: "The fact that South Vietnam no longer exists does not diminish the sacrifices made by Captain Landers and the 58,000 plus names on the wall, for they had a duty and they met that duty. I assure you that neither of these awards were passed out often or cheaply especially to foreigners. Freedom isn't free. Citizens of a free nation enjoy their freedom because of men and women like Captain Landers."

Also at the dedication ceremony was Walter O'Shea, a nephew of Ed Landers, who recalled: "Edmond was a true soldier, a paratrooper, who had served in one of the U.S. Armies élite airborne units, the 101st Airborne Division, "The Screaming Eagles", and who served the last few months of his life in combat with the men of the 1st Infantry Division, in the Republic of South Vietnam. Before leaving for Vietnam in February 1968, he gave me the peaked cap of his officer's green uniform. On it was a large golden eagle, the symbol of a commissioned officer in the United States Army. This particular item was something that he knew I would have given anything to have possession of. His last words to me before he left were 'look after this for me until I come home'. Unfortunately, he never did return home again, alive."

Edmond John Landers was born in the village of Oola, County Limerick, in 1937 the youngest of a family of four boys and three girls. After a year working as a barman in Kilburn, London, Ed Landers returned to Ireland and joined the FCA, serving in the Pallasgreen Battalion and the 3rd Field Supply and Transport Company, at Sarsfield Barracks in Limerick City. He emigrated to the US in May 1957, living first with his sister, Mary Dewald and her family in Vacaville, California. While there he worked for the Pacific Gas and Electric Company until May 1958, when he was called up to serve two years mandatory National Service in the US Army. After basic training in Fort Ord, California, he was assigned to the 82nd Airborne Division, at Fort Bragg, North Carolina. He qualified as a Senior Paratrooper and was honourably discharged in April 1960 as a Specialist 4. He immediately re-enlisted for a further three-year term, quickly made sergeant, served over two years in Japan and Okinawa, and on return to the US in March 1963 became an American citizen. The following month Ed was selected as an officer candidate and when he graduated was placed eighth out of over 111 other students. On receiving his commission to the rank of Second Lieutenant, Ed was assigned to the 101st Airborne Division at Fort Campbell, Kentucky, where he qualified as a Master Paratrooper.

While on one of his few trips home to Ireland, while stationed in Japan, Ed met Teresa Murphy, the sister of his brother John's wife. They were married on 1 January 1964 in Tipperary town and after a honeymoon in Ireland the couple returned to the US where their only child, Chantelle, was born in May 1965. After a brief stint in Korea and Germany Edmond Landers was promoted to Captain in early 1967 and in September received written orders for a twelve-month tour of duty in Vietnam beginning in February 1968. Ed and his family returned to Ireland in December 1967 and in early February 1968 he left Shannon Airport en route for Saigon, via the USA, London and Germany. He arrived at Tan Son Nhut Airbase, Saigon on 29 February 1968, and reported to a replacement centre at Lai Khe, where he remained for a few days awaiting confirmation of his orders and subsequent assignment. The 1st Infantry Division, the Big Red One, was tasked with securing Tan Son Nhut Airbase and for the conduct of operations in and around Saigon. Capt. Ed Landers was assigned to the division's 2nd Battalion, 18th Infantry Regiment, based at the Thu Duc Water Treatment Plant. The 2nd Battalion operated both within and outside the Capital Military District of Saigon, Gia Dinh Province, in III Corps Tactical Zone. During his tour Ed Landers served through two major military campaigns, the Tet Counteroffensive (30 January-1 April 1968) and Counteroffensive Phase IV (2 April-30 June 1968).

Capt. Landers first appointment was as Battalion Intelligence Officer, or S-2. His code name was Darkness 2 and in that capacity he took part in many of his units field operations, as part of a Combined Divisional Operation code named "Resolve to Win." This operation, over a twenty-eight day period, from 1 March-7 April, involved twenty-two battalions from the US 1st, 9th and 25th Infantry Divisions, assisted by battalions of the ARVN, in operations in Saigon and five surrounding provinces. Two months after his arrival in Vietnam, Ed was assigned a Rifle Company. On 12 April he was appointed Commanding Officer of Company A, 2nd Battalion, 18th Infantry, based at the Thu Duc Electrical Power Plant. Earlier that month, on 8 April, the Big Red One had embarked on the largest operation of the war to date. The two-phase operation code-named "Certain Victory" involved all US military and Allied troops within III Corps Tactical Zone. The objective of Phase-One of the operation was to prevent re-supply and replacements to enemy forces already inside III Corps TZ and to prevent further infiltration of VC and NVA units into the area, especially the capital Saigon. In order to achieve the mission objective, extensive Reconnaissance in Force and Ambush Operations were conducted throughout the Tactical Zone. (Phase-One ended on 31 May, after fifty-four days, and was immediately followed by Phase-Two.)

On 15 May Alpha Company under the command of Capt. Edmond Landers (Call sign: Darkness Alpha 6) was engaged in military operations against NVA and VC forces in Gia-Dinh Province. The Company, which consisted of HQ element CP and 1st and 3rd Platoons, was conducting a reconnaissance in force mission near the village of Thu Duc, in the Thu Duc district, northeast of Saigon. They were supported by A Troop 7-1 Air Cavalry light fire teams and artillery. Earlier that morning Capt. Landers had stood down the 2nd Platoon and tasked it with maintaining security at the unit CP in his absence. At 0700 hours A Company departed its CP at the Thu Duc Electrical Power Plant, and moved on foot along the railroad tracks heading northwest until they reached Highway 1. They turned west on Highway 1 and crossed a bridge, which was held by ARVN troops. Normally a US Military Adviser was stationed with the ARVN, but he was not at the bridge when A Company crossed, so no information was passed to indicate there was any enemy activity or suspected activity in the immediate area. The company continued to move west along the highway until they reached a trail running northwest. They moved up the trail for about 500 metres and deployed with two platoons in line, heading east. Up to this point the company had made no contact with the enemy and there was no indication of any enemy activity. They had only moved about 300 metres east when initial contact was made.

While moving through an area of thick vegetation, the unit was suddenly subjected to intense small arms, machine gun and RPG fire from a large Viet Cong force. Three men were killed and five wounded. Capt. Landers sent a contact report to Battalion HQ and requested support fires and medical-evacuation. The VC occupied a series of well-concealed and strongly fortified bunkers and all approaches to their positions were covered by integrated patterns of fire. At the time of the initial contact Capt. Landers courageously led his men forward through the intense hostile fire. He ignored enemy rounds hitting all about him as he moved from position to position, checking casualties and adjusting friendly artillery fire upon the well-entrenched VC. Landers then led an assault across an open rice paddy, and from this forward position he was able to direct effective fire on four enemy bunkers. He then directed evacuation helicopters into the area to promptly extract his wounded. Once again he reorganised his men and they continued the assault, again coming under heavy effective fire from concealed underground bunkers. They fought through the area destroying numerous enemy bunker positions. A Company then continued its advance.

At approximately 1530 hours, as Capt. Landers and his men were again moving forward, Ed spotted several Viet Cong positioned in a pagoda about to open fire. He shouted to his men to take cover, but before he could reach safety he was hit in the chest and mortally wounded by a sniper located in a spider hole. He died from his wounds minutes later. The sniper was subsequently killed in the ensuing firefight. Two other men were killed, including Capt. Landers' radio man. The leader of the First Platoon, Lieutenant David Chapman, and his RTO and FO were also wounded. Lt. Chapman said: "Captain Landers was about fifteen metres in front of me laying next to another man. I could see that they were both dead. Another officer was between me and Captain Landers. He had only been wounded. I tried to get over to him but when I moved the shooting started again. I could see rounds hit all three of them. I shot back but I did not know where the shots came from. Every time I tried to move they opened up again. Just about that time, Colonel Waldrop came on the radio and I informed him of the situation. I still could not move without getting shot at. The gun-ships came in, which kept the V.C. hard-down while I made my way back to the rest of the guys."

The Battalion commander, Lieutenant Colonel Max Waldrop, was in the air in his command helicopter directly over the action. He realised his troops were in very serious trouble, with the commander on the ground, Capt. Landers, seriously wounded and the Platoon Leader 1st Platoon and his Artillery FO also wounded. He called for a replacement commander to be inserted on the ground to regain control of the situation and evacuate the wounded and the dead. He then ordered his chopper to set down, Just before he left Col Waldrop was informed that Capt. Landers was dead. Waldrop then made his way to the med-evac area and assumed command until reorganisation of the company was complete and all troops wee accounted for. After about an hour on the ground Lt-Col Waldrop handed over command to a subordinate officer, who assumed command for the remainder of the action. The rest of A Company then pulled back, and air and artillery strikes were called in and pounded the battle area. A Company continued the engagement until relieved by reinforcements later that evening. Captain Landers body had been removed from where he fell to the rear of the battle area. During the day long battle 2nd Battalion lost Captain Ed Landers and nine other men killed and thirteen wounded. The bodies of thirty-two enemy soldiers were found in the area.

For his actions on the day he died Ed Landers was posthumously awarded the Silver Star. His citation reads: "For gallantry in action while engaged in military operations involving conflict with an armed hostile force in the

Republic of Vietnam. His selfless concern for the welfare of his men and gallant efforts undoubtedly saved numerous friendly lives and contributed significantly to the defeat of a large Viet Cong Force. Captain Landers unquestionable valour in close combat against numerically superior hostile forces is in keeping with the finest traditions of the military service and reflects great credit upon himself, the 1st Infantry Division and the United States Army." He was also awarded the Purple Heart for "Wounds Received in Action", resulting in his death, and the Bronze Star for "meritorious Achievements Against Hostile Forces" from 29 February to 15 May 1968. These medals, plus six other awards, were presented to his widow, Teresa, in the US Embassy, Dublin, in September 1968. The ceremony was held by the then US Ambassador to Ireland, Leo J. Sheridan, and the US Defence Áttache, Colonel Joseph F. O'Connor.

Edmond J. Landers was both a dedicated family man and a professional career soldier. On the day he died he left behind a young wife and a daughter, who was just twelve days away from her third birthday. In a letter to his widow after his death, his Battalion Commander, Lt-Col Max Waldrop stated, "I find it difficult to write to you as it reminds me of Ed and that black day of 15 May. As I've said before, not only did I lose an outstanding Company Commander, I also lost a friend along with several other fine soldiers."

In a letter written to Ed Landers nephew Walter O'Shea, LTC Max Waldrop (Retd), Edmond's commander in Vietnam, recalled his service with Capt. Landers and said, "In my dealings with Ed, I found him to be an honest man. He was a brave soldier, courageous and completely unselfish. He was an intelligent and competent officer. One of his outstanding characteristics was his concern for his men. He worried more about their welfare than he did about his own. I found Ed to be calm when things started popping and he was cool under pressure. It was a distinct pleasure for me to have known him, and an honour to have served with him. If I had to do it all again I would choose Ed to be a member of my team."[1]

## CHAPTER 14

# THE YEAR OF
# LIVING DANGEROUSLY

O n 20 January 1969 eight years after he lost to John F. Kennedy, Republican candidate Richard M. Nixon was inaugurated as the thirty-seventh US President and declared " … the greatest honour history can bestow is the title of peacemaker. This honour now beckons America … " He was the fifth President coping with Vietnam and had successfully campaigned on a pledge of "peace with honour". By November the Nixon administration had introduced the concept of "Vietnamisation" to the war. This entailed re-equipping the ARVN so it would be able to stand alone against the communists, allowing a gradual US withdrawal. The level of US involvement in the ground war began to drop throughout the year and while the intensity of the fighting did not reach that of the Tet Offensive the fact that thousands of Americans were still dying continued to divide America. In April 1969 peak US troop strength stood at 543,000. Two months later the first of the promised troop withdrawals began, as 25,000 men of the 9th Infantry Division were withdrawn from Vietnam. Between 18 September and 15 December another 40,500 men – primarily the 3rd Brigade, 82nd Airborne and the 3rd Marine Division were withdrawn. At the end of 1968 the US troops in Vietnam, whatever their view of the war, were a cohesive force, but the morale and discipline of American troops declined in 1969 as the futility of the ground war and the beginnings of US withdrawal became more obvious. After an intense ten-day battle in May, infantrymen of the 101st Division (Air Mobile) took a ridge in the A Shau Valley that they had dubbed Hamburger Hill. Having fought bravely and suffered significant losses, the soldiers were bitter when the site was soon abandoned. In America the anti-war movement became stronger and more and more troops began to wonder why they were there risking their lives when the people and the politicians back home were giving up on the war. Slogging through the jungle, fighting a war nobody cared about soon affected combat effectiveness. Simple survival of their twelve-month tour of duty became the only motivation for many soldiers. Incidents of insubordination, mutiny, "fragging" of officers, drug use, racial tensions, and other serious problems increased. The professional soldiers of 1965-67 had gone to be replaced more and more by draftees who did not want to be the "last GI to die in Nam."[1]

For many soldiers in Vietnam there was no war. (Only about 50,000 of the 500,000 or so Americans in-country, were in combat at one time.) Many soldiers never saw any of it in the giant rear base camps and beaches. Even for them, though, there was fear, depression and anxiety. The fear of what could happen, the depression of being part of an unpopular violent conflict, the anxiety of being away from wives, sweethearts, friends and family for a whole year. Their fears and anxieties manifested itself in the abuse of drugs and the refusal to carry out orders. While Nixon preached peace, the war escalated; Cambodia was invaded in 1970, Laos in 1971, and the bombing and killing kept going on and on.[2]

Despite the withdrawals and the scaling down of the American war 1969 was a bad year regarding casualties and 9,314 Americans were killed in Vietnam. Thomas P. Noonan, an Irish American with family roots in Woodside, was posthumously awarded the Medal of Honour for heroism during February 1969 in Vietnam. He was born in 1943, in Brooklyn, New York, and grew up in Woodside, Queens. He has a playground in Thomas Hill Park, Sunnyside, Queens, named in his honour. Tom Noonan enlisted in the US Marines in December 1967. His education could have granted him an almost immediate commission when he joined the Corps, but he preferred to serve as a rifleman and was ordered to Vietnam in July 1968, where he was assigned duty as a mortar man with H&S Company, 2nd Battalion, 27th Marines, 1st Marine Division. In August, he was reassigned to the 3rd Marine Division where he saw combat as a rifleman and M-79 man with Company G, 2nd Battalion, 9th Marines.

Tom was promoted to lance corporal in January 1969 and was mortally wounded on 5 February 1969, while participating in action against NVA troops south of Vandegrift Combat Base, headquarters for the 9th Marines.[3] Operation Dewey Canyon was the last major offensive by the Marines during the Vietnam war. It took place from 22 January through 18 March 1969 and involved a sweep of the NVA-dominated A Shau Valley by the 9th Marine Regiment reinforced by elements of the 3rd Marine Regiment. The Marines encountered stiff resistance throughout the conduct of the operation, most of which was fought under triple canopy jungle and within range of NVA artillery based in Laos. Marine casualties included 130 killed in action and 932 wounded, while the USMC reported 1,617 NVA killed, the discovery of 500 tons of arms and munitions, and denial of the valley as a NVA staging area for the duration of the operation. The Marines claimed the operation as an overall success.[4]

On 5 February the men of Company G were moving out of its location southeast of Vandergrift Combat Base as part of the incursion into A Shau Valley. It was early in the monsoon season, so the dense foliage, the intermittent rains and the slippery mud hampered the progress of the Marines. As the men moved slowly down the hillside through the slippery mud the lead element walked into a concealed enemy position. The North Vietnamese opened fire, wounding four men. Further up the hill the rest of the Marines were stuck by the impossible terrain and the hail of NVA fire. No one could reach the wounded. Lance Corporal Noonan took upon himself the task of rescuing his wounded comrades. He moved carefully down the slippery slope and nearing the wounded, took cover behind some rocks to shout encouraging words to the wounded Marines, assuring them that help was on the way. Tom Noonan raced across the fire-swept area, locating the most seriously wounded man and dragging him backwards to shelter. Enemy rounds hit Tom, knocking him to the ground. Despite his own wounds, Lance Corporal Noonan got back up and resumed dragging the wounded Marine towards the cover of the rocks from which he had earlier encouraged the men. Before reaching its shelter, enemy fire hit him again. Inspired by Noonan's example, the rest of the platoon charged the enemy, pushing them back and reaching the wounded. All four survived, but Tom Noonan did not. He was the only fatal casualty.

Tom Noonan's citation describing the events said that as a group of Marines "commenced a slow and difficult descent down the side of the hill made extremely slippery by the heavy rains, the leading element came under heavy fire from a North Vietnamese army unit occupying well-concealed positions in the rocky terrain." When four wounded comrades were cut off, "repeated attempts to recover them failed because of the intense hostile fire. L/Cpl. Noonan moved from his position of relative security and, manoeuvring down the treacherous slope to a location near the injured men, took cover behind some rocks. Shouting words of encouragement to the wounded men to restore their confidence, he dashed across the hazardous terrain and commenced dragging the most seriously wounded man away from the fire-swept area. Although wounded and knocked to the ground by an enemy round, L/Cpl. Noonan recovered rapidly and resumed dragging the man toward the marginal security of a rock." Noonan was mortally wounded when hit again by enemy bullets before he could reach the rock. He died, the collar of his wounded comrade's fatigue shirt still grasped in his hands in a valiant attempt to save a friend.[5]

March was a bad month for the Irish in Vietnam. Before it was over three Irish soldiers – Brian McCarthy, Seán Doran and Peter Nee – would be dead. Specialist 4 Brian McCarthy was killed in action on 15 March 1969. Born in The Bronx, NYC, in 1945 to an Irish (Cork) father Brian's tour of duty had begun on 2 July 1968 with the 1st Infantry Division. Brian was a teacher in New York and could have become an officer, but only wanted to do his two years national service and return to the job he loved most – teaching. He had a cousin, Bob Fitzgerald, from Connecticut, serving in Vietnam at the same time, but neither were aware of each other's presence in-country. Brian McCarthy survived many fire fights in his eight months in South Vietnam, but was killed from multiple fragmentation wounds from an explosive device in Long Binh on 15 March.[6]

Corporal Seán Doran was killed by small arms fire on 28 March in Tay Ninh, fifteen days after arriving in-country. Born in Dublin in 1948 he lived at Lennox, California, and was drafted in 1968 and posted to the 25th Infantry Division. He was twenty years old when he died.[7] The enemy's use of Cambodia as a sanctuary led to an increased emphasis on American operations in Tay Ninh province and the 25th Infantry Division conducted many patrols in their theatre of operations near Saigon. The patrols were anxiety-ridden because of the many mines and booby traps planted by the enemy and the sudden prospect of deadly ambush. Seán Doran was on one of these many patrols when he was killed in action.[8]

Lance-Corporal Peter Nee was killed from multiple fragmentation wounds on 31 March in Quang Nam while serving with the US Marines. He had enlisted on 15 April 1968 and arrived in Vietnam on 30 September 1968 and was assigned to the 5th Marine Regiment, 1st Marine Division. Born in Connemara, Co. Galway, in 1947, Peter Nee had emigrated to the US and lived with his cousin, John Glynn in the Savin Hill neighbourhood in Cambridge, Massachusetts. His sister, Margaret, said he didn't have the chance to go to secondary school in Ireland, but he did go to High School in Boston and worked at night. She said he intended going to College and liked science and law. Margaret noticed in his letters that Peter told his mother he would send more money home only that so much was taken up with his schooling. Peter also felt that he should serve the country where he would have many opportunities. His mother always kept a poem he wrote to her at her fireplace – a sad, almost prophetic poem.[9]

*The brown leaves of Autumn are*
*settling on my path,*
*Soon my footprints will be gone,*
*Forgotten no longer in view.*

*I walk slowly along this path,*
*thinking of the past;*
*things I've done; people I've known;*
*places I've been.*
*My eyes, oh, how little they have seen,*
*now I realise they were blind.*
*My ears have never heard the sweet music*
*of a waterfall, but instead heard and*
*instead heeded the furing call of night.*
*My mind was not a mind but a canyon*
*where thoughts and ideas bounded*
*from wall to wall.*
*My heart was not a heart but a bowl,*
*which when filled, cracked and*
*allowed its contents to flow away.*
*How much have I contributed to life? Nothing!*
*Why must a man travel onward without*
*knowing where he is going?*
*Why all of a sudden does he realise that*
*The things he valued in life are valueless?*
*The things he believed in he finds he*
*never really believed in at all.*
*Why does he find this out when it's too late?*
*The sun slowly descends behind the mountain,*
*the valley is quiet.*
*Crouched behind a fallen tree,*
*A young man awaits for eternity.*
Peter Nee.

Soon after his arrival in Vietnam Peter Nee was wounded in action and then returned to his unit, soon making squad leader with 1st Platoon, Hotel Company, 2nd Battalion. Radio-man Jay Petersen* said, "During the short period from January to March I came to know him as a friend as well as a mentor. I had a grandmother who was Irish (Monaghan) and that was one small thing we had in common. Peter was a squad leader when I arrived in the field. Although not my squad leader he was still concerned about the well being of all the members of the company. His humour was something that always attracted people to him. He had the ability to correct you with a quick command and a little humour to make it easier to absorb. On more

---

*     Jay A. Petersen is now an attorney at law in California.

than one occasion I recall being told I was a real stupid piece of shit and when it came from Peter I almost felt good about it. Because I was assigned to do a job for which I had not trained, I was often subjected to Peter's witty correction." Despite having no training as a radio operator Jay Peterson had been assigned as 1st Squad radio operator and in this position he regularly met the other squad leaders, including Peter Nee.

In March 1969, in a prelude to Operation Muskogee Meadow, which was to begin on 7 April, the 5th Marines moved into positions in the Arizona Territory. The Arizona was a triangle of land, which was defined by the Song Vu Gia river on the north, the Song Thu Ban on the south and a mountain range on the west. The Arizona was a highly contested area. By the end of March Hotel Company were near the east side of the Phu Binh (2) On 31 March Company H was moving north towards Phu Binh (1) with 1st Platoon on point. As Peter's squad approached a treeline, a thick line of bamboo trees, which are used to separate rice paddys, an explosion occurred. Peter Nee was killed instantly. Several of his comrades were also killed and wounded by the explosion. Jay Petersen said, "The platoon commander and I were almost next to him when it occurred and we were the second and third to arrive. We immediately called for a corpsman up. Peter was killed instantly, however, a couple of his squad members were alive. They were evacuated along with Peter and the other KIA within minutes of the explosion." Jay Peterson believed the explosion was from a B40 rocket fired by NVA troops, as Peter was too careful to be killed by a booby-trap. One NVA was killed and another captured shortly after with a rocket launcher. "My belief is that Peter and his squad were hit by a RPG. Peter was always so careful. Given the close proximity of the rocket crew … it is more than likely that they had fired the round, got Peter and were preparing to get a second round off.

"My most vivid memory of Peter was that he liked ice cream bars that would often be sent out with re-supply. I believe they are called ice cream sandwiches. Every once in a while we would get a bunch of ice cream bars shipped out to us by re-supply chopper loaded in metal ice chests.  Peter was constantly saying in his Irish accent that we would be getting ice cream with the next re-supply as if saying it with a positive attitude would make it happen. The day he died with got ice cream with the re-supply."[10] Another comrade, Tom Klein, said, "I think of Peter often as I think we were kindred spirits – he the poet and me the dreamer."[11] Peter Nee was buried in the remote Famine graveyard in Ard Caiseal, Connemara, on the western seaboard of Ireland, facing the country for which he died.

Both the NVA and the VC had suffered enormous losses in 1968-69, but their strength in I Corps held steady at approximately 50,000 troops. The communists had simply shifted away from big-unit offensives to more limited sapper and rocket attacks on American bases and conventional guerrilla operations against the ARVN and Vietnamese villagers. The grunts could hardly tell that the war had changed as they stumbled into booby traps and traded shots with the NVA and VC.[12] In May 1968 the 1st Cavalry (Airmobile) Division and the 101st began probing the A Shau Valley as the US Marines prepared to leave the troublesome I Corps area. The first US Marine redeployments started in mid-1969, and by the end of the year the entire 3rd Marine Division had departed to be replaced in the I Corps area by the 101st Airborne and 1st Cavalry. In early 1969 the 101st Division was deployed in Thua Thien province in the northern I Corps region operating against the NVA infiltration routes through Laos and the A Shau valley. The A Shau valley was a thirty-mile-long natural funnel near the Laotian border in northwest South Vietnam, and was one of the most important VC and NVA supply and staging routes. Nicknamed "Ah Shit Valley," this was the setting for some of the war's bloodiest operations. The valley consists of rolling terrain covered by eight-foot high elephant grass. It is protected by a rim of triple-canopied hills, one of which was Hill 937 — which would soon become known as Hamburger Hill. Because it was so inaccessible, this was key terrain for guerrillas, and one of Hanoi's major supply lines into the South for much of the war. From May 1968 through February 1969 the Screaming Eagles conducted Operation Nevada Eagle, successfully denying the rice crop of Thua Thien province to the enemy. On 1 March the 101st Airborne was recommitted, this time in a series of operations, to clear the valley and reopen temporary airstrips abandoned years earlier. Firebases were set up along the edge of the A Shau and the 101st used helicopters to occupy key locations. Again, supply dumps were uncovered, but little contact with the enemy was made.[13]

First Lieutenant John Driver was killed in an ambush in Thua Thien province on 17 April while serving with the 101st Airmobile Division. He was a natural leader and is still held in great esteem by many who served with him in both the 1st Cavalry and the 101st Airborne. John Driver was a career soldier, a veteran of a 1965-66 tour in the Ia Drang with the 7th Cavalry. After completing his first twelve-month tour of Vietnam, John travelled to Ireland in late 1966 to visit his family. When he returned to the US John was selected for commissioning and went to Officers Training School and underwent airborne training in Fort Benning, Georgia, the home of the US Army infantry. He was commissioned second lieutenant on 12 February 1968, no mean feat for a non-national in the United States. Phil Dean, one of John's classmates at the time, recalled how Driver blended humour with his soldiering: "A few weeks into the class it was John's turn to serve as student company commander. On his first morning John took the report from the first sergeant and delivered the sharpest British salute I have ever seen. The officers went berserk. John said he sometimes forgot which army he was in. The other candidates loved it and loved him."[14]

At Christmas 1968 John again returned home to Ireland bringing with him his new wife of four months, Marie, to meet his family in Ringsend. It was a joyous re-union, but no one knew it would be John's last visit.[15] He began his second tour of duty in Vietnam on 17 January 1969 with Bravo Company, 2nd Battalion, 501st Regiment, 101st Airborne Division. While the 1st Brigade of the Screaming Eagles was in Vietnam since 1965, the remainder of the division did not arrive until December 1967. In 1968 the 101st took on the structure and equipment of an airmobile division – making the transition from parachutes to helicopters. Combat veteran and author of *The 13th Valley*, the 1982 classic of the Vietnam war, John M. Del Vecchio, stated that the "One Oh One" was "the most elite-sized unit in the war".[16] A military unit tends to have a character of its own, an identity comprised of its history and traditions and of the personality of its leaders. A squad becomes an extension of the squad leader, a platoon that of its platoon leader and platoon sergeants; and the company, the body of the captain who leads it. The ethos of the 101st was purposefully directed and devised from the style, zeal and *espirit de corps* of the airborne of WWII – firebases were named after WWII locales and slogans, Bastogne, Carentan, Eagle's Nest, Ripcord, etc. By the time the division had become airmobile most of the troops were no longer hard-core jump-qualified paratroopers, though most of the senior officers and leaders were.[17]

When John Driver took over as Platoon Leader of 1st Platoon, B Company, 2/501st, Bravo Company was under the command of Captain Pierce Graney (now Colonel Graney, retd), who described Driver in 1999 as: "the best lieutenant in the company … a superb soldier … tremendously disciplined … a natural leader," and as having a "great sense of humour."[18] Sergeant James Duke remembered that, "Lt. Driver was one of the most influential people in my life and at the time he came into the company, a real godsend. Sergeant Martin and 'C' were two others but they were made in the American mode but Lt. Driver was by far was the best of the best, a true professional solider. The first time I saw Lt. Driver we had just came in from the boonies* and were waiting at Firebase Birmingham that day before being trucked down to the road to Firebase Boyd, which was our station when we were not in the bush. We had ground our packs near the mess area, which was a bulldozed off table fifteen feet or so high above the heli-

* Airborne troops called the jungle boonies and referred to themselves as boonierats.

copter pad and supply area for the fire base. I was sitting at a mess table when the battalion jeep driver came by and sat down and started talking to me. The first thing he said was that Lt. Julien was going to Second Platoon and a new guy was talking over First Platoon and was going to bust my balls. About that time someone else from my platoon came by and said that we were getting a new platoon leader and Julien was going to Second.

"I knew that Capt. Graney (Bravo company commander) had considered me one for his most insubordinate NCOs and would bust me in a second, but I had been in-country for over five months and an experienced squad leader that he could not find in someone else in the company. What he needed was somebody who could crack this misbehaving squad leader. I had something to think about so I got up from my table and walked over to the ledge and was looking down at the lower level when I saw Graney, Pue, Julien and this new guy all walking together talking as they walked my way. All at once Capt. Graney saw me looking down at them and he stopped and ever so slightly pointed up at me and you could see the eyes of the others follow his point. Then he said a few other words to this older new guy that was in the group of officers I knew so well. He then shouted up to me to form up First Platoon, which I did and we had a short but very formal change of command. Funny thing was that Second Platoon never had a formal change of command when Julien took over that same day from Lt. Welsh who was now our new XO.

"Once Lt. Driver was in charge we gave orders for all to pick up our packs and load up in a deuce-and-a-half truck so we could be trucked down the hill to the area where we were to make camp for the night. We all did just that but when we got to the location where we were to camp some of us climbed off the truck near the front where it was easy to get out of the back bed of the truck. Lt. Driver was in the back and the others back there with him couldn't get out of the truck. He told me to have the driver and shotgun helper to get out of the truck and let down the tailgate. I said to them 'The L-T would like it if you two would get out and let the tail-gate down.' They never moved a muscle but Lt. Driver exploded, 'You two get your bloody asses out of that damn truck and let down this tailgate, NOW.' There was nothing but elbows and assholes from the two in the truck as they ran back to the rear of the truck. At that time I said really loud, 'Boys it looks like we have a real L-T this time,' and I said it loud enough so he could hear it, too. We all took the position up for the night and afterwards a dozen or so of us gathered around and in the waning light we asked questions about Africa and his first tour of duty with the 1st Cav. He was honest, easy to talk to, and the guys fell in love with him almost instantly and for me getting my balls busted, it never happened. It was just like I said in the tailgate incident we had a real L-T. He never said one harsh word to me and only at one time later on in 'the Valley' did he ever say anything harsh to me and that was because he thought I was getting a little too harsh on another NCO in my squad."[19]

Pat O'Leary arrived in Vietnam on 21 November 1968 and departed exactly a year later. Pat remembered John Driver arriving as a lieutenant to his company: "Lt. John Driver was assigned to our company – Bravo 2/501st Infantry. John Driver was probably one of the best soldiers that ever put on a uniform." Pat O'Leary was born in Staten Island, NYC. His mother was from Kilkeel, Co. Down and his father from Philadelphia. "My Mom was a war bride, born in Kilkeel, Co. Down in the northern part of Ireland. My dad was born in Philadelphia. His dad came over from Ireland and joined the US Army during WWI to become a US citizen. While in the Army he met his wife, a US Army Nurse, Mary Lawlor. She was born in the USA, but her parents were both from Ireland. My Dad (Jeremiah) was stationed in Kilkeel just before D-Day and that is where he met my Mom Josephine Hudson. My Mom worked up in Belfast at Langford Lodge for the 8th Air Force as a switchboard operator. I volunteered for Military Service. What I did was I had a deferment from the draft so I went down to my Draft Board and dropped the deferment and 'pushed up' my draft. I could have avoided military service altogether. My older brother is a Vietnam vet and my Dad was a Combat Medic with Patton's 3rd Army, assigned to the 5th Infantry Division. Not serving in the Army never crossed my mind. My brother Jere (Jeremiah) was a truck driver stationed in Saigon. He was with MACV. He arrived in Vietnam just in time for the big party – the Tet Offensive of 1968. He did Tet and I did Hamburger Hill. He was home one month and I went over. My poor Mom what she must have gone through, and Dad.

"My Mom's family had a bit of a history with the IRA. I had a great uncle that was a Battalion Commander. I was raised with a deep understanding of the 'troubles' and what was going on in the northern part of Ireland in the 1960s. One day I was sitting on the side of a hill and Driver walked past me. I looked up at him and said 'Hey, L-T, what the heck are you doing here in Vietnam, you should be back in Ireland fighting with the IRA.' Well he did not say a word, but … he stopped and if looks could kill, I was dead about one thousand times over. The 'eye to eye' exchange took all of about ten seconds. From that moment on I knew John Driver was different. He was a leader, a man's man and the best solider I ever met – a true hero. I was there with him the day he died, doing what he loved to do – soldier. We were stopped along a trail in the very dense, steep jungle mountains of I Corps. Suddenly an ambush was sprung by the enemy. At this point training kicks in and you get low and start putting out fire. All this happens within seconds to short minutes. After the first few seconds of firing I witnessed Lt Driver run down the trail at full speed directly at the enemy position. I did not actually see him get hit. After the smoke cleared we learned of his death. A good man and a great soldier was lost. Lt John Walsh came back out to field to replace Driver and was also killed a short time after."*[20] (Lt John Walsh, an Irish-American from Long Island, New York, was killed in action on 22 April.)

On 17 April 1969 B Company was conducting an advance-to-contact mission against enemy forces. John Driver was reading a letter from his wife in the A Shau when his platoon's OP blew their claymore mine as they came under attack from NVA troops. Lt Driver grabbed his M16 and ran towards the sound of firing, closely followed by his radio man, Clyde Crossguns. Crossguns wrote: "I followed closely behind, the buzz of AK rounds did sizzle past the ears over the helmet, between the legs, under the arms. I looked but could not find (Driver), but suddenly I found that heroes do die." John Driver had been hit in the head and lay mortally wounded. William "Tiny" Kaufman was the artillery RTO that day and said he "rushed down a hill in the A Shau Valley to respond to an enemy attack. As AK-47 bullets zinged around us, John went around a tree and the fire shifted toward us. I was pinned behind the tree and continued firing at the enemy. John moved towards the enemy as AK fire bounced off my tree. The firefight continued intensely for a few minutes, and when the gunfire stopped I came out from behind the tree to find my good friend John had been shot in the face and lay dying. I tried to do something, but it was too late. I knelt beside my friend as he died, and then we wrapped his body up and carried him to a waiting chopper … John was one of the friendliest, kindest and closest officers with his enlisted men that I ever knew. I trusted him and would have followed him anywhere."

Clyde Crossguns said, "I don't remember the first time I met Driver, but what I later remember is that he became a prominent part of my service in Vietnam. I served from November 1968 to 1969. I am an enrolled member of the Blackfeet Tribe of Montana, and the great, great, great, great grandson of the last official Chief of the Blackfeet Tribe, White Calf, who died in 1903 in Washington, D.C., as well as the great, great, great, great, grandson of Chief Mountain Chief, whom the U.S. Army was looking for to

---

* After his army service Pat O'Leary followed his father's footsteps into the NYPD and became a Police Officer, retiring after ten years to become a High School teacher/coach. He is now a College Football Coach at the College of the Holy Cross in Worcester, MA. His brother, Jere, served thirty years with the NYPD

arrest or kill when they massacred Heavy Runner's Band commonly known as 'Baker's Massacre' in 1869 on the Marias River near present day Shelby, Montana. As for Driver, I will always hold a special place for him in heart, he is a source of strength and pride for me even now. I don't recall a whole lot of memories of Vietnam for some reason, other than walking point many times for Driver, and later I believe Driver requested that I be his RTO. As a point man and under Driver's leadership, we seemed to be so very constant in fighting the NVA, but I felt safe which is weird as point men don't usually last very long.

"I however, vividly remember the day Driver was killed. As an RTO I felt it was my duty to stay in close proximately to Driver, in fact I stayed near him almost twenty-four hours a day. I don't recall many conversations with him, as he seemed generally quiet most of the time. On this day April 17th, 1969, he appeared even more quiet, and distant. We were on NDP (Night Defensive Perimeter) for three days, which certainly is out of the norm, and we figured the CO Graney was looking for a fight. He was a gung-ho officer that would volunteer our company for extended stays in the bush, even when the Battalion CO asked him if wanted to be extracted.

"Many times I listened to the Battalion CO and B Company CO radio communications, where Graney would decline, and ask to extend our stay. I do know that the company CO looked up to Driver and respected him. It seemed our platoon was always walking point, many times with me out front. Under Driver we found many NVA weapons cache. Several times Chinook helicopters were needed to remove these mortars rounds, AKs, SKS rifles, claymore mines, 122 mm rockets, RPGs, etc. Under Driver's leadership I believe the NVA tactics where disrupted more than once.

"Going back to that day, our platoon (1st) had an OP (outpost). Specialist James Irvin was one of them. Driver was sitting with his back against a tree in our perimeter I believe reading a letter from his family – wife, I think. Our OP detonated their claymore mine as the NVA were probing our perimeter. I know they hit one NVA as I viewed his wounded body later. As soon as the claymore went off, Driver jumped up, grabbed his M16 and was off. He went down into that ravine where his squad had the OP. I had to release the D rings off my radio to remove the main bag of the rucksack and grab my M16, which didn't take very long. Then I followed Driver hoping to catch up to him down into this ravine. Driver had a few steps on me because of the initial delay. As I ran the NVA small weapons fire was intense, their tracer rounds, of white and green, were hitting all around me. I knew they could see the whip antenna of my PRC25 radio. I finally reached the low point of the ravine, hit the ground behind a small tree, while continually taking fire.

"Meantime, the Company CO was calling Driver on the radio, 6 his call sign, 16 Driver's call sign, and my call sign was 16 kilo. I called 6 back stating that I couldn't find 16, but a few moments later I turned around and lying directly behind me no more than ten feet was Driver. He suffered a fatal wound, a rifle shot through his right eye, and was in his death throes. On that day, Driver gave no thought to his own personal safety but ran into this hail of fire to assist members of his platoon's OP. Later, the rest of his platoon came charging down into this ravine. Our platoon suffered 1 KIA (Driver), 2 WIA's: Charles Hyatt; Donnie Vaile – also a Blackfeet Tribal Member, who had joined us a couple of weeks prior, on an in-country transfer from the 4th Division. Charles was hit three times – once in the wrist, once in the ankle, and very badly in the stomach, and Donnie was hit through his right thigh – both are living. I and Hyatt walked point many a time, backing up each other under Driver.

"The NVA had us in a horseshoe ambush, which they used more than once. Their wounded NVA soldier was killed by one of our guys with a 45 pistol. I was sobbing like a baby after finding Driver, and seeing Hyatt (my best friend), and hometown friend (Vaile) wounded, I was going to shoot the wounded NVA myself, but I could see all the holes in him caused by the claymore mine and I couldn't bring myself to do it even at the urging of the CO's radio support personnel, but one of them completed the suffering of this NVA with his 45 pistol. Later on, three of us carried Driver's body up into the NDP perimeter, with me supporting Driver's head and shoulders.

"I always felt angry that the CO didn't call in gunships, artillery, or air strikes after the NVA were running away after they had attacked us. The CO had three days to plan this, and he knew the NVA would come after us in our NDP. Driver always treated me as a person with dignity and as a good soldier (an American Indian), which I know other officers didn't care if I lived or died. In fact Driver's replacement later replaced me as his RTO, and put me back on point. Sadly Lt. Walsh was killed almost two or three days later. I will always remember John 'Cecil' Driver for his courage and unselfishness, and have visited him at the Vietnam Memorial Wall in D.C. in September of 2002."[21]

Sergeant Brian Scott said, "I knew Lt. Driver and he was far and beyond the most competent, easiest to deal with, and bravest officer I ever encountered in my life. One sensed as soon as they met him that he was one of the 'best of the best' soldiers. The other thing that struck me about him was that he truly respected the on-the-bottom grunt, as he treated us all with a dignity that I rarely saw with any other officer. I myself recovered his body and it was one of the few times that I had to make a real effort not to cry in front of those in my charge."[22]

John H. McCammon served in Vietnam, 1968-9, with the Screaming Eagles. "Lt. Driver was one of my training officers at Ft. Lewis, Washington, and we ended up in the same company in Vietnam at LZ Sally. LZ Sally was 2nd Brigade Headquarters. It was a moderately sized firebase and landing zone northwest of Hue and there were a variety of different units stationed there. He (Driver) was always one of my favourite officers, even though I was just a lowly sergeant and didn't really know him on a personal basis. I found him as somewhat reserved and on the quiet side, and very professional. Some of us enlisted men were in awe of him and I tended to imagine him as a kind of adventurous solder of fortune. After his death I had a part in writing his sympathy letter (I was company clerk) and was very saddened by his passing because of my respect for him. To my knowledge he was always courteous and fair to others and his death was a great loss to me."[23]

In respect to his wife Marie's wishes Lieutenant John Driver was buried in Arlington Cemetery. Back home in Dublin Don Driver remembered his older brother, Jim, driving towards him as he walked home from work that Saturday morning. There were very few cars on the roads in Dublin at the time and Don thought it strange to see his brother pulling up to him. Jim told him the sad news that Marie had rang earlier to tell them of John's death. John Driver's son, Jack, was born two months later and in 1971 Marie brought him to Dublin to meet the Driver family. John's father talked all the time about his son and kept his photograph and Purple Heart on his barbershop wall in Ringsend until it was sold in 2005. When he died, John's letters were placed in the coffin with him.[24]

In 2000 John Driver was honoured by his former US Army comrades at a special ceremony in Washington DC. His older brother, Jim Driver, was presented with a special plaque in his brother's memory by the lieutenant's former commander, retired Lieutenant General Harold Moore. "On April 17, 1969, 1st Lieutenant John Cecil Driver made the ultimate sacrifice for this country, by giving his life so that others could gain freedom," Gen Moore told the 5,000 people attending the ceremony. "God bless Lieutenant John Cecil Driver and God bless his family. He, and they, will never be forgotten by his fellow soldiers, and by a grateful nation who was honoured and blessed by his presence." Jim Driver said: "I was overwhelmed. It was a very emotional occasion for me. I realised for the first time that he had not given his life for nothing." Jim said it was the first time he had travelled to the United States and the first time he saw his brother's name engraved on the plinth that carries the names of the 58,000 American servicemen and women killed in the Vietnam War. "I touched the wall and rubbed my fingers along his name. It was very moving for me," he said. "I got a phone call from John Howard who was Lieutenant Colonel and who was in London. He tracked me down through directory enquiries. "He said: 'I fought alongside your brother in Vietnam.' He told me they were going to honour John at a ceremony in Washington and asked me would I like to come."[25]

The operation to clear the A Shau Valley continued. On the morning of 11 May Company B, 3rd Battalion, 187th Infantry of the 101st Airborne, moved cautiously up the north slope of Hill 937 in a routine search-and-locate exercise. Little did they know that when the NVA opened up on them it would take another nine days before the position, dubbed "Hamburger Hill," was finally taken. US losses totalled seventy dead and 372 wounded. To take the position, the 101st Airborne eventually committed five infantry battalions, about 1,800 men, and ten batteries of artillery. The 7th and 8th Battalions of the 29th NVA Regiment suffered 630 dead discovered on and around the battlefield, including many found in makeshift mortuaries within the tunnel complex, and an unknown number of wounded that likely totalled most of the remainder of the two units.[26] Pat O'Leary was with Bravo 2/501 as "we approached Hill 937 from the south west side. We did hit only light resistance getting to the top, still much more resistance than normal but light compared to the main battle. The main battle was mainly to the north west side of the mountain, with the 3/187 (Black Jack Battalion) taking all the heavy casualties (40 KIA - 300 WIA). The movie *Hamburger Hill* was about this battalion. We were basically in support with two other battalions, or possibly three, making the total four. There were one or two ARVN battalions involved. They attacked from the west. We did stay on top of Dong Ap Bia for approx. ten days as I recall. We would recon in force and try to mop up. Every night we were mortared and rocketed."[27]

The repercussions of the battle were more political than military. Questions raised by the media concerning the necessity of the battle stirred controversy for weeks after the fighting ended. These issues flared up again when the new commander of the 101st, Major General John W. Wright, quietly abandoned the hill on 5 June and the operation to clear the A Shau was abandoned. The debate over Hamburger Hill reached Congress, with particularly severe criticism of military leadership by Democrat Senators Edward Kennedy, George McGovern, and Stephen Young. In its 27 June issue, *Life Magazine* published the photographs of 241 Americans killed in one week in Vietnam, considered a watershed turning point in the war. While only five of these were casualties on Hamburger Hill, many Americans had the perception that all the dead were victims of the battle. The controversy of the conduct of the Battle of Hamburger Hill led to a reappraisal of US strategy in Vietnam. As a direct result, to hold down casualties, the battle spelled the end of major American ground combat operations and US troops never again initiated large-scale actions.[28] Due to these operations by the 101st much of the NVA ability to attack the Thua Thien province was destroyed and I Corps became reasonably pacified. However, it was too late. America had decided to leave and the communists only had to bid their time.

US coastal patrols had the dangerous task of stopping sea-borne infiltration by communist junks along South Vietnam's 120,00 square miles of coastal waters. Falling under the jurisdiction of the US 7th Fleet, Task Force 115 (TF 115) and Operation Market Time became a key element in America's fight to interdict the flow of arms and supplies from North Vietnam along the southern coast. From surveillance bases at Vung Tau, Qui Nhon, Da Nang, An Thoi and Nha Trang, Task Force 115 operated in nine coastal patrol areas – from the DMZ in the north to the "Brevie" line in the Gulf of Thailand. At any one time, there were 50,000 sampans, junks and trawlers in South Vietnamese waters. With Coast Guard cutters forming barrier patrols at both ends of the coast, each patrol area was assigned a destroyer escort or minesweeper. Further in to the coast any suspect craft that got through had to contend with heavily armed WPB Coast Guard Point class cutters stopping it and demanding to see registration and identity papers. Finally, PCF Swift Boats patrolled the shallower in-shore waters. By the beginning of 1967 the communists were no longer trying to use the sea-borne infiltration routes as the Ho Chi Minh Trail was at full swing, but the endless patrols continued. Only during the 1968 Tet Offensive did maritime traffic increase, but by this time the US Navy was well ready for it.[29]

Martin Doherty was killed in action while serving with the US Navy in December 1969. He was born in 1949, in Brooklyn, New York, to Irish-born parents. His brother, Joseph, recalled that: "In April of 1949 Mary Kate Doherty, delivered a son Martin Stephen Doherty, with the help of Moses, in Brooklyn N.Y., USA. Moses was Dr. Otto Moses a Polish Jewish doctor whose arm was tattooed with the serial number of a death camp inhabitant of World War II. In true Irish tradition Martin Stephen was named after his maternal and paternal grandparents respectfully. His father Michael Stephen Doherty was a native of Swinford, Co. Mayo, and his mother Mary Kate O'Brien was born in Cloonacat, Co. Galway. Both parents lived in Ireland and immigrated to the US where they met. Mom left home at the age of eighteen during the Depression around 1930. There is little known of my dad's coming over but they did meet in the country. Martin attended St. Teresa of Avila Church and Elementary School, where Martin became Marty. At about the age of ten he procured a job selling the diocesan paper

The Tablet in the vestibule of the church where he was baptised. This entailed being there at 6am every Sunday morning through the end of the 12:20 mass. He didn't miss many days during two years of cold, wet, snowy, or sunny days. He went on to deliver telegrams for Western Union on a bicycle throughout the Flatbush area of Brooklyn for several years, under similar weather conditions. He was not afraid of work or many other things. After Marty graduated from Erasmus Hall High School in 1966 he joined the work force in NYC. He enlisted in the US Navy in May 1967 as the Vietnam 'conflict' was worsening." Marty was following in the footsteps of his older brother, Joe: "After I graduated High School I joined the US Navy in 1966, a year before Marty. While Mom didn't go wild over it, she did sign the necessary papers as I was under the legal age of eighteen to join. Some of our Irish neighbours, Bill and Seán O'Malley, had joined the Navy years prior and received excellent training that carried into their civilian lives. The military service was just one way of gaining education and training for those unable to afford college courses, but yet possibly learn a trade for the future." (Joe Doherty was based at a military airfield south of San Francisco as an Air Traffic Controlman.) The Doherty's valued their Irish heritage and Mary Kate had a high regard for education, hard work, honesty, and religion and instilled those values in all of her children.

"After boot camp and radar specialist school Marty joined the fleet for service aboard two different destroyers in the Pacific Ocean. At some point he volunteered for duty with the US Naval Coastal and Riverine Forces (Swift Boats) patrolling the river and coastal waters of Vietnam. Being accepted for duty in these special operations forces meant additional training in and around Coronado, CA. The training included jungle survival, escape and avoidance, and other specialised training. While there he became close associates with several other 'Swiftees.' After this training he was granted a shore leave before being assigned to a unit in South Vietnam. He relayed a story about how during the training for how to intercept boat traffic on the rivers of Vietnam, part of looking for Viet Cong or contraband, that one of the role players on the suspicious ship pulled a pistol and shot him point blank in the face. It was supposed to be a blank, but apparently there was enough powder in the charge to send him to sick-bay with numerous facial wounds. He wondered if this was an omen, but didn't dwell on it.

"I recall he told me about an incident on that shore leave. He was crossing a street in Brooklyn when a cop stopped him and gave him a ticket for jaywalking ... an unheard offence in that area of Brooklyn. (Jaywalking is crossing a roadway in the middle of the street, not at the corner, or crossing against the light at the intersection. Naturally one does this only when it is safe, and this is such a low level event a cop writing a ticket for this has very little to do. The 'fine' was just a few dollars and was rarely followed up on.) Marty had his military ID and even a copy of his orders, which he showed the policeman. The officer gave him a ticket and told him he had x number of days to take care of it, or it would become a more serious offence. Marty took the ticket, saying, 'By that time I'll be in the jungles of Vietnam. If the ticket is still on file when I get back in a year, I'll worry about it then and be grateful.' At that he walked away. To Marty it was 'when I get back.' He was always sure of himself, in a positive way and it showed that Marty had a sense of priorities in that the jay walking ticket was a mere nothing compared to going to Nam, and that he would take care of it when he got home.

"During his tour in Vietnam he served on a number of Swift boats from several different bases. He didn't write much about conditions or activities. The conditions were spartan at best, but probably better than being in the jungles themselves. From what I've gathered the Swift Boats had a crew of about six and their special operations included landing special forces units behind enemy lines and retrieving same. They also conducted 'psych-ops' against enemy forces, sometimes going upriver alone playing messages over PA systems. The nature of these messages varied. Other missions would include going upriver alone or followed by another swift boat specifically to draw fire.

These 'reconnaissance missions' were meant to gauge the strength or size of the opposing land forces. In other words, lets send a boat up the river and see how much fire they can draw, and from where. Upon drawing fire the 'Swiftee's' could call in support fire or return their own limited fire-power. Just about all their operations were classified.

"Sometime in mid-November 1969 I received the most revealing letter yet from Marty. He explained some of the functions that he as an E-4 (NCO) Radarman performed aboard these small riverine craft. I recall he wrote that during operations his job was to 'crouch in a small hatch in the bow of the boat with an M-60 machine gun and an M-79 grenade launcher, hiding behind some sand bags and return enemy fire'. Obviously his skills and knowledge of radar and radar sets didn't matter too much during these times. The particular day he wrote this letter must have been a slow day, or he had some other premonitions on his fate. After we were notified of his passing, the funeral and all, I spoke with many of his friends and my immediate family. It seems that he wrote many letters that day, some mentioning his duties, some not, but all written the same day in mid-November. It was unusual that any two of us would get a letter the same day, but this time he was writing letters to many close friends.

"Marty was killed in action on December 4, 1969. I had been discharged from my tour of duty and at home in Brooklyn with Mom and younger sister, Anne, the evening the official notification came. Mom was devastated, and the rest of us weren't much better. Even the neighbours were on edge, when they saw the official car parked on the street. Many of them also had sons serving in Vietnam, and when the official car is on the block it could be anyone getting the notification. Family and friends just hold their breath as they walk home to see if the armed forces chaplain and medic are at their home."[30]

Martin Doherty's tour of Vietnam began on 19 June 1969 and he served on board PCF-42 and PCF-50, Coastal Division II operating out of An Thoi, South Vietnam as a 3rd Class Radarman. Swift Boats (PCFs) played a major part in stopping the flow of weapons into South Vietnam by patrolling the rivers and canals. He volunteered for river patrols. Marty was always known as a good-humoured guy, ready with a joke. With a crew of six it took a special breed of sailor to fight from the decks of a Swift Boat, as the patrols were strenuous and the casualties high. A total of fifty sailors were killed serving on Swift Boats during the war; Martin Doherty being the youngest to die. Deprived of their speed and manoeuvrability in the constricted tributaries, and with just a quarter inch of armour for protection, the Swifts were easy targets for rockets and other heavy weapons. After the completion of a psych-ops mission on the Dam Doi river, on 4 December 1969, PCFs 50, 56 and Vietnamese Navy PCF 3805 came under intense B-40 rocket, automatic weapons and small arms fire near An Xugen. The lead boat, PCF-50, took a B-40 hit head-on in the pilothouse, killing the bow gunner, Martin Doherty, and wounding the officer in command and the helmsman. A second B-40 hit close aboard to port, wounded two additional crewmen on the fantail. The VNN PCF took a B-40 hit low on the port bow and another on the port side of the pilothouse, killing the USN adviser and seriously wounding two crewmen. PCF-56 received a B-40 near miss that wounded one.[31]

"Mary Kate always believed in doing what was right, and if that meant her sons joining the military then so be it. After Marty's passing I'm not so sure she ever accepted his fate in the same spirit. It must be hard to have a son pass before the parent, and Mary Kate lived with that anguish for years. As for burial arrangements Mary Kate did not hesitate, Marty was going to be buried in the local church cemetery in Kilkerrin, Ireland. No national cemetery, Marty was going to Ireland. The US government made all travel arrangements and her brothers in Ireland made whatever arrangements were necessary there. After the funeral procedures in our own local parish church we set off to Ireland. I travelled as the official representative (escort) of the detail, Mom as the next of kin. We flew into Shannon airport. The coffin was draped with the US flag as it was deplaned and placed into the 56 Chevy Hearst that Keevany Funeral Home had sent to meet us. I rode in the hearse and Mom got into another car for the family setting off for the Kilkerrin church. "At some point I glanced in the rear view mirror to see a line of cars following us that seemed to go on forever. Apparently the whole area knew Mary Kate's boy was coming home to a place he had never known. As we drove the roads I was very impressed how the farmers or anyone within sight of the road, upon seeing the hearse would stop whatever they were doing, doff their hat, make a sign of the cross and bow their heads. Most impressive on that journey was the two Irish Army soldiers standing on a corner in a town centre, it may have been Tuam, I'm not sure, upon seeing the flag draped coffin came to attention and rendered the smartest salute I had seen in years. Military respect for a fallen brother, unknown to them.

"When we did arrive at the parish church in Kilkerrin a crowd met us. We escorted the casket inside for the evening, said a few prayers and travelled on to Cloonacat. The family members and friends who had dug the gravesite had some last minute alterations to take care of that evening. The coffin was longer and wider than the gravesite, so they changed clothes and got to the shovels again. The US caskets were larger than the local ones, so much so that Mom purchased three sites side by side. One-plot-and-a-half for Marty and the other for when her time came. She knew she was going to return to Ireland and live out her 'retirement years' there. She told me years later that she would rather be there, next to him, than in the family plot, just a few yards away. The church was packed to overflowing the next day. After the services we went to a nearby pub, where if I recall correctly Mary Kate paid for some beverages especially for the men who dug the grave and a few others … in fine Irish tradition." When Martin Doherty's father, Michael, passed away in New York Mary Kate returned to Cloonacat, County Galway, where she chose to live out her final days in the home that was built about the time she left Ireland. Joe Doherty wrote: "In the late 1970s Mom did finally return to her family home, the one that was completed the year she left for America. She passed away and was buried next to her son, as was her wish, in 1984. Myself, I visit the church and graveyard each time I am fortunate enough to get to Ireland. The church has a few pews and stained glass windows in Marty's remembrance, courtesy of my Mom. The relatives are still warm and caring. The gravesite is watched over with its US Navy plaque and occasionally someone plants a small US flag there. On my last visit just after the US Memorial Day holiday in late May 2005 the small US flag was there, honouring the Yank."[32] .

## CHAPTER 15

# AND THE BAND PLAYED
# WALTZING MATILDA

While the 1st Royal Australian Regiment had fought well as part of the US 173rd Airborne in the opening year of allied intervention the difficulties in integrating the Australians with American units became so great that as 1 RARs tour of duty came to a close in June 1966, Australian commanders and political leaders in Canberra were forced to seek a solution. Their answer was for the Australians to be allocated a province of their own in which they could operate as an autonomous unit with their own field commander. The Australians were allocated Phuoc Tuy province in III Military Region, just south east of Saigon. Now they would have to rise and fall on their own talents, as no blame could be attached to the Americans or the ARVN.[1] Between June 1966 and November 1971 Australian Forces-Vietnam conducted their own, largely successful, counter-insurgency (COIN) campaign in Phuoc Tuy province. An area of about 150,000 square miles, Phuoc Tuy comprised a central plain, bordered to the west by the "impenetrable" Rung Sat Special Zone, to the north and east by the VC-dominated hills and to the south by the sea. It was a known centre of VC activity, but the Australians had experience of fighting communist guerrillas in Malaya, and they brought to Vietnam skills that added a new edge to the anti-communist forces operating there against the VC.

The first task confronting the Australian force, a two- (later a three-) battalion group was to dominate the central plain. This was achieved by occupying a prominent hill feature known as Nui Dat, close to Binh Ba in the middle of the province and constructing a firebase for US and Australian artillery. Their range protected infantry patrolling about 17,000 yards, beyond which Australian SAS operations took place.[2] 5 and 6 Royal Australian Regiment were the first two infantry battalions to arrive at the new base at Nui Dat. The base was set in a mature, French-owned, rubber plantation, which had been captured in battle by 5 RAR. The population of

Phuoc Tuy was a mix of long-established South Vietnamese families and North Vietnamese (mostly Catholics) who settled there in 1955 after the French pulled out. The latter were more supportive of the Australians while the more established residents tended to view the Aussies with ambivalence or outright dislike and distrust. Principal economic activities of the province were fishing and rice cultivation, though there were also large rubber plantations in the area. The VC was very active and well organised, having operated substantial forces against the government since 1959. To control Phuoc Tuy the Australian Army undertook substantial restructuring of its Vietnam command. Beginning June 1966 the 1st Australian Task Force, in command of Phuoc Tuy, had infantry, artillery, engineers, commandos, armour and signals units, with the required back up of medical and logistics units. With these changes complete Australian involvement in Vietnam grew to a force of some 4,500 men, of whom about 1,000 were conscripts. The Australian Air Force and Navy also served with distinction in both combat and humanitarian roles and won high praise from the United States.[3]

In Australia, with the undertaking of a direct military role in Vietnam the army moved to a general state of war training. As the flow of National Servicemen increased further battalions were raised to accommodate the rapidly expanding army. Militarily and economically the early 1960s were uncertain times for Australia so the government had no problem in introducing two years National Service for all twenty-year old males. Conscription was a controversial issue of the Vietnam War and in 1964 the Australian government implemented a National Service Scheme. It became known as the "Lottery of Death," as many young Australians who were being unwillingly sent to Vietnam and forced to fight and kill, couldn't even legally vote or drink alcohol at home. In 1966 Vietnamese Premier Marshall Ky visited Australia, facing protests wherever he went. Later in the year President Johnson became the first US President to visit Australia. He too faced demonstrations. In Sydney the New South Wales Premier Askin told his driver to "Run over the bastards!" when protesters lay in front of his and Johnson's car.[4]

The Australian Special Air Service Regiment was also deployed to Vietnam. The SASR was modelled on the original British SAS and also drew on the traditions of the Australian WWII commando units, which were active in the South Pacific. Based at Campbell Barracks, Swanbourne, Perth, Western Australia, they have been widely regarded as one of the better special forces units in the world; ranking alongside the British SAS/SBS and US Navy SEALs. The SASR's participation in Vietnam began when 3 Squadron deployed as part of the 1st Australian Task Force in April 1966. The SASRs role in Vietnam was to act as the "eyes and the ears" of the Australian Task

Force through conducting reconnaissance patrols throughout 1 ATFs area of responsibility. At least one Irishman, a Tipperary native, served with 3 SAS on its first deployment in Vietnam.[5]

As in Borneo the SASR operated closely with the New Zealand SAS, with a New Zealand SAS troop being attached to each Australian Squadron. SASR Squadrons rotated through Vietnam on one year long deployments until the last Squadron was withdrawn in October 1971. During its time in Vietnam the Regiment was extremely successful in the reconnaissance role. Due to their cunning and field craft members of the Regiment became known as "Phantoms of the Jungle" to Vietnamese communist forces. The SASR also worked with US SEAL Teams and Green Berets.[6]

The Australian battalions sailed off to South Vietnam, much as they had in WWI and WWII, from Circular Quay, in Sydney Harbour. However, individuals and reinforcements often flew to Vietnam. Pat Landers arrived in South Vietnam, in December 1967, as a reinforcement for D Company, 7 RAR. Born in Lackaroe, Youghal, Co. Cork, Pat emigrated to Australia from London, where he was working as a barman, in 1964 on the ten pound system. Pat immediately found work on the railway lines in Sydney. He knew he would be soon conscripted and rather than wait to be drafted he joined the Australian Army in 1966, signing on for a three-year term. Pat knew he probably would be sent to Vietnam and in fact was told so by the recruiting sergeant. On completion of his basic training Pat applied for the infantry, as did many of his friends. He found the Australian army training very professional. In late December 1967 Pat Landers was assigned as a reinforcement to D Company, 7 Royal Australian Regiment.[7] RAR was formed as a new infantry battalion in September 1965 and had begun its tour of Vietnam in April 1967. He flew from Sydney to Saigon with about 120 other reinforcements. Pat remembered it was the loneliest time of his life, "sitting with my pack and my rifle and no one to see me off". He arrived at the Nui Dat base to the 1st Australian Reinforcement Unit.7 "The Dat" was home for Aussie soldiers in Vietnam, a place where soldiers could rest and sleep comfortably with minimal danger. However, it was one they seldom occupied. The tents were sandbagged to waist height for protection against enemy mortar fire. Each soldier was assigned a defensive trench in case of attack and a modified defensive routine saw the perimeter carefully guarded. There were showers and primitive but hygienic toilets, huts for some of the senior personnel, orderly rooms, kitchens, company "boozers," power and some water supply. It had rudimentary sporting facilities, with chopper pads providing a venue for impromptu football matches. A basic open-air cinema screened relatively new movies, while the Australian Forces Overseas Fund, provided entertainment in the form of popular home bands and singers. During operations, about 100 administrative personnel occupied the base. As companies rotated through the cycle of operations, Nui Dat was an infrequently visited, but welcome safe haven.[8]

A reinforcement, or rio, to an infantry unit was not a regular member of the unit. He was usually a replacement for men who had been killed or wounded. As a reinforcement he had a completely different experience to men who had trained with a battalion, who had marched off to war with them, and fought with them from the beginning of their tour. Replacing one of the original guys he was immediately under pressure to fit into the unit and perform. The rio needed to appreciate the tactics of the particular unit, and get to know his fellow soldiers in a climate of suspicion, and extreme stress. This was emphasised if a man ended up as a rio in more than one unit, as did Pat Landers. However, Pat had no trouble fitting in with both battalions. However, some reinforcements were not up to scratch, and this could lead to problems for the veteran troops. Pat recalled one reinforcement setting up claymore mines on a night defensive operation. Despite clear identification markings "front toward enemy" the new guy pointed the claymores in the wrong direction towards his own troops. The next morning the reinforcement was put on a helicopter and flown out to the rear.

Pat Landers recalled that there were no Vietnamese, aside from ARVN interpreters, on their bases, and after the photographs taken by the Australian freelance photographer Gabriel Carpay in October 1966, which was central to what became known as the "water torture case" there were no journalists allowed with Australian forces. Australian troops rarely worked in close proximity to US infantry, although they worked together on the same operations. While the Americans had Vietnamese working on their bases, and subsequently came under accurate mortar attack with information supplied from inside, the Australians were more security conscious and rarely let locals on their bases. There were only a handful of Americans on Australian bases, mainly helicopter pilots. (The US Army Aviation Corps supported the Australians in four main ways – airmobile insertions, light fire team support, casualty evacuation and operational re-supply.)

Soon Pat Landers was out on jungle patrols. He said: "We had many close shaves in Vietnam. I remember one time I was a forward scout for our platoon. We were following a track through the jungle. It was something like a cow track we have back home. The jungle on both sides of the track had very thick overgrowth and visibility was bad as the track twisted through the jungle. As I rounded one bend on the track I came face to face with an NVA soldier. We both opened fire at the same time. I hit him in the chest with two bullets. He missed me but he had fired three rounds from his

AK47 rifle. I actually took the spent round out of the chamber of his AK47 to keep as a souvenir, which I still have today.

"On another occasion we were practically surrounded by enemy troops. That's when we thought it was all over. Only for American helicopter gunships we would have had it. We always left a letter in base camp to be sent home in case of our death. The jungle is a beautiful place to be in – in peacetime. We patrolled through beautiful plantations of rubber trees and coffee plants. On one occasion I was machine gunner, because at this stage our gunner had been killed and I qualified in training for scouting, so I became our M60 machine gunner. While patrolling I screamed Jesus! Dropping my m.g., and my trousers, to find two red ants stuck on top of my dick. The pain I will never forget. My mates almost pissed themselves laughing! That's another of the hazards we faced in the jungle. Another time I had just finished my two hours 'sentence' (guard duty) and went back to my hutchie, looking forward to four hours sleep. I put my hand on the groundsheet and quickly removed it. There was an army of chomper ants on the move and my hutchie was in its path. I got a lot of bites on my hand as it was covered in blood when I pulled it out. There were also snakes, wild pigs and scorpions to contend with, but the dirtiest bastards of all were the leeches. Especially during monsoon seasons, as several areas of the jungle were flooded. Often we were waist deep in water areas that the maps showed dry. This all changes when the clouds roll in around 3 p.m. every evening with thunder and lighting, and boy does it come down for five or six hours. The enemy were most active during monsoon as they thought we wouldn't be patrolling but we were trained in the jungle of southern Queensland, in a place called Canungra, which was very like the jungle in Vietnam, so we were well used to the hardship of jungle warfare."[9]

The Australians were involved in constant patrolling activities in Phuoc Tuy. This was to maintain a high profile among residents of the province and to deny the enemy its supply points within the villages.[10] "I remember," Pat said, "one village search we were on. I had the most unusual experience. The village was enemy held, so there was a lot of shooting before we eventually took the village. I remember entering one house after kicking down the door. I entered the house and was faced with a statue of the blessed Virgin, a candle lighting in front of it and at least six bullet holes had struck all around the statue. I stopped for a few seconds and looked, not believing what I was looking at and said maybe there is a God after all. But, then I thought, how could He let this war happen.

"On another occasion we were briefed before leaving base camp that there were a lot of enemy activity in the area and expect to go in 'hot,' which means under fire. As we land the helicopters swoops in, but doesn't stop as normal, but hovers one meter off the ground. You jump out, but thanks to American gunships, which were blasting the area, we all got off safely. Not long afterwards we were moving downhill into a valley when we came under heavy enemy fire. We had walked into an enemy ambush. Fighting back to gain control of the situation we had twelve men wounded. The enemy used rocket-propelled grenades. It took us one hour to drive them off and gain control and take the hill on the opposite side of the valley. We found it was an enemy camp. We recovered no enemy bodies but a lot of blood trails leading away from the camp so they must have had heavy casualties to break off contact and run."[11]

Pat celebrated his twenty-second birthday in March and in June was entitled to five days leave after serving six months. Leave was in Vung Tau, further south, which was where the Viet Cong also took R and R. Previously the beach resort for wealthy French and Vietnamese holidaymakers, Vung Tau provided a haven for both sides. Beaches, bars, women, entertainment and relaxation were all a diversion to the war a few miles away. After nine months service troops were entitled to another five nights R and R in Bangkok. Pat never met any other Irishmen while in Vietnam, though he did meet several Englishmen.[12]

Vietnam for the Australians was a section, platoon and company commander's war, one of bushcraft, silence, endurance and the ultimate reliance on your fellow soldier. The threat of contact with the enemy was always present. Private Pat Landers was a forward scout for about four months and an M60 machine gunner for about six months. As a forward scout (pointman) he preferred the Australian SLR to the American M16, which had a habit of jamming in wet weather. However, he preferred the American C-rations to that of the Australians. "The C-rations had four cigarettes in every pack and far better food than the rice, dog biscuits and bully beef we were issued. We carried about five bottles of water and filled them up from the rivers. We popped in a blue tablet to kill the bacteria, then a white tablet to kill the taste of the blue tablet." By the time 7 RAR arrived in Vietnam the VC had become more sophisticated. "Gone were the punji pits, though I did see one once in a village. They used more landmines and tripwires." While they tried to continue their normal way of life the villagers were subject to taxes, kidnapping and violence from the Viet Cong who often incorporated the villages as part of their administrative infrastructure. "The VC came into the villages and always abducted and killed a village chief and a child. They cut their throats as a warning to hand over food. We usually came in to clean up. It happened quite a few times, and it was always a village chief and a child."[13]

On 23 January 1968 7 RAR and 2 RAR moved to the Bien Hoa area in "expectation of an attack", leaving 3 RAR to defend Phuoc Tuy province. A week later the Tet Offensive broke out. The two battalions were involved in heavy fighting east of the huge American Bien Hoa/Long Binh base complex and at Fire Support Base Andersen. Having recovered from their shock the American and ARVN forces eventually broke the enemy strength forcing them to flee Saigon. The Australians were deployed to the east of Saigon to intercept and engage the escaping communist forces. In the ensuing fighting twenty Australians were killed.[14]

The annual rotation of units took place in May and June 1968 with 2 RAR and 7 RAR returning home to Australia, their places taken by 1 and 4 RAR. The "First" was undertaking its second tour of duty, having been the original battalion committed in 1965. In April 7 RAR began rotating home. Members of the Battalion who had arrived as reinforcements during the tour and who had not completed their twelve months, stayed on with the incoming 1st Battalion. Pat Landers had only four months in-country and could not go home with 7 RAR. Instead he was sent to HQ for a few weeks. "I was mad to stay, but they were having none of it." Pat was reassigned to A Company, 3 RAR, just in time for Operation Toan Thang (Phase 1). A combined American and Australian operation the purpose was to maintain the post-Tet pressure on the enemy and to drive all remaining NVA/VC troops from III Corps and the Saigon area. The constant patrolling was designed to maintain a high profile and make life less tolerable for the enemy, though Pat found it very stressful. "Often you could be out for six weeks at a time, with three days rations. We were re-supplied by American choppers. Then back for two or three days and back out again. The worst was the severe pressure and stress of patrols – not knowing whether you would stand on an anti-personnel mine, or hit a trip wire, or walk into an enemy ambush. One position I hated travelling was Ass End Charlie. You were sniper's bait.[15]

"I remember one morning we moved into ambush at 6 a.m. on a track leading through the jungle. I had set one claymore mine strapped on to a tree about 20 metres in front of me. I had the press plunger in my hand, which explodes the mine when pressed. About 1 p.m. the corporal told us an American platoon was moving up the track. At exactly 2.55 p.m. I saw the bushes part, as the track was partly overgrown. An NVA soldier appeared, and stopped in front of the claymore mine. He had his AK47 on his shoulder. He turned around and waved his hand to call up his mates. Two more arrived. The reason for this was two of our troops were resting – one was aboriginal, and one English. I think the NVA mistook the aboriginal for one of them. I blew the claymore mine at this stage. Then all hell broke loose. Result, three dead NVA and blood trails leading away from the contact. I visited one of the soldiers in Adelaide last year (2006). He said 'I am glad you blew that mine because we would not be here now.' We had a good laugh about it and a few drinks. It was nice to be remembered."[16]

During May 3 RAR and 1 RAR, with Australian and New Zealand artillery support, were deployed to Bin Duong Province and set up Fire Support Base Coral, in an attempt to block withdrawal and re-supply routes for communist forces attacking Saigon. Coral was intentionally sited on a major enemy trail just inside the western edge of War Zone D, 20 km north-west of Bien Hoa. On 13 May troops from the NVA 7th Division launched a surprise attack on Coral. The battle, which consisted of several actions, went on for twenty-six days, being the biggest unit level battle of the Vietnam War that involved Australians. On 26 May the battle widened as a large force of NVA attacked Fire Support Base Balmoral, five kilometres from Coral. Balmoral came under heavy ground and mortar attacks from a battalion sized enemy force. Four Australians were killed in the barrage — two from A Company and two from D Company. The barrage was followed up with a ground assault the brunt of which fell on D Company. With support of Centurion tanks from the 1st Armoured Regiment, the NVA were repelled.[17] "The mortars scared the shit out of us," Pat said. "One of the scariest things are the mortars coming at you in the middle of the night. You will hear them being let off and they whistle through the air and can land anywhere amongst you. We had several casualties this way.[18] Our foxholes were filled with water from the constant rain. We put up our tent behind the foxholes. When the mortars landed quite near we jumped into the water filled holes. A mortar round landed right on our tent. Everything was destroyed. Even our mess tins had shrapnel holes. We were very lucky, but I suppose it's the luck of the draw."[19] A sweep of the perimeter at first light found six enemy dead, discarded weapons, ammunition and equipment. Two nights later the NVA returned with more mortar attacks and a ground assault through a gap blown in the A Company perimeter wire. Small arms fire from A Company's forward weapons pits halted this assault before it reached the wire and the enemy threw his main attack force into a major thrust against the base. Tanks, artillery, mortars and helicopters were needed to repel the attack. Forty-two bodies were counted the next morning. In addition, seven prisoners and a large amount of equipment were captured. By the time the Australians returned to their base at Nui Dat some twenty-six of their number were dead and 110 more wounded.[20]

Through September and into October Pat Landers was involved with A Company in protecting engineer land-clearing teams as they bulldozed wide blazes through acres of primary jungle both between and on the periphery of the Nui Thi Vai and Nui Dinh hills. He returned to Nui Dat on 2 October where he remained for a few days until A Company began intensive patrolling during Operation Capital. On 19 October, in heavy rain and thick jungle, A Company clashed with a company-sized enemy force. The resulting battle resulted in two Australians killed and five wounded for the death of seven VC. These were the last two fatalities for A Company and for the remainder of the operational tour 3 RAR remained at Nui Dat and maintained base patrolling, road convoy protection and security duties.[21]

In November 3 RAR was replaced by 9 RAR, the most recently raised battalion of the Royal Australian Regiment.[22] During 3 RAR's tour of active service it took part in twelve operations covering four provinces. On 20 November 3 RAR returned as a full battalion on HMAS *Sydney*. Freemantle was the first port of call where soldiers proceeding on leave in Western Australia disembarked. On 2 December the remainder of the Battalion disembarked at Adelaide and marched through the city with fixed bayonets as they were expecting trouble from anti-war protesters. "They threw dye and paint and the usual names," Pat said. "We were none too happy, but there was nothing you could do about it. We were giving three months leave, then it was back to spit and polish to put us back into line." Pat Landers served out his remaining time in the army and then went to work in the mines for six months before returning to Ireland in 1970. Pat said: "I liked my time in the Army. The discipline was hard to take at first, but it saved my life in the jungle of Vietnam."[23]

As one Irishman was leaving with 3 RAR another Irishman was arriving with 9 RAR. George Nagle, from 33 Barron Park, Clonmel, Co. Tipperary, arrived with 9 RAR on 20 November. Born in 1946 George served with the 12th Infantry Battalion, Irish Defence Forces, which had two companies based in Clonmel Barracks. He served two tours with the Irish UN Peace Force in Cyprus, before emigrating to Australia in 1967. George worked in a factory for a few months until he volunteered for the Australian Army in August 1967.[24] After a period of familiarization in-country, 9 RAR commenced Operation King Hit One, a cordon and search of the village of An Nhut on the road between Baria, the provincial capital, and Dat Do, resulting in one enemy killed, several VC suspects detained and the seizure of weapons, equipment and medical supplies. On 1 January 1969 the Battalion deployed on Operation Goodwood which was a 1st Australian Task Force (1 ATF) reconnaissance-in-force operation into a likely enemy base area east of Saigon. The object was to interdict VC movement from the Hat Dich to the Long Binh-Bien Hoa military complexes. The operation was characterized by short savage contacts against the VC in well-sited bunker complexes and Main Force enemy units.[25] On 6 January Private Nagle suffered fatal fragmentation wounds to his body when struck by a claymore mine in an extended contact with the enemy. He was twenty-three and the first

Irishman to die serving with the Australian forces. He had been only in Vietnam for three months. His widowed mother, Mrs Ellen Nagle, was told her son would be buried in Vietnam or Australia, but if she desired her son's ashes would be sent home.[26] His body was eventually retuned to Ireland for burial.[27] His family had to pay for his remains to be repatriated to Tipperary. Though this was common practice at the time the Australian Ambassador recently apologised to the Nagle family on behalf of the Australian Government for making them do that.[28]

Back in Australia the protest movement was gathering huge momentum. In the beginning the war was well supported and overwhelmingly popular, but the introduction of conscription and the deaths of the first National Servicemen had turned many Australians against participation. In August 1969 the Morgan Gallup Poll found that fifty-five per cent of Australians wanted their troops brought home from Vietnam.[29] For Australia 1970 was the military turning point in the Vietnam commitment. The US had begun a phased withdrawal of ground troops in 1969, so Australia followed suit. In April, attempting to appease the moderate elements of the protest movement, the government announced one battalion of Australian troops, 8 RAR, would be withdrawn at the due time in November and not replaced. The May changeover of two battalions took place as usual that year. 7 RAR was back for a second tour arriving in February 1970. 7 RAR occupied the same area of Nui Dat as it had on its first tour of duty and took it over from the same battalion, 5 RAR. The base had developed further and continued to do so in 1970 and 1971. Many of the recreational and administrative facilities were made more substantial. Two factors dominated this tour of duty: mines and ambushes. The Viet Cong had recovered many of mines from the Australian barrier minefield that had run from the Horseshoe east to Phuoc Hai on the coast. These mines, supplemented by other improvised mines used by the enemy, caused many of the casualties suffered by 7 RAR. Enemy capacity within Phuoc Tuy province had been diminished by constant Australian operations and the need for food became a dominant issue for the VC. Frequent small ambushes around the villages in the eastern half of the province became the routine, while at the same time a company was constantly in depth searching for the bunkers of the elusive enemy.[30]

The conflict was not just an infantry war. The Australian Armoured Corps provided welcome transport and protection in their M113 armoured personnel carriers and Centurion tanks. The tracked armoured carriers were the work-horses of the ATF and were employed in both cavalry and armoured personnel carrier roles. The M113 weighed ten tons, was amphibious, and armed with a .50 calibre heavy machine gun mounted in front of the command hatch on top. The behemoth could carry around ten infantrymen inside its belly and could churn across flooded rice paddys at ten to twenty miles an hour. The "track," or "carrier" crews were kept to a tight schedule of infantry insertions, convoy protection and a multitude of other tasks, which included reconnaissance in force and perimeter defence.[31] David Doyle, born in Dublin into a family of fifteen children, was living in Belmont, New South Wales, when he enlisted in June 1969. He joined B Squadron, 3 Cavalry Regiment, in Phuoc Tuy province shortly after completing basic training. B Squadron 3 Cavalry Regiment had been in Vietnam since May 1969. Trooper David Doyle was a driver and signalman on an APC. He was killed accidentally on 31 July 1970 when the vehicle in which he was riding backed up to a helicopter and the blades struck him. He was nineteen.[32] His commanding officer wrote he "he reversed his vehicle in close to a helicopter off-loading some equipment. Apparently not appreciating just how close the helicopter was the driver, Tpr Doyle, walked along the top of the carrier and straight into the whirling rotors. He died almost immediately and his body was removed to Vung Tau at 0830 hours and the OC had a replacement driver sent out to Sharon. The OC to conduct an immediate investigation."[33] The following month the Commander 1st Australian Task Force (1 ATF), Brigadier William G. Henderson, joined officers and men of B Squadron 3rd Cavalry Regiment, for a memorial service to Trooper David Doyle. The non-denominational service was attended by about 140 men, many of whom were relieved briefly from operational commitments so they could return to the 1 ATF base for the commemoration of their fallen comrade.[34] David's body was brought home to Australia and buried at Belmont Cemetery. His mother Mrs Kathleen Doyle wrote: "He was such a beautiful young boy in so many ways." David's brother, also served in Vietnam.[35]

Another Irishman serving with the Australian forces, Sergeant Robert Fleming, died of a brain haemorrhage at the 24th US Evacuation Hospital, Long Binh, on 9 November 1970. He was twenty-four and lived in Melbourne, Victoria. He had emigrated with his family from Northern Ireland and enlisted in November 1963 when he was seventeen. He was a sergeant at twenty-two. Bob Fleming served an earlier tour in 1965/66 with 1 RAR. When he died he was serving with 1st Australian Reinforcement Unit, based in Nui Dat. He was survived by his wife, Kerrie and daughter Cheryl. The Flemings were married at Kingscliff, New South Wales, on 15 March 1968. Mrs Fleming, who lived in Uki, NSW, "was a bride at eighteen, a mother at nineteen and a widow at twenty". Robert Fleming's body was brought back to Australia for cremation.[36]

In February 1971 large areas of Phuoc Tuy were handed over (in terms of operational responsibility) to the South Vietnamese forces. However, they proved unwilling and unable to fill the gap left by the Australian Task Force. In March 1971 Sgt Thomas Birnie, serving with 2 RAR, was killed in Phuoc Tuy. He was the last known Irishman to die in Vietnam. Thomas Birnie was born in Belfast, in 1940, the youngest son in a family of seven children. In his late teens, he enlisted in the British Territorial Army, serving in Belfast as a corporal with the Royal Military Police until he emigrated to Australia in 1961. After spending some time in South Australia and Victoria, he joined the Army and was posted to Brisbane and 2 RAR. He was a natural athlete and played rugby union for Power House in Melbourne and the Army team, usually as five-eighth. He met and married a girl who was also from Belfast, Joan Carr, and had a son, Mark. Tom Birnie had served an earlier tour of Vietnam, 1967-68, as platoon sergeant of 4 Platoon, B Company, 2 RAR, during which he was wounded, although not seriously. Before he returned to Vietnam for his second tour Tom went on a family holiday to Rollingstone Beach, near Townsville, at Christmas 1969. It was the last holiday the family had together. Tom left for Vietnam in May 1970. Ten months into his second tour Tom Birnie, the "soldier poet," was killed in a "friendly fire" incident returning from patrol on 25 March 1971. He was thirty-one and was survived by his wife, Joan, and young son, Mark, in Townsville. His body was brought back to Australia for cremation. A month before he died Tom sent his wife a prophetic poem he had written called *The Long Hill Home*. The last stanza said:

> *I stand atop the long hill home*
> *With wife and son, we three alone;*
> *And far away in the jungle's mould*
> *The bones of my youth lie stiff and cold*
> *Never to walk the long hill home* [37]

After an afternoon contact, a platoon from B Company harboured for the night near the banks of the Suoi Soc river. At first light, the platoon sergeant, Tom Birnie, led a small patrol across the stream to reconnoitre to the east of the platoon's night position. It was expected that he and his patrol would rejoin the platoon by returning along the same route. In the course of the patrol Sgt Birnie found signs of the enemy crossing the stream and, after seeking permission from the platoon commander, he followed this track and crossed the stream. After a short distance, he and the patrol came under fire, and the sergeant was seriously wounded. Unbeknown to Birnie, the stream followed a circular path around the platoon position and the patrol had actually approached their own troops from the opposite direction. One of the sentries, not expecting movement from this direction, assumed that it was the enemy and opened fire. Although Tom Birnie was quickly evacuated he died of wounds at 1 Australian Field Hospital in the early hours of 25 March.[38]

On 30 March 1971 Prime Minister McMahon announced further cuts in the Australian forces in South Vietnam, including the withdrawal of the tank squadron, RAAF Canberra bomber squadron and some Caribou transport aircraft. The government announced the rest of 1 ATF would be withdrawn by Christmas in line with the American withdrawal policy. In May the two-battalion changeover occurred, but the new arrivals were destined not to serve their full twelve-month tours of duty in Vietnam. 1 ATF pulled out over Christmas-New Year, while 1 ALSG remained to complete technical details of the withdrawal. Unfortunately, when the Australians withdrew from Phuoc Tuy the VC quickly regained the upper hand. By early 1972 the Australians were all but gone from Phuoc Tuy province, leaving the AATTV as the sole representative of the Australian Army. The AATTV, known as "The Team," was the first and last Australian unit serving in Vietnam and was awarded four Victoria Crosses, the American Meritorious Unit Commendation and the Vietnamese Cross of Gallantry with Palm Unit Citation. On 19 December 1972 the officers and warrant officers of the AATTV arrived back in Australia, ending ten years of involvement in Vietnam.[39] Between July 1962 and December 1972 46,852 Australians served in Vietnam. The final count was 496 killed and 2,398 wounded. While it is unknown how many of the serving men were Irish natives, four Irish-born soldiers died serving with Australian Forces Vietnam. The whole Vietnam adventure had cost the Australian government about $A500 million.[40] It had divided the nation like never before. Vietnam involvement and National Service were two of the main reasons the Liberal-Country Party lost the 1972 election and no Australian government since has felt tempted to reintroduce conscription for whatever reason.[41]

## CHAPTER 16

# WAR IS OVER

From 3-5 October 1970 US President Richard Nixon arrived in Ireland to visit his ancestral home in Timahoe, Co. Kildare. There were anti-war protests at the US Embassy in Dublin and one protestor managed to splatter him with an egg as his cavalcade drove through O'Connell Street. In an effort to win the war before completing the troop withdrawals Nixon had illegally invaded and was illegally bombing neutral Cambodia. This programme of destruction, kept secret from the American public and carried out without the permission of Congress, killed thousands and opened the door to the Khmer Rouge nightmare and Pol Pot's Year Zero. In March 1970 Cambodia's neutralist Prince Sihanouk was overthrown by a pro-American clique headed by Prime Minister Lon Nol. He demanded that the communists leave his country. When the communists did not leave Lon Nol, at the urgings of the Americans, asked for US assistance. The change in government in Phnom Penh removed the long-standing fear of violating Cambodian neutrality, and Nixon, hoping that a war in Cambodia would divert Hanoi's energies from the battle for South Vietnam, moved. On 29 April US and ARVN troops moved into Cambodia to destroy communist sanctuaries in the south of the country. Much to Nixon's delight they found huge caches of arms and ammunition, but the elusive communist headquarters was not found. The attacks on the sanctuaries could now be justified in terms of sustaining a friendly Cambodian government as well as easing the pressure on South Vietnam. The last US troops were withdrawn from Cambodia at the end of June and on 22 December Congress prohibited the use of US forces in Cambodia or Laos.[1]

On 3 August *Newsweek* announced: "five years of warfare against the US has so badly depleted Viet Cong ranks that today an estimated seventy-five per cent of the combat troops in main-force units are North Vietnamese ..."[2] But by now few Americans cared or believed in the war. Many returning veterans became vocal critics of the war. Irish-American novelist Tim O'Brien was born in the small town of Austin, Minnesota. He graduated from college in 1968 with a BA in political science, but was soon drafted. O'Brien was against the war, but reported for service and was sent to Vietnam with what has been called the "unlucky" 23rd Infantry (Americal) Division due to its involvement in the My Lai massacre in 1968. He was assigned to the 3rd Platoon, A Coy, 5th Battalion, 46th Infantry, as an infantryman. O'Brien's tour of duty was 1969-70 and he was wounded in action in July 1969. When he returned to the US he took up journalism and wrote his war memoir *If I Die in a Combat Zone* in 1973, which became one of the great anti-war classics.[3]

Another novelist of Irish extraction is James Webb, whose *Fields of Fire* (1978) is considered by many to be the classic novel of the Vietnam War. Webb is descended from Scotch-Irish settlers and both sides of his family have a strong citizen-soldier military tradition that predates the Revolutionary War. His father flew B-17s and B-29s during WWII, cargo planes during the Berlin Airlift, and was a pioneer in the United States missile programme. He was a vocal critic of Defence Secretary McNamara's leadership methods, which eventually caused him to retire from the Air Force, partially in protest of the manner in which the Vietnam War was being "micromanaged by the political process". James Webb graduated in 1968, but chose a commission in the US Marine Corps. He served with the 5th Marine Regiment, where as a rifle platoon and company commander in the An Hoa Basin he was awarded the Navy Cross, the Silver Star, two Bronze Stars, and two Purple Hearts. He later served as a platoon commander and as an instructor in tactics and weapons at the Marine Corps Officer Candidate School, and then as a member of the Secretary of the Navy's immediate Staff, before leaving the Marine Corps in 1972.[4]

Brian McGinn, the man responsible for the website *The Irish on the Wall*, served in Vietnam from 1969-70. Brian McGinn was born in New York City to emigrant parents from Monaghan and Sligo. His father, Michael McGinn from Swann's Cross, Co. Monaghan, played Senior Football in New York with Co. Fermanagh. He was a five-year veteran of World War II, including service with New York's famed "Fighting Irish" NY 69th Regiment. After his mother's death in 1951, Brian and his sister Sheila were raised and educated in Ireland. Brian attended St. Mary's College, Dundalk, graduating in 1964. After his return to New York, he was employed in the News Bureau of *Life Magazine* while enrolled as an evening student at New York's Hunter College. In 1968, Brian was drafted and trained as an intelligence specialist at Fort Bragg, NC. From 1969 to 1970, he was assigned to the 519th Military Intelligence Battalion, operating in Vietnam. His military awards include the Joint Services Commendation Medal. After his discharge, Brian completed his BA degree under the GI Bill and was re-employed by *Time-*

*Life* in 1972. In 1998 Brian McGinn set up *The Irish on the Wall* website to honour the forgotten Irish of the Vietnam War. Brian McGinn died on 20 July 2005, aged fifty-nine.[5]

With America thoroughly sick of the war the time was now coming when the Saigon government would have to stand, or fall, on its own merits. American help would be limited to advisers, Army helicopter units, and the fixed-wing airpower of the Air Force and the Navy. Starting in July 1969 with the 9th Marines, the entire 3rd Marine Division had moved to Okinawa by that November.[6] During August, redeployment of both ground and air units accelerated. As Marine strength declined, allied staffs through-out Military Region 1 drafted their fall and winter campaign plans. With fewer allied troops available and with the monsoon rains sure to restrict air support of operations deep in the mountains, Americans and South Vietnamese alike prepared to commit their regular units alongside the Regional and Popular Forces in major pacification efforts in the lowlands. At the same time III MAF modified its operating methods to get the most out of its remaining Marine air and ground forces. The plan would guide operations from September 1970 through February 1971. Mostly restating earlier directives, the plan called for a balance between offensive actions against base areas and protection of population centres, with an increased emphasis on efforts to eliminate the Viet Cong and their administrative apparatus at the village and hamlet level. The plan directed III MAF essen-tially to continue what it already was doing: to protect the Rocket Belt; to cooperate with the Government of Vietnam in pacification activities; and to continue its drive against enemy bases in the Que Son Mountains.

Lieutenant General Lam soon committed all the ARVN forces in Quang Nam to support pacification. On 22 October, he launched Operation Hoang Dieu. Lam also arranged for III MAF to cover areas in the northern and western fringes of the populated region of Da Nang and in the Que Son Valley and for the Korean Marines to conduct saturation operations in two portions of their TAOR. Within each command's zone of responsibility, troops would fill the countryside around the clock with small-unit patrols and ambushes. They would cooperate with police and local officials to cor-don and search hamlets, concentrating on about eighty known VC-infested communities. In an attempt to restrict clandestine movement of communist personnel and supplies, the allies would set up check points daily at a chang-ing series of positions on major roads. Operation Hoang Dieu initially was planned to last thirty days. In fact, it continued through November and into the first days of December.[7]

On 20 November 1970 Sergeant Arthur Fisher, US Marine Corps, died from multiple fragmentation wounds in a landmine explosion in Quang

Nam Province during one of these operations. Arthur Fisher was born on 31 July 1942, in Portrush, Co Antrim. He was twenty-eight and single when he died. Arthur Fisher lived at North Tonawanda, New York, and joined the USMC in 1968, beginning his tour of duty in Vietnam on August 24 1970. Arthur is buried in St Pancras, Islington and Finchley Cemetery, London.[8] At time of writing Arthur Fisher is the last known Irish-born soldier to die with US forces in the conflict.

Nixon's withdrawals had reduced the number of American military men in South Vietnam by half, to about 270,000, from the April 1969 peak of 543,000. The invasion of Cambodia had bought some time, but had brought such an outpouring of antiwar protest that Nixon had no choice but to accelerate the rate of withdrawal. By April 1972, there were to be fewer than 70,000 Americans in South Vietnam, virtually all advisers and aviation and support personnel. The Vietnamese communists were rebuilding and enlarging their Cambodian bases and preparing for an all-out offensive to win the war. In the hope of postponing the inevitable showdown for at least two more years, Creighton Abrams sent the ARVN into Laos along Route 9 from Khe Sanh in February 1971 to seize the road centre at Tchepone and sever the Ho Chi Minh Trial. The result was ominous, a debacle in which more than 3,000 South Vietnamese troops died. The showdown could not be put off much longer.[9]

US domestic opposition to the war increased, especially after the invasion of Cambodia, leading to nationwide student protests and tragedy at Kent State University when four students were shot and killed by the Ohio National Guard.[10] In South Vietnam the last US major military operation took place on 5 September 1971 when the 101st Airborne in conjunction with the ARVN 1st Division initiated Operation Jefferson Glenn in Thua Thien Province. American battle deaths for July 1971 were sixty-six, the lowest monthly figure since May 1967. In early November, President Nixon announced that American troops had reverted to a defensive role in Vietnam. Meanwhile, US troop levels fell from 280,000 to 156,000. American casualties were also down: 1,386 killed compared to 4,204 in 1970. But these losses gave little comfort to troops arriving to an army whose morale was at an all-time low. Men escaped into marijuana and heroin and other men died needlessly because their comrades were "stoned". Some units were on the verge of mutiny, and the increase of "fragging" of officers and noncoms increased. The signs of demoralisation were evident by the time of Westmoreland's departure in mid-1968 and they worsened under Creighthon Abrams because, while he attempted new tactics, he continued Westmoreland's attrition strategy and kept pushing US soldiers into the bunker-complex killing grounds the NVA prepared. The battle for

Hamburger Hill was a prime example. Fifty-five Americans died fighting for this fortified hill only to see it quickly abandoned after its capture.[11]

On 14 April the last US Marines left Vietnam; elsewhere throughout the country, other American units departed almost daily. Yet the security situation in the south was improving daily. The Viet Cong had been irretrievably weakened by the Tet Offensive and without Viet Cong help the politburo could no longer conduct a guerrilla war; its strategy had to be changed to conventional invasion.[12] On 30 March 1972 Hanoi began a full-scale offensive against South Vietnam. The NVA, now equipped with Russian T54 tanks and 130mm guns, eventually committed fourteen divisions and several independent regiments. Although nearly all US ground combat forces had been withdrawn the offensive was blunted and then defeated by the ARVN and US tactical firepower. The NVA sustained 120,000 casualties while the ARVN, with fewer losses and good reserves had actually increased in numerical strength. The NVA's ability to continue the offensive was greatly hampered by the resumption of air strikes on logistic targets in the North. For the first time Hanoi was facing possible defeat. The North offered to restart negotiations with all previous American concessions still on the table. The US bombing of the North was halted and Hanoi gained a six-month respite.[13]

From October 1972 until the cease-fire in early 1973, the entire scope of the war changed. As peace rumours increased, combat action rose. Both sides began final land-grabbing and consolidation operations.[14] As the US war wound down John Dullahan, from Dundalk, County Louth, was one of the few Irishmen left in Vietnam. "You always read about loud Americans blundering about in the jungle and getting picked off by super stealthy Viet Cong or NVA. There has been so much bullshit written, or shown on film, about Vietnam. The reality was somewhat different – we whispered to each other the entire time we were on patrol (up to two weeks), and just before these unexpected clashes, we would hear the NVA talking to each other as they walked along, giving us an edge in the ensuing firefight. By the way, during the Tet Offensive in early 1968, the VC was annihilated, so after that time there was only NVA, infiltrated from the North, to contend with. We mostly knew each other by first names or duty positions. (I was 'the FO' for forward observer.) Many of the guys I was with were KIA, but I still don't know their last names, so I can't look them up when I visit The Wall*

---

* The Vietnam Memorial Wall in Washington carries the names of 58,203 Americans who died in the Vietnam War from 1956 to 1975. Located in Constitution Gardens, near the Lincoln Memorial, it is the most visited site in the United States. It is intended as a human memorial rather than a war memorial and is credited with changing much of America's perspective on the war and returning veterans.

here in Washington. Nevertheless when there I feel their presence and share the sense of loss of the children and wives to whom they never returned."[15]

John Dullahan was born in Dundalk, in 1945 and as a teenager joined the FCA, the Irish Army's part-time reserve. As a member of the 8th Battalion's shooting team he won the 2nd Brigade individual full-bore competition in 1966. John emigrated to America in 1967 and worked as a house-painter while living with his older brother Pat in Montclair, New Jersey. (Pat Dullahan had emigrated in 1961; served three years in the 101st Airborne Division, then joined the police force, made detective, and later became a lawyer. He died in 1992.) John Dullahan was drafted in September 1968 and after basic training at Fort Dix, NJ, volunteered as a paratrooper and took pre-airborne advanced infantry training at Fort Gordon, Georgia. After airborne training in Ft. Benning, Georgia, he was assigned to the 82nd Airborne Division, Ft. Bragg, NC. John went to Officer Candidate School (OCS), and was commissioned a 2nd Lieutenant, Field Artillery, at Ft. Sill, Oklahoma, in June 1970.

In January 1972 he was sent to Vietnam. From January to August 1972, John Dullahan served as an artillery forward observer with the 7th Cavalry Regiment, 1st Cavalry Division. The job of an artillery forward observer was both highly responsible and dangerous. John's job was to become so familiar with his surroundings he could confidently call in air or artillery strikes when enemy positions were located. If he made one mistake – one miscalculation – fellow soldiers could be hit by friendly fire. John arrived in Vietnam as most Americans were leaving.[16] By the beginning of 1972 there were only about 156,800 American troops left in Vietnam. Throughout the period of the incursions into Laos and Cambodia (1970-71) the US armed forces were shrinking in size as Nixon's government did its best to bring the boys back home and end direct US involvement in Vietnam. The majority of US troops remaining were support elements. The 101st Airborne Division began pulling out on 31 January, leaving the 3rd Brigade, 1st Cavalry Division, and the 1st Aviation Brigade in the vicinity of Saigon, while the 196th Infantry Brigade remained on the perimeter of Da Nang. In the whole of I and II Corps Tactical Zones there was less than the equivalent of a division of American personnel left. Many US bases had been closed down or handed over to the ARVN. All Allied troops, except for two reduced Korean divisions, had also departed.[17]

"I arrived and departed Vietnam as an individual replacement. I went to a replacement unit in Saigon for about three days before shipping out to the 1/7th Cavalry … People would occasionally kid me good-naturedly about my brogue, which is still intact after all these years of minimum contact with Irish people. I enjoyed my tour in Vietnam. We operated out of firebase 'Melanie' about 40 km north of Saigon. The infantry company where I was assigned went into the field by helicopter (legs hanging out the door with no safety straps). After insertion, the company split up into separate platoons, and I always went with the company commander. Each platoon would establish a base where it would stay for about a day and send out 'lites' (a squad carrying only weapons, ammo, and water) to intercept the NVA supply lines and small units trying to get to Saigon.

"When in the field I looked forward to getting up in the morning, scraping a small trench in the ground with my finger, throwing a couple of heat tablets in, and making a canteen cup of tea. It took a while to get used to all the loud noises from birds and other creatures of the night. The heat was intense and hardly a square inch of clothes was not saturated with sweat. We carried enough food, water, and ammo for about four days. Then we had a 'log' (logistics) day when the choppers brought in supplies, including mail. We felt safe in our positions because we set tripwire booby traps on the trails leading to our positions. Sometimes an animal would set one off, and sometimes a small group of NVA would do the same. Of course, the same thing sometimes happened to our 'lites.' I replaced a FO who was with a lite when it blundered into an NVA camp, setting off their booby traps. The FO lost his legs and the platoon leader was killed."[18]

The 3rd Brigade, 1st Cavalry, saw minor action at the beginning of the NVA Easter Offensive in 1972, but it was soon relieved by the ARVN 18th Division and pulled back to the Bien Hoa-Long Binh-Saigon complex. The Easter Offensive did nothing to halt the withdrawal of US troops and in August the 1st Battalion, 7th Cavalry (part of Task Force Gary Owen) and the 3rd Battalion, 21st Infantry left, leaving just 25,000 American troops in-country.[19] On 11 August America's final ground troops, a defence force around the Da Nang airbase, where the very first US ground troops had been deployed, left for home. From August 1972 to January 1973, John Dullahan served as the Senior Adviser to the South Vietnamese 104th Artillery (175mm) Battalion. As Vietnamisation continued the ARVN activated three 175mm gun battalions for service in Military regions I, II, and III. Of these units, the 104th Artillery Battalion was the first to receive guns supplied directly from the United States rather than guns transferred within the country from departing American units. During the last three years of American involvement, efforts were concentrated on preparing the Vietnamese to defend their country without active American participation. John Dullahan left Vietnam in January 1973, one of the last Americans going home.[20]

The last American operations of the war in Vietnam were mainly waged by the US Air Force. From 1961 to 1973 the USAF flew over one million missions in which over 8,500 aircraft were shot down and 1,300 airmen killed or missing. A tour of duty for aircrew consisted of 100 missions and like the ground war the air war became more brutal and protracted than the Americans had expected. The USAF was the service of choice, theirs or the government's, for many Irishmen during the Vietnam conflict. John Oman, from Dublin, served with the USAF in the Vietnam theatre. He emigrated to the US in November 1954 and joined the air force the following year. He spent the next thirty years in the USAF as a Flight Engineer. John spent 443 days in Vietnam, Laos and Cambodia, during which he flew 206 combat missions.[21] Mike Curran was born in London to Irish emigrant parents. His father was from Waterville, Co. Kerry, while his mother was from Garryspillane, Co. Limerick. The family later emigrated to Boston. Mike joined the US Air Force in 1962 and served in USAF Munitions, from February 1963 to September 1992. He served in Vietnam from 1966-7, and then Thailand and Vietnam in 1973.[22] Seán McGovern, from Belfast, was thirteen when he emigrated with his family to New York in 1961. After high school he signed up for a four-year term in the USAF. Seán served one tour of duty in Turkey, which lasted fifteen months. He returned to the US where he spent another nine months then volunteered to go to Vietnam. Seán served eleven months in Cam Ranh Bay and Ton San Nhut in 1971 and 1972 with 483rd Supply Squadron, and one month in Thailand. His younger brother, James (Seamus), born in Enniskillen, Co. Fermanagh, joined the US Navy after graduating from high school. He served four years in the USN with many world-wide deployments, including a tour of duty in the Gulf of Tonkin.[23]

In October Hanoi finally agreed to the American peace proposals but then became more intransigent at the negotiating table, frequently going back to points agreed. This caused great frustration to Nixon and Kissinger, who were under enormous domestic pressure to settle at any price. In mid-December the peace talks broke down and the B-52 bombers were unleashed again. From 18-29 December around the clock surgically precision bombing raids were conducted against Hanoi, Haiphong and other northern targets. Within eleven days the North's defences were shattered and the whole anti-aircraft system was breaking down. After 1,242 surface-to-air missiles were fired the USAF was free to roam the skies over North Vietnam with impunity. To get the Americans out of the war Hanoi signed the ceasefire agreement.[24] Nixon was delighted. He had proved ruthless in his use of strategic bombers as a military, diplomatic and propaganda weapon, boasting to the American public that he "bombed Hanoi back to the conference table." On 12 February the first American POW in North Vietnam was released, to be followed by the remainder over the next four weeks. With the signing of the ceasefire on 25 February 1973 and its effective date on 28 February 1973, the United States involvement in Vietnam came to an end. On 23 August 1973 the last US ground combat battalion in Vietnam, 3rd Battalion, 21st Infantry, left the country.[25] The Paris Agreement of 1973 removed the advisers and the residual American military forces propping up the Saigon side, while leaving the NVA in the South to finish its task. Nixon and Kissinger convinced themselves they were not condemning their Saigon surrogate. They reasoned that they could hold Hanoi at bay with the threat of American air power. However, within two years South Vietnam had fallen.[26]

Throughout 1973 and 1974 communist forces built up their strength in the south and a number of severe battles were fought. In December 1974 Hanoi began an offensive to gauge ARVN strength. The ARVN had no reserves and was unable to switch forces or supplies from one region to another. The soldiers of the south were also weary, demoralised, and lacked the motivation of their enemies and in spite of Nixon's guarantee to South Vietnam, political pressures ensured that the US Air Force would play no part in its defence. The South Vietnamese government pleaded for arms and money, and though President Ford was willing to provide some assistance, Congress refused every funding request. The North could see the writing on the wall and the NVAs overwhelming success prompted the politburo to begin a more ambitious offensive. In March 1975 an all-out drive was ordered to end the war once and for all. Cities and provinces fell one after another as the ARVN disintegrated and within weeks the NVA was at the gates of Saigon. On 9 April the evacuation of American citizens and some Vietnamese began as the NVA closed in on the city. On 21 April President Thieu resigned and fled the country, as sixteen communist divisions surrounded the capital. He was replaced by Tran Van Huong, who resigned a week later. Off the coast, US Navy Task Force 76 began the final evacuation of US citizens by helicopter on the morning of 29 April. The evacuation from city rooftops ended that evening but that at the US Embassy continued until 0430 the following day. Two US Marines were killed in a communist rocket strike on the primary LZ near the American military compound at Tan Son Nhut airbase on April 29. They were the last Americans killed in Vietnam. The two were killed by a direct hit on their bunker. They were L/Cpl Darwin Judge, Iowa, and Cpl Charles McMahon, Massachusetts. The last Americans, eleven US Marines used to secure the Embassy, left at 0753. At 10.15 am, on 30 April, President Minh said he was ready to transfer power to avoid further bloodshed. Frantic crowds tried to storm the US Embassy in order to be airlifted out. At midday, communist forces entered Saigon. The Vietnam War was over.[27]

The war cost America dearly – 46,360 US servicemen died in battle, while more than 10,000 died from non-combat related causes and a further 200,000 were wounded. Australia lost 496 killed and 2,398 wounded. Over 5,000 South Koreans also died in Vietnam. The ARVN lost over 230,000 while that of the NVA and VC were 1,100,000. Civilian losses, North and South, were staggering – possibly four million. Through *The Agence France Presse* (French Press Agency) news release of 4 April 1995 the Hanoi government revealed that the true civilian casualties of the Vietnam War were two million in the north, and two million in the south. Military casualties were 1,100,000 killed and 600,000 wounded in twenty-one years of war. These figures were deliberately falsified during the war by the North Vietnamese communists to avoid demoralising the population.[28]

It is hard to determine how many Irishmen served in Vietnam during the conflict, but it is thought over 2,000 men served in the American forces and another several hundred in the Australian forces. Because most had given a US or Australian address, they were not registered as Irish. To date, it is known that twenty-one Irishmen and one Irishwoman were among US military deaths in Vietnam; an additional four Irishmen died serving with Australian forces; one died serving with the South Vietnamese police; one was lost over Laos while serving with the Canadian Army and one died serving with the CIAs airline, Air America.

# BETTER TIMES THAN THESE

When Saigon fell on 30 April 1975 it was renamed Ho Chi Minh City in honour of the communist leader. Most Americans and many South Vietnamese believed that there would be instant and indiscriminate mass liquidations, after the "liberation." Doubtless, many old scores were settled, but the majority of those connected with the US and South Vietnamese regimes had to report for basic re-training. Unhappy with the new communist regime, almost one million Vietnamese fled the country in the late 1970s. In 1979 Ireland accepted 500 of these "boat people." In America and Australia Vietnam veterans were a source of embarrassment. Everyone wanted to forget about the war and it was not until a decade later that the veterans and their families began to accept that the war they had fought was not of their doing.

In 1995 the end of the long US embargo against Vietnam signalled the start of a bilateral trade agreement and convinced many that the war era between America and Vietnam had been finally laid to rest. The "Bamboo curtain" that had been imposed after the fall of Saigon in 1975 began to lift. Foreigners were allowed to visit some parts of the country and slowly many American and Australian war veterans began to make the trek back to the country where they had spent a year of their young lives. Today if you walked around Ho Chi Minh City you are likely to bump into an American or Australian veteran of the war. Some, like the veterans of Peace Trees Vietnam, returned to uproot mines and plant trees, while others came to cry for dead friends or look for lost ones.[1]

Mick Coyne went back to Vietnam in 2000. He admitted that he was frightened to return. "At first I was apprehensive but my family persuaded me to do it – they knew it would be good for me." Michael was amazed at how warmly he was received. At the Cu Chi Tunnels he met with Viet Cong veteran Le Van Tung who shook his hand and said: "I never knew Irish fought in the war. Only Americans. We hated the soldiers, but now we have left that all behind and only have good feelings." Mick Coyne has different feelings than when he was a young idealistic soldier in Vietnam. "You were in there protecting capitalism. The French couldn't do the job so the Americans took over. The emotions I feel are a mix of shame, anger and I think the people should be compensated in a big way. I don't think an apology will put things right." Mick Coyne is a committed socialist. He had returned to Ireland in 1970, "went to England in 1973 and came back here (Ireland) in 1979. When I was in England, I joined the Workers Revolutionary Party and when I came home, I set up the Socialist League in Dublin. The struggle I was interested in was that of the working class in every country". Ultimately he remains proud of his role in the war. "I am proud to be a veteran. I'm proud because of what I learnt from the experience and what I've been able to pass on." He lives in Jenkinstown, Co. Meath, and remains actively involved in veterans associations.[2]

Tom Kelly returned to Ireland in 1970 and became a successful dairy farmer in Roscommon. He regularly visits America where his three sons live, one of whom also served in the US army. Tom firmly believes that the cause that he and other veterans fought for was right. He feels that the South Vietnamese would have a much brighter future if America had won. He also points to the changes in Vietnam and its dependence upon American trade, and dollars sent home from those South Vietnamese who managed to escape from Vietnam: "I was both spat on and clapped on the shoulder for my service in Vietnam, but I always thought what I did was right ... Certainly wouldn't encourage you to talk about it. The protesters get the airwaves. It was a little humiliating. My mind has never changed about the Vietnamese people. They were very nice people. I have absolutely no grudge against them and I think it is very sad. I wish we had won the war for them. If the political will was there Vietnam would be free today."[3]

Mike Flood returned to New York in 1970. "Coming back from Vietnam was pretty tough. I didn't know how to handle it. The biggest part of Vietnam for me was coming home. The disrespect was terrible. It was brutal. It wasn't until ten or fifteen years later that we got any recognition. While I'm glad I did it, I wouldn't want to do it again. In any event, I am glad that time heals, and I am ever so thankful that I had the opportunity to be part of the 2nd Battalion, 1st Marines." Mike lives in Long Island, New York.[4] He drives a 4x4 emblazoned with the US flag; MIA sticker; Kildare flag; and a 2nd Battn, 1st Mar. Div. insignia. He maintains that you could not do this after returning home from Vietnam. "The disrespect for the flag was awful. The American flag was a source of embarrassment. If you had it on your truck like this it would be thrashed. Now it's different. Everywhere you look around the American flag is there." Mike still bears the scars of war mentally and physically. "I thought the guys I went to Vietnam with, that we would all come home together. But within months they were all dead. I became hardened, angry and bitter. You had to, to survive." Like most veterans Mike readjusted to society in the same way veterans handled combat – by their own efforts and with the help of their friends and families. However, the memory of those days and events remain long after their passing. Mike often thinks of the young dead Vietnamese he pulled from a spider hole. "It was just another dead body at the time. I pulled him out and left his body there for someone else to bury. It was not my job. I didn't care. You become brutalised to these things. But a few days later we passed the same spot and his body was still there. We expected his guys to come along and bury him, but they didn't. I often think about him now and say a little prayer."[5]

Ed Somers returned to Ireland in 1967 where he managed a number of businesses including a shop, a pub, and a haulage business. He feels that the allied action in Vietnam "was the right thing to do. We wanted to help the Vietnamese, and we wanted to protect them, and to stop North Vietnamese aggression." As with many other allied soldiers, Ed feels that until the late 1960s the Allies were winning the war. "It was just so badly handled." Ed's views of the war have since changed. "I realise now the awful bombing that went on and the mass destruction of cities and villages; not by us but by the people who came after us. It was totally and utterly wrong." However, he makes a point of not blaming soldiers. "Soldiers are only tools of a government. Government policies were absolutely appalling and wrong. War is the ultimate obscenity; there is no glory in it, only suffering."[6]

Gerry Duignan said: "I came back to Ireland and through farming and the land, I rehabilitated myself. I had a huge amount of stories in me, good ones and bad ones, but I found no one to tell them to. Where were you in Vietnam, they would say, it's a terrible place. And I would say, no, it's a beautiful place." Gerry had a unique time in Vietnam, spending nearly four years there. He made many Vietnamese friends and said he never met a family that had not lost a relative at the hands of the Vietnamese or the Americans. "They accepted it then, but I don't think now that it need ever have happened."[7]

Vietnam did nothing to dispel John Dullahan's love for the military life. From March 1973 to May 1976, on a NATO assignment, he was attached to 45 Medium Regt, Royal Artillery, British Army on the Rhine, in Paderborn, West Germany. He returned to the US in 1976. After graduating from Cameron University, Oklahoma, he studied German at the Defence Language Institute, Monterey, California. From February 1979 to June 1983 he was attached to the German Army in Gissen, Germany. After attending Arabic language training in the US, John was assigned to the UN

Truce Supervision Organization (UNTSO) as a UN Observer, from June 1985 to December 1986. He served six months in Damascus, Syria, under the command of Commandant Seán Brennan, Irish Army. He served six months each in Southern Lebanon and on the Sinai Peninsula with UNTSO. He returned to the US in 1987 and served two years in the Defence Intelligence Agency, Washington, DC; and a further three years on the Joint Staff, Pentagon, as the East European Action Officer on General Colin Powell's staff. John travelled to almost all the former Warsaw Pact East European countries, just after their communist regimes collapsed, to arrange military-to-military contacts. He retired as a lieutenant colonel from the US Army in August 1992 and as a Department of Defence employee, travelled to Iraq in the late 1990s as a UNSCOM inspector. John returned for a six month tour in 2003 as a member of the Iraqi Survey Group (ISG) targeting the Iraqi Intelligence Services as well Iraqi regime safe houses in Baghdad. His youngest brother, Jim, also emigrated to the US at seventeen in 1979, making three of four brothers from the Dullahan family who were paratroopers in the US Army. Jim became the youngest sergeant in the 82nd Airborne Division. He later joined the Special Forces and had numerous assignments in various countries before retiring as a lieutenant colonel in 2005. Terry, the only brother to remain in Ireland, won the All Army individual rifle falling plates competition, at the Curragh, while serving with the FCA in 1976.[8]

John Barnicle: "(Vietnam) I'm not sad I done it, but wouldn't wish it on anyone. I wouldn't do it again." John left the army in 1970 and flew civilian helicopters in Australia for eight years. He first came to Ireland in 1974, for a holiday, because for three months of the year it was too hot to work in Australia. "I met more cousins here than I did in America," he said. John loved the Irish culture and the relaxed atmosphere and moved to Ireland in 1979. He worked with Irish Helicopters, then started up his own company, Celtic Helicopters, and took up Irish citizenship. He now lives in Ireland.[9]

John O'Sullivan made a career of the Army. He retired as a major in 1982 and went to work as a pilot with the US Army Avionics Research and Development Activity, Fort Monmouth, New Jersey. Interviewed in 1972 when applying for American citizenship John said the US was "definitely doing the right thing in fighting in Vietnam", and said "dissenters would not be welcome over there". Summing up his military career he said, "I just did my job." John returned to Ireland to live and still flies helicopters.[10]

Pat Nee's return to Boston was anticlimactic. "I returned to Southie, a place that has always welcomed Marines with open arms. I've heard that Southie lost seven times the national average, per capita, for men killed in combat in all the wars Americans have fought." Pat's views on the war are as clear as the day he landed in South Vietnam in 1965. He maintains the Americans were fighting a war of liberation. "There is no doubt in my mind – Vietnam was a war we could have won."[11] Pat, like many returning servicemen, became involved in veterans affairs as a member of the South Boston Veterans Group. Southie has one of the first Vietnam Veteran's Memorial's in the country. The South Boston Vietnam Veteran's Memorial sits in the M Street Park in South Boston. The twenty-five veterans from the area listed on the monument had come to the park sometime during their childhood. The idea for building the monument came while some veterans had gathered to remember three of their friends who had been killed in 1968 while serving in Vietnam. It was the tenth anniversary of their deaths. The three were part of a group of six friends that joined the military together after finishing high school. The surviving friends began to reminisce about other members of their community that had given their lives in Vietnam. By the time they were done, they had counted twenty-five fallen friends and neighbours. In remembrance to them, they decided to build a memorial. The memorial was built with funds raised from the community and $30,000 donated by the City of Boston. It was dedicated on 13 September 1981. The guest speaker at the dedication was author and war veteran James Webb. At least ten of the men listed on the Memorial have an Irish-American background.[12]

"I lost a lot of good friends in Vietnam," Pat Landers said, "but that's war. We had a few lads completely crack and had to be sent home. Even to this day soldiers are suffering PTSD and depression and I am one of them. A large amount have died of cancer and suicide. Cancer caused by Agent Orange that was sprayed to kill vegetation in the jungle to make it possible to spot the enemy from the air. We had to patrol these areas. In January 2007 one of my best mates hanged himself in Australia. I flew out for the funeral. We had joined up together and trained together. They call it the 'war that goes on killing' even though its all over. I served a twelve months tour of duty in Vietnam. The loneliest day of my life was at Sydney airport leaving for Vietnam. Coming home I still had no one to meet me off the ship, but that's life. I wish I had never been to Vietnam, but I would like to go back and see Vietnam, now. I am told now it is a beautiful place to take a holiday. A lot of front line soldiers suffer from PTSD and depression. I myself suffer from PTSD and depression since the war and am on medication for the rest of my life."[13]

John Barrett said: "I am proud of my service. Am I glad I did it? Yes. Would I do it again? Probably, not. I know that's a contradiction, but I was young then. I believed in the American way. I have no regrets about doing my duty. I had chosen to make America my home. America is a great country and was good to me. I became a citizen and I am very proud of my American passport. I go back three or four times a year. I had a good life after." However, John became disillusioned on his return to America after his tour of duty in the summer of 1967. "I was very disappointed in the Chicago riots. I had given two years of my life to protect these beatniks who took over the city. I lost a lot of faith in America. I never told anyone I served in Vietnam. I came back to Ireland in uniform and went to a local dance hall where I was spit at as a warmonger." John had an uncle who was severely wounded in the First World War and was able to talk to him about his experiences. He travels a lot but has no desire to return to Vietnam. "A lot go back, but no I have no desire to go back." John Barrett returned to live in Ireland in 1981.[14]

American and Australian intervention in Vietnam ended in 1973. Two years later Vietnam was united by force of communist arms. For the thousands of Irish-Americans and Irish-Australians who served there the war is over, but the memories, good and bad, are still alive.

# GLOSSARY OF TERMINOLOGY

| | |
|---|---|
| **Airmobile** | Helicopter-borne. Those who jump from helicopters without parachutes. |
| **Airborne** | Parachutist. Those who jump from airplanes with parachutes. |
| **AK-47** | Kalashnikov AK-47. Russian originated, but produced in many other eastern-bloc countries. The most widely used assault rifle in the world. |
| **A.O.** | Area of Operation. |
| **Arty** | Artillery. |
| **ARVN** | Pronounced Ar'-vin. Army of the Republic of Vietnam. |
| **B40** | A communist block rocket-propelled grenade launcher. |
| **B52** | An American heavy bomber. |
| **C-4** | A powerful plastic explosive. Often used for cooking as well as detonation. |
| **C.C.** | Company Commander. |
| **C. & C.** | Command and Control (helicopter). |
| **Chi-Com** | Chinese Communist. Used in conjunction with an object this denoted manufactured in Communist China. |
| **Chinook** | A large twin-rotor cargo helicopter, CH-47. |
| **Chopper** | Helicopter. |
| **Claymore** | Anti-personal mine with one-pound charge of C-4 behind 600 steel balls. |
| **C.O.** | Commanding Officer. |
| **C.O.S.V.N.** | Communist Office of South Vietnam. Thought to be located in the Parrot's Beak area of Cambodia. It was never found. |
| **C.P.** | Command Post. |
| **D.E.R.O.S.** | Date Estimate Return from Overseas. The day a serviceman is scheduled to go home. |
| **D.M.Z.** | Demilitarised Zone. |
| **Dust-Off** | Medical evacuation by helicopter. |
| **E-1** | Private One. The lowest army pay grade. |
| **E-2** | Private Two. E stands for enlisted. Pay grades run from E-1 to E-11. |

| | |
|---|---|
| **F.O.** | Forward Observer. |
| **Fragging** | To wound or kill a person with a fragmentary grenade, usually a noncom or officer. |
| **Grunt** | An infantryman. |
| **Gook** | Korean word for person. Used for any Oriental human being. |
| **H.E.** | High Explosive (Artillery). |
| **H.&I.** | Harassment and Interdiction (Artillery). |
| **K.I.A.** | Killed in Action. |
| **Klick** | Kilometer. |
| **LAW** | An American shoulder-fired, disposable 66-mm rocket. |
| **L.P.** | Listen Post. Where a fire team went outside the perimeter in order to give advance warning of any probe or attack. |
| **L-T** | Lieutenant. |
| **L.Z.** | Landing Zone. |
| **Medevac** | Medical evacuation by helicopter. |
| **M.I.A.** | Missing in Action. |
| **M-16** | A gas operated, air cooled automatic/semi-automatic assault weapon. The standard rifle of US military. |
| **M-60** | The standard American light machine gun. A gas operated, air cooled, belt-fed, automatic weapon. |
| **M-79** | An American single-shot 40-mm grenade launcher. Called a blooper, or thumper. |
| **N.D.P.** | Night Defensive Position. |
| **O.P.** | Observation Post. Manned during daylight hours to watch for enemy movement. |
| **Point/pointman** | The first man on patrol. The Australians referred to the pointman as a forward scout. |
| **R. & Rr** | rest and relaxation. |
| **R.O.T.C.** | Reserve Officer's Training School. |
| **R.T.O.** | Radio-Telephone Operator. |
| **S.K.S.** | A communist Simonov 7.62 semi-automatic carbine. |
| **Slick** | Huey helicopter. |
| **Tigerland** | US Army training camp located at Fort Polk, Louisiana, part of the US Army Advanced Infantry Training Centre. |
| **W.I.A.** | Wounded in Action. |
| **X.O.** | Executive Officer. |

# NOTES

## Chapter 1 Good Morning, Vietnam

1.   Neil Sheehan, *A Bright Shining Lie*, pp. 155-9.
2.   'Major Peter Dewey, America's First Vietnam Casualty,' Gary Linderer, *Behind the Lines*, 6 September 2005.
3.   Ed. Sir Robert Thompson, *War in Peace,* p.180.
4.   'The Jungle Doctor,' Edward T. O'Donnell. *The Irish Echo*, April 9-15 2008.
5.   John Cooney, *The American Pope: The Life and Times of Francis Cardinal Spellman*, p. 242.
6.   Sheehan, *A Bright Shining Lie*, p. 189.
7.   Thompson, *War in Peace*, p.194; Scott Brodie, *Australia in the Vietnam War*, p. 22.
8.   Michael Sallah and Mitch Weiss, *Tiger Force*, pp. 19-20.
9.   Thompson, *War in Peace*, pp. 181-2.
10.  Brodie, Australia in Vietnam, p. 30.
11.  Author interview and correspondence with Canice Wolahan, January/May 2007.
12.  Thompson, *War in Peace*, p. 182
13.  Author, Wolahan.
14.  Ibid.
15.  Kurt Jensen, *USA Today*, 8/5/2003.
16.  Author, Wolahan.
17.  Ibid.
18.  Ed. Jonathan Reed, Nam. *The Vietnam Experience 1965-75*, p. 6.
19.  Thompson, *War in Peace*, p. 182.
20.  Ibid, pp. 182-3.

## Chapter 2 The Green Machine

1.   Kevin Kenny, *The Irish in America*, p. 221, p. 226.
2.   Ibid, pp. 221-2; Donald Harman Akenson. *The Irish Diaspora. A Primer*, p. 257.
3.   James Durney, *The Far Side of the World. Irish Servicemen in the Korean War 1950-53*, p. 107.
4.   Reed, *Nam*, p. 27.
5.   Patrick Nee, *A Criminal and an Irishman. The Inside Story of the Boston Mob and the IRA*, pp. 21-2, pp. 29-30.
6.   Ibid, pp. 57-8.
7.   Author interview with Mike Flood, October 2006.
8.   James Bradley, *Flags of Our Fathers*, pp. 70-1, p. 78.
9.   Nee, *A Criminal and an Irishman*, p. 82.
10.  Ibid, p. 81-2.
11.  Author correspondence with Pat Nee, November 2007.
12.  Nee, *A Criminal and an Irishman*, pp. 83-4.
13.  Timothy J. Kutta, *The First Marines in Vietnam*.
14.  Nee, *A Criminal and an Irishman*, pp. 86-91.
15.  Ibid, pp. 111-2; Author, Nee.
16.  Author, Nee.
17.  Ibid.
18.  Author interview with Pat Nee, February 2008.
19.  Reed, *Nam*, p. 33.
20.  Katcher, Philip. *The American Soldier*, pp.168-70.
21.  Sheehan, *Bright Shining Lie*, pp. 525, 527.
22.  Michael Casey, Clark Dougan, Dennis Kennedy and Stanton Shelby. *The Vietnam Experience. The Army at War*, p. 168.
23.  Author interview and correspondence with Martin Hennigar, March 2007/February 2008.
24.  *The Green Berets*, Wikipedia, sourced March 2008.
25.  Author, Hennigar. One evening in March 2007 the day after talking to Martin about the time he met Larry Feehan in Vietnam I was watching RTE's travel programme *No Frontiers* when it featured the same Larry Feehan talking to the presenter Ryle Nugent in upstate New York. (The programme was about travel in

upstate New York and North Vietnam – hence my interest – and what got my attention was a Munster rugby flag on display when presenter Ryle Nugent arrived at the Mohonk Natural Preserve.) I immediately telephoned Martin who was as surprised as I was.

26. 'The Builders of Cam Rahn Bay', 35th Engineer Group News Bulletin, vol i, no. 16, 15 February 1968.
27. Author, Hennigar, January 2008.
28. Letter of appreciation for Martin Hennigar, 9 February 1968, Capt. Lawrence Gralla, CO Company A, 577th Engineer Battalion. Copy given to the author by Martin Hennigar.
29. Author, Hennigar.
30. Reed, *Nam*, p. 11.
31. Medal of Honour Citations, sourced online May 2005.
32. *The Irish Times* 8 December 1966.
33. Reed, *Nam*, p.13.

## Chapter 3  A Rumour of War

1. Reed, *Nam*, p. 32a.
2. Author interview with Tom Kelly, January 2006.
3. RTE interview, *Green Fields of Vietnam*, 2004; Address by Tom Kelly as Chairman, Irish Veterans Memorial. IVM is a project undertaken by Irish veterans and their friends to establish a Memorial to all those Irish men and women who served, and especially those who died serving, over the last 100 years or more.
4. Ibid.
5. 173rd Airborne.com, sourced February 2007.
6. Author, Kelly.
7. Robert Manning, ed. *The Vietnam Experience*, p. 29.
8. Author, Kelly.
9. 173rd Airborne.com.
10. John M. del Vecchio. *The 13th Valley*, p. 126.
11. Tom Mangold and John Penycate. *The Tunnels of Cu Chi*, p. 163.
12. Brodie, *Australia in Vietnam*, p. 38.
13. Author interview and correspondence with Ed Somers, September 2006.
14. Author interview with Dan Danaher, September 2006.
15. Author, Somers; Vanessa Connolly interview with Ed Somers from *Airborne All The Way*.
16. Brodie, *Australia in Vietnam*, pp. 38-40.
17. Author, Somers; Connolly, *Airborne All The Way*.
18. *Canberra Times*, 3 October 1992.
19. Connolly, *Airborne All The Way*.
20. Author, Danaher.
21. Brodie, *Australia in Vietnam*, p. 70.
22. Somers, RTE; Somers, author; Manning, *Vietnam Experience*, pp. 28, 31.
23. Connolly, *Airborne All the Way*.
24. Mangold and Penycate, *Tunnels of Cu Chi*, p. 44.
25. Mary Francis Ryan, *The Enniscorthy Echo*, 7/9/2005.
26. Mangold and Penycate, *Tunnels of Cu Chi*, pp. 43-4, 54.
27. Miles Dungan, Distant Drums. *Irish Soldiers in Foreign Armies*, p. 172.
28. Mangold and Penycate, *Tunnels of Cu Chi* p.56; Dungan, *Distant Drums*, p. 172.
29. Author, Danaher
30. Ibid.
31. Mangold and Penycate, *Tunnels of Cu Chi*, p. 58.
32. Somers, RTE.
33. Author, Danaher.
34. Ibid.
35. Brian Finch. *Vietnam Revisited*, p. 25.
36. Author, Danaher.
37. 173rd Airborne.com.
38. Kelly.
39. Somers, RTE.
40. Author, Somers.
41. Ibid.
42. 1 RAR Unit History, p.35.
43. Author, Somers.
44. Author, Danaher.
45. Author, Kelly.

**Chapter 4 Under the Red Duster**
1. Author interview with Michael Cahill, September 2006.
2. *Encyclopaedia Britannica*, p. 406.
3. Author, Cahill.
4. Manning, *Vietnam Experience*, p.80.
5. Sheehan, *A Bright Shining Lie*, pp 680, 777.
6. Author, Cahill.
7. Austin Williams. 'The Star and the Sickle. A study of Soviet-Vietnamese Relations during the Vietnam War.'
8. Author, Cahill.
9. Author interview and correspondence with John Dobbin, July/August 2008.
10. Ibid.
11. 12th Tactical Fighter Wing Association.
12. Author, Dobbin.
13. Ibid.
14. CBC Archive, sourced online August 2008.
15. Author, Dobbin.
16. Merchant Navy Association, sourced online August 2008.

**Chapter 5 Other Days May not be so Bright**
1. Manning, *Vietnam Experience*, p. 8.
2. Author correspondence with John Jennings, January 2007.
3. Manning, *Vietnam Experience*, p. 8.
4. Letter of recommendation 20 December 1965 written by Captain Robert G. Canady, copy given to author by John Jennings, Long Island.
5. Sheehan, *Bright Shining Lie*, pp 569-70.
6. Ibid, p. 570.
7. Reed, *Nam*, pp 68-9.
8. Sheehan, *Bright Shining Lie*, p. 570.
9. The Irish on the Wall website.
10. Author interview with Don Driver, September 2006.
11. Paddy McGarrigle. 'John C. Driver, A Soldier's Story.' *An Cosantoir*, May 1999.
12. Ibid, p. 13.
13. Harold G. Moore and Joseph Galloway, *We Were Soldiers Once and Young*, pp. 375-6.
14. Ibid.
15. Ibid.
16. Ibid.
17. Sheehan, *Bright Shining Lie*, p. 572.
18. Reed, *Nam*, p. 37.
19. Moore and Galloway, *We Were Soldiers*, pp. 375-6.
20. Reed, *Nam*, pp. 69, 63.
21. Canadian Vietnam Veterans Memorial, Windsor, Ontario.
22. Gar Pardy and Donald J. Byrne. 'Canadians in Vietnam.'
23. John Prados. 'Operation Masher. The Boundaries of Force.' *The VA Veteran* February/March 2002.
24. Irish on the Wall.
25. Sheehan, *Bright Shining Lie*, p. 581.
26. Ibid.
27. Prados, 'Operation Masher.'

**Chapter 6 First Blood**
1. *Irish Evening Press*, 28 March 1966.
2. Tom Kelly, RTE.
3. Irish on the Wall.
4. Author correspondence with Bill Lee (USMC retd), September 2006.
5. Legend has it that Brian Coll wrote the song, but I believe it was songwriter Johnny McCauley. Several Irish singers have recorded the *Blazing Star of Athenry* and it is still a popular song in the Irish bars in North America.
6. Author interview, Canice Wolahan.
7. Author interview, Ed Somers.
8. Author correspondence with Rory O'Connell, November 2006.
9. Charles D. Melson. *The Marine Corps in Vietnam*, pp 6-7.
10. Sheehan, *Bright Shining Lie*, p. 634-5.
11. Ibid, p. 535-7; Philip Jones Griffith, *Vietnam, Inc.*, p. 35.

12. Author, O'Connell, November 2006.
13. 1st Battalion, 4th Marines, Operation Reports 010001 to 312400, March 1966.
14. Sheehan, *Bright Shining Lie*, p. 638.
15. Author, O'Connell, November 2006.
16. Author, O'Connell, March 2008.
17. 1st Batn, 4th Marines, Operation Reports 010001 to 312400, August 1966.
18. Author, correspondence O'Connell, November 2006.
19. Author interview and correspondence Rory O'Connell, October 2006; correspondence March 2008.
20. Author, O'Connell, October 2006.
21. 1st Batn, 4th Marines, Operation Reports 010001 to 312400, August 1966.
22. Author, O'Connell, September 2008.
23. 1st Batn, 4th Marines, Operation Reports 010001 to 312400, August 1966.
24. Author, O'Connell, October 2006.
25. *Stars and Stripes* report 'Marines batter N. Viets trying to destroy tanks,' by Wallace Beene. Undated copy sent to author by Rory O'Connell.
26. Author, O'Connell, November 2006.
27. Undated reports from *Clare Champion*, copy sent to the author by Rory O'Connell.
28. Author interview with John Barrett, February 2008.
29. Ibid.
30. Reed, *Nam*, p. 83.
31. Ibid.
32. Sheehan, *Bright Shining Lie*, pp. 568-9.
33. Allan R. Millett. Semper Fi. *The History of the United States Marine Corps*, p. 576.
34. Reed, *Nam*, p. 160.
35. Sheehan, *Bright Shining Lie*, p. 617.

### Chapter 7  Journal of a Plague Year

1. 'Casualties - US vs NVA/VC,' Ray Smith 2000, sourced online August 2007.
2. Manning, *Vietnam Experience*, p. 54.
3. Brian McGinn, 'Encounters with the Irish on the Wall.' *Irish Echo*, 1999.
4. Irish on the Wall; After action reports: 1st Battalion, 22nd Infantry, 3 May 1967.
5. Manning, *Vietnam Experience*, p. 57.
6. Personal letters and reminiscences, Smith family, Cavan.
7. Ibid.
8. Pat Doyle, 'Irish on the Wall,' *Irish Emigrant* 18 April 2005.
9. Millet, *Semper Fi*, pp. 584, 58.
10. Irish on the Wall.
11. Warren, *American Spartans*, pp. 224-5.
12. Author correspondence with Rory O'Connell, November 2006.
13. Ibid.
14. Irish on the Wall.
15. Jack Schulimson. 'The Marine War: III MAF in Vietnam, 1965-1971.'
16. McGarry, Patsy, *Irish Times*, 14 November 1998.
17. McGinn, 'An Irishman's Diary.'
18. Irish on the Wall.
19. Eds. David and Marian Novack, Eds, *We Remember. The Vietnam stories of the men of the 2nd Battalion, 1st Marines*, pp. 447, 423.
20. Jim Belshaw. 'The Fighting Irish on the Travelling Wall,' 1999.
21. Novack, *We Remember*, p. 377.
22. Ibid, p. 373.
23. Sallah and Weiss, *Tiger Force*, pp. 54-5.
24. McGinn, 'An Irishman's Diary,' *Irish Times*, 28 May 2001.
25. Ibid.
26. Manning, *Vietnam Experience*, p. 59.
27. McGinn, 'An Irishman's Diary,' *Irish Times*, 28 May 2001.
28. Irish on the Wall.
29. Gary Hart, correspondence with author, September 2006, and account of action on Vietnamtripledeuce.org.
30. Author correspondence with Jim Gebhardt, September 2006.
31. Brownwater Navy Vietnam.com; Reed, *Nam*, pp. 288b, 293.
32. Irish on the Wall.

33. Thompson, *War in Peace*, pp 183-4; Sheehan, *Bright Shining Lie*, p. 717.
34. Diarmaid Ferriter, *The Transformation of Ireland*, p. 578.

**Chapter 8 Training Days**
1. Warren, *American Spartans*, p. 188; Richard Holmes, ed. *The Oxford Companion to Military History*, p. 941.
2. Melson, *Marine Corps in Vietnam*, p. 6.
3. Author correspondence with Rory O'Connell, March 2008.
4. Melson, *Marine Corps in Vietnam*, p. 6.
5. Ibid, p. 60.
6. Author, O'Connell.
7. Author interview with Mike Flood, April 2008.
8. Warren. *American Spartans*, pp. 192-5.
9. Ibid, p. 202.
10. Ibid.
11. Author interview with John Barrett, May 2008.
12. Author interview and correspondence with Martin Hennigar, June 2008.
13. Author correspondence with Pat Landers, February 2008.
14. Brodie, *Australia in the Vietnam war*, pp. 63-4.

**Chapter 9. Choppers and LZs**
1. Reed, *Nam*, p. 225a.
2. Author interview with John O'Sullivan, March 2007; author interview with John Barnicle, April 2006.
3. Helicopters in Vietnam. Sourced online April 2006.
4. Author, Barnicle.
5. Robert Mason. *Chickenhawk*, p. 19.
6. Author, Barnicle.
7. Vietnam Helicopter Pilots Association, 2004.
8. Sheehan, *Bright Shining Lie*, P. 763.
9. Author, Barnicle.
10. Ibid.
11. David T. Zabecki, 'The Battle for Saigon.'
12. Author, Barnicle.
13. Zabecki, 'Battle for Saigon.'
14. Author, Barnicle.
15. Brownwater Navy, sourced online April 2006.
16. Author, Barnicle.
17. Author interview John O'Sullivan, April 2007.
18. 174ahc.org, sourced April 2007.
19. Author, O'Sullivan.
20. 174ahc.org.
21. John O'Sullivan Archive, untitled newspaper reports.
22. *Trenton Evening Times*, 5 May 1971.
23. O'Sullivan Archive, untitled newspapers.
24. Ibid.
25. 174ahc.org.
26. Distinguished Service Cross Citation. General Order no. 3869, 21 August 1970, O'Sullivan Archive.
27. Peter S. Sorenson, 3 May 1970. 'NVA loses 135 in Nghia Hanh attack.'
28. Author, O'Sullivan.
29. O'Sullivan Archive, untitled newspapers.
30. General Orders – Legion of Valour – January 1972.
31. Author, O'Sullivan.

**Chapter 10. Tour of Duty**
1. Russ Anderson, *Stars and Stripes*, 8 April 1968.
2. *Time* Archives 15 August 2008; *Irish Times* 18 August 1970.
3. Interview Michael Coyne, RTE.
4. Author interview with Michael Coyne, January 2007. Michael Coyne has given interviews to RTE and many Irish local, national and Irish-American newspapers. His story in this book is an extension of many of these interviews with updates he gave to the author.
5. Manning, *Vietnam Experience*, p. 130.
6. Author, Coyne.
7. Manning, *Vietnam Experience*, pp. 130, 134.

8. Author, Coyne.
9. Ibid.
10. Coyne, RTE.
11. Author, Coyne.
12. Coyne, RTE.
13. Ibid.
14. Author, Coyne.
15. Ibid.
16. Author interview with Sean Levins, March/April 2007.
17. Author interview with Mike Flood, October 2006.
18. Novack, *We Remember*. Mike Flood, James Kirk, 'Bronx Reunion,' p. 287.
19. Author correspondence with Jim Kirk, October 2006.
20. Ibid.
21. Author interview with Mike Flood, April 2008.
22. Millet, *Semper Fi*, p. 592.
23. Novack, *We Remember*. Mike Flood, 'Time Heals Almost Everything,' pp. 120-1.
24. Author interview with Mike Flood, October 2006.
25. Author interview with Anne Flood, April 2008.
26. Copy of original telegram, given to author by Mike Flood.
27 Mike and Anne Flood; copy of original telegram, given to author by Mike Flood.
28. Anne Flood, correspondence with author, June 2008.
29. Author interview with Gerry Duignan, December 2006.
30. Author correspondence with Gerry Duignan, November 2006.
31. Ibid.
32. Ibid.
33. Mangold and Penycate. *Tunnels of Cu Chi*, p. 143.
34. Author, Duignan.
35. Ibid.
36. Duignan, correspondence, November 2006.
37. Dungan, *Distant Drums*, p. 172.
38. Author, Duignan.

## Chapter 11 Sand in the Wind

1. Holmes, *Oxford Companion to Military History*, pp 954-6; Millet, Semper Fi, p. 592.
2. Ibid, pp. 592-4.
3. Griffiths, *Vietnam Inc.,* p. 135.
4. Thomas L. Johnson and Mary R. Himes 'Historical Account of the Military Police Corps Regiment Assault on the American Embassy Tet –1968.'
5. Information given to author by Michael Fanning, Below the Radar.
6. The battle for the US Embassy is based on Lt Col Jack Schulimson, Leonard Blasiol, Charles R. Smith, and Capt. David A. Dawson. *U.S. Marines in Vietnam: 1968, the Defining Year,* pp. 642-4; and Johnson & Himes, 'Military Police Corps Regiment Assault on the American Embassy.'
7. Reed, *Nam,* pp. 369-72; Griffiths, *Vietnam Inc.,* pp. 122, 125.
8. George McArthur. 'He Wouldn't Stay Behind. Chaplain dies at front with his men.' *Seattle Times*, Seattle WA, 20 February 1968.
9. Sheehan, *Bright Shining Lie*, pp. 722-3.
10. Ibid.
11. Ferritter, *Transformation of Ireland*, pp. 576-9, p. 804.
12. Reed, *Nam*, p. 352.
13. Reed, *Nam*, p. 401.
14. Frank R. Miller, Jr. *Public Safety During Combat: A positive lesson from Vietnam*, p. 3.
15. Essay by Kyra Heiker. Trooper Michael Murphy Scholarship. 1996.
16. Irish Times, 26 May 1968.
17. The 9th Infantry Division Index. Sourced online September 2006
18. 'Remembering the Irish who died in Vietnam,' *Connaught Tribune*, 4 December 1998.
19. *Irish Times*, 13 September 1968.
20. Reed, *Nam*, pp. 504-7.
21. Christopher Podgus. 'Eight Names On The Wall Belong To Women.' *The VVA Veteran*. Special Commemorative Issue, November 2002.
22. Irish on the Wall.
23. *Irish Times*, 13 September 1968.
24. Podgus, 'Eight Names On the Wall.'

25.    Author interview Stanley Bancroft, January 2007.
26.    Brian McGinn, 'An Irishman's Diary,' 29 May 2000.
27.    Sheehan, *Bright Shining Lie*, pp. 720, 726.
28.    McGinn, 'An Irishman's Diary.'
29.    *Leinster Leader*, June 1968; *Cork Examiner*, 19 December 1968.
30.    1st Cavalry Division Homepage.
31.    Reed, *Nam*, pp. 384a&b.
32.    Ibid.
33.    Sandra Scanlon. 'That bitch of a war: Lyndon B. Johnson and Vietnam,' *History Ireland*, May/June 2008.

### Chapter 12 Air America

1.    *Irish Times*, 18 December 1968; Author correspondence with Joe Hennessy, June 2008.
2.    *Cork Examiner*, 19 December 1968.
3.    Reed, *Nam*, p. 478; Author, Hennessy.
4.    *Cork Examiner*, 19 December 1968.
5.    McCarthy family/Declan Hughes, July 2008.
6.    Correspondence and interview, Joe Hennessy, June 2008.
7.    On 2 June 2001 The Central Intelligence Agency commended CAT/AA for its work in Southeast Asia: "During the hottest days of the Cold War, the aircrews and ground personnel of Civil Air Transport and Air America gave unwavering service to the United States of America in the worldwide battle against communist oppression. Over the course of four decades, the courage, dedication to duty, superior airmanship, and sacrifice of these individuals set standards against which all future covert air operations must be measured. From the mist shrouded peaks of Tibet, to the black skies of China, to the steaming jungles of Southeast Asia, the legendary men and women of Civil Air Transport and Air America always gave full measure of themselves in the defence of freedom. They did so despite often outdated equipment, hazardous terrain, dangerous weather, enemy fire, and their own government bureaucracy. Their actions speak eloquently of their skill, bravery, loyalty, and faith in themselves, each other, and the United States of America."
8.    *Air America*, by Joe Hennessey. Joe Hennessy's *Air America* has been described as a remarkable piece of literature on the workings of the company during the Southeast Asia conflict. It is reproduced here in full with several updates from the author. Charlie Weitz has also read this chapter and with Joe Hennessy has congratulated me on my research, which included this: "at its height the CIA operations in Laos tied down the bulk of two NVA divisions, which would otherwise have been available for deployment in Vietnam." Joe's reply was: "I have never before seen this written and I don't think any Air America pilot ever even considered that as a result of their actions they kept two NVA divisions, what you might say otherwise engaged to partake in the Vietnam episode."
9.    CAT/Air America Memorial; Joe Hennessy said of Bernardo L. Dychitan: "No one seems to know who this man is. He could have been a German with an Italian mother working for some foreign aid agency. The only sure thing is that he was not a tourist, not if he was travelling on an Air America (Laos branch) airplane."
10.    Joe Hennessy, correspondence July 2008. According to correspondence from Wayne Knight this caused a big change in the way Air America allowed ammunition to be loaded on their aircraft.

### Chapter 13 Darkness Falls

1.    This chapter is based mainly on the work 'Profile of Service. Edmond John Landers. Captain/Infantry. United States Army,' by Walter S. O'Shea. Researched and compiled by Walter S. O'Shea, Tipperary, Ireland. March 2001. Revised June 2002 / December 2003 / June 2004 / August 2005 / March 2006.

### Chapter 14 The Year of Living Dangerously

1.    Reed, *Nam,* p. 401.
2.    del Vecchio, *The 13th Valley*, p. iii.
3.    Medal of Honour Citations.
4.    Charles D. Melson. *The Marine Corps in Vietnam*, pp 45, 52.
5.    Medal of Honour Citations.
6.    Irish on the Wall.
7.    Ibid.
8.    Manning, *Vietnam Experience*, p. 80.
9.    *Connaught Tribune*, 4 December 1998.
10.    Jay Petersen Tribute to Peter Nee, by kind permission of the author.
11.    Author correspondence with Tom Klein, September 2006.
12.    Millet, *Semper Fi,* pp. 601-2.
13.    Reed, *Nam*, pp. 386-7.

14. Declan Power. 'Born and bred in Dublin ... but he fought and died in Vietnam.' *Sunday Mirror* 30 June 2002.
15. McGarrigle. 'John C. Driver. A soldier's Story.' *An Cosantoir*, May 1999.
16. del Vecchio, *The 13th Valley*, p. x.
17. Ibid, p. 126.
18. *An Cosantoir*, p.13.
19. Author correspondence with James Duke, June 2006.
20. Author correspondence with Pat O'Leary, June 2006.
21. Author correspondence with Clyde Crossguns, June 2006.
22. Author correspondence with Brian Scott, June 2006.
23. Author correspondence with James McCammon, May 2005.
24. Author interview with Don Driver, July 2006.
25. *Irish Examiner*, April 2000.
26. Reed, *Nam*, pp. 385-7.
27. Author, O'Leary.
28. Reed, *Nam*, pp. 385-7.
29. Ibid, pp. 136-9.
30. Author correspondence with Joseph Doherty, October 2006/February 2007.
31. Author correspondence with Terry Boone, September 2006.
32. Author, Doherty, February 2007.

## Chapter 15 And the band played Waltzing Matilda

1. Brodie, *Australia in Vietnam*, pp 54, 56.
2. Reed, *Nam*, p. 244.
3. Brodie, *Australia in Vietnam*, p. 61.
4. Ibid, p.143.
5. Australian SAS Regimental History/Ed Somers.
6. SASR History.
7. Author interview with Pat Landers, September 2006.
8. David Webster and Ross Ellis. 7 RAR, *Through a Soldier's Lens. The two tours in Vietnam 1967-68 & 1970-71.* p. 18, 126.
9. Author correspondence with pat Landers, February 2008.
10. Brodie, *Australia in Vietnam*, p. 70.
11. Author correspondence with Landers.
12. Author interview Pat Landers, January/March 2007.
13. Ibid.
14. Brodie, *Australia in Vietnam*, p. 75.
15. Author, correspondence with Landers, February 2008.
16. Author, Landers, March 2007.
17. Maj. R. F. Stuart. ed. *3 RAR in South Vietnam 1967-68.* pp. 35-6.
18. Author correspondence with Landers, February 2008.
19. Author, Landers, January 2007.
20. Stuart, *3 RAR*, pp. 35-6.
21. Author, Landers.
22. Brodie, *Australia in Vietnam*, p. 78.
23. *Irish Times*, 17 July 1968.
24. Brodie, *Australia in Vietnam*, p. 78.
25. *Irish Times*, 17 July 1968.
26. Author, Landers.
27. *The Australian* (Special Edition.) '500. The Australians who died in Vietnam.' 18 August 1988.
28. Author correspondence with Declan Hughes, February 2007.
29. *The Australian* (Special Edition) 3-4 October 1992.
30. Webster and Ellis, 7 RAR, pp. 188, 240.
31. Sheehan, *Bright Shining Lie*, p. 243.
32. *Australian, 500*.
33. Ibid.
34. Ibid.
35. Series AWM 95 Australian Army Command Diaries RAAC. Item no. 2/5/16. Item B Squadron, 3rd Cavalry Regiment.
36. Australian War Memorial.
37. *Australian, 500*.
38. Ibid.

39.  Lt Col Robert C. Stevenson, 'Not so Friendly Fire: An Australian Taxonomy for Fratricide.' Land Warfare Studies Centre. March 2006. Working Paper No. 128, p.30.
40.  Brodie, *Australia in Vietnam*, pp. 83-8.
41.  Reed, *Nam,* p. 245.

**Chapter 16  War Is Over**
1.  Reed, *Nam*, pp. 448a, 480a.
2.  *Newsweek*, 3 August 1970.
3.  Tim O'Brien.net.
4.  James Webb.com.
5.  Irish on the Wall.
6.  Melson, *Marine Corps in Vietnam*, p. 53.
7.  ehistory archive U.S. Marines in Vietnam. *Vietnamization and Redeployment, 1970-1971*. Graham A. Cosmas and Lieutenant Colonel Terrence R Murray, USMC, sourced May 2008.
8.  Declan Hughes, IVMP.
9.  Sheehan, *Bright shining Lie*, pp. 570-1.
10.  Holmes, *Oxford Companion to Military History*, p. 956.
11.  Ibid, pp. 572-3.
12.  Thompson, *War in Peace*, p. 184.
13.  Ibid, pp. 214-5.
14.  Reed, *Nam*, p. 538.
15.  Author correspondence with John Dullahan, April 2006.
16.  Ibid.
17.  Reed, *Nam*, p. 487.
18.  Author, Dullahan.
19.  Reed, *Nam*, pp. 486-7.
20.  Author, Dullahan.
21.  Irish on the Wall.
22.  Ibid.
23.  Author correspondence with Sean McGovern, September 2006.
24.  Thompson, *War in Peace*, pp. 184-5.
25.  Reed, *Nam*, p. 487.
26.  Sheehan, *Bright Shining Lie*, pp. 784-5.
27.  Reed, *Nam*, pp. 560-3.
28.  *The Agence France Presse*.

**Epilogue  Better Times than These**
1.  David McNeill. 'Spoils of War.' *The Irish Times Magazine*, 14 May 2005.
2.  Michael Coyne, RTE; author interview January 2007.
3.  Tom Kelly, RTE; author interview August 2006.
4.  Novack, *We Remember II*, p. 12; author interview, September 2006.
5.  Author interview with Mike Flood, April 2007.
6.  Ed Somers, *Enniscorthy Echo* 7 September 2005.
7.  Gerry Duignan, RTE; Dungan, *Distant Drums*, p. 180.
8.  Author interview with John Dullahan, April 2006.
9.  Author interview with John Barnicle, April 2006.
10.  Untitled newspaper reports, January 1972, John O'Sullivan Archive.
11.  Nee, *A Criminal and an Irishman*, p. 92.
12.  Jason M. Pratt, 2nd Lt, USMC. 'South Boston Vietnam Veterans Memorial,' sourced online January 2008.
13.  Author correspondence with Pat Landers, February 2008.
14.  Author interview with John Barrett, May 2008.

# SOURCES

## BIBLIOGRAPHY

**Books**

Akenson, Donald Harman. *The Irish Diaspora*. A Primer. Belfast 1996.

Bradley, James, with Powers, Ron. *Flags of our Fathers*. London 2000.

Brodie, Scott. *Australia in the Vietnam War*. NSW 1990.

Casey, Michael. Dougan, Clark. Kennedy, Dennis and Shelby, Stanton. *The Vietnam Experience. The Army at War*. Boston 1987.

Cooney, John. *The American Pope: The Life and Times of Francis Cardinal Spellman*. New York 1984.

Cosmos, Graham A. & Murray, Lt Col. Terence. *Vietnamization and Redeployment, 1970-1971*.

Del Vecchio, John M. *The 13th Valley*. New York 1982.

Dungan, Myles. Distant Drums. *Irish soldiers in foreign armies*. Belfast 1993.

Ferriter, Diarmaid. *The Transformation of Ireland 1900-2000*. London 2004.

Griffiths, Philip Jones. *Vietnam Inc*. London 2005.

Holmes, Richard, ed. *The Oxford Companion to Military History*. NY 2001.

Katcher, Philip. *The American Soldier. U.S. Armies in uniform, 1775 to the present*. London 1990.

Kenny, Kevin. *The American Irish. A History*. New York 2000.

Mangold, Tom and Penycate, John. *The Tunnels of Cu Chi*. London 1985.

Mason, Robert. *Chickenhawk*. London 1984.

Melson, Charles D., *The Marine Corps in Vietnam*. London 1988.

Millett, Allan R., *Semper Fidelis. The History of the United States Marine Corps*. New York 1991.

Moore, Lt. Gen. Harold G. and Galloway, Joseph L. *We Were Soldiers Once ... And Young*. London 2002.

Murphy, Jack. *History of the US Marines*. New York 1984.

Nee, Patrick, with Farrell, Richard and Blythe, Michael. *A Criminal and an Irishman. The inside story of the Boston Mob and the IRA*. Dublin 2006.

Novak, David and Marian, eds. *We Remember. The Vietnam stories of the men of the 2nd Battalion, 1st Marines*. Lexington, Virginia 1993.

Novak, David and Marian, eds. *We Remember II. The Vietnam stories of the men of the 2nd Battalion, 1st Marines*. Rockbridge Baths, Virginia 2003.

Pemberton, Gregory, ed. *Vietnam Remembered*. Sydney 1990.

Reed, Jonathan, ed. *Nam. The Vietnam Experience 1965-75*, 2 Vols. London 1987.

Sallah, Michael and Weiss, Mitch. *Tiger Force*. London 2006.

Sheehan, Neil. *A Bright Shining Lie*. London 1990.

Schulimson, Lt Col Jack, Blasiol, Leonard, Smith, Charles R. and Dawson, Capt. David A. *U.S. Marines in Vietnam: 1968, the Defining Year*. Washington DC 1997.

Stuart, Major R. F., ed. *3 RAR in South Vietnam 1967-1968*. NSW 1968.

Warren, James A. *American Spartans. The U.S. Marines: A combat history from Iwo Jima to Iraq*. New York 2005.

Webb, James. *Fields of Fire*. New York 1978.

Webster, David and Ellis, Ross. 7 RAR, *The Two Tours in Vietnam 1967-68 and 1970-71. Through a Soldier's Lens*, 7th Battalion, The Royal Australian Regiment Association. NSW 2004.

**Papers**

'A Bronx Reunion in Nam.' Jim Kirk and Mike Flood. *We Remember. The Vietnam stories of the men of the 2nd Battalion, 1st Marines*.

Australian Army Command Diaries RAAC. Series AWM 95.

'Born and bred in Dublin ... but he fought and died in Vietnam.' Declan Power. *Sunday Mirror*, 2002.

'Canadians in Vietnam.' Gar Pardy and Donald J. Byrne.

'Eight Names On The Wall Belong To Women.' Christopher Podgus.

'He Wouldn't Stay Behind. Chaplain dies at front with his men.' George McArthur. 1968.

'Historical Account of the Military Police Corps Regiment Assault on the American Embassy Tet –1968.' SSG Thomas L. Johnson and Mary R. Himes, United States Army Military Police Corps Regimental Museum, 1983.

'IRAs role in Vietnam.' Danny Conlon, *Sunday Mirror*, 11/3/2007.

'John C. Driver. A Soldier's Story.' Cpl Paddy McGarrigle, *An Cosantoir*, 3/5/1999.

'Major Peter Dewey, America's First Vietnam Casualty.' Gary Linderer, 2005

'Not so Friendly Fire: An Australian Taxonomy for Fratricide.' Lt Col Robert C. Stevenson. 2006.

'Operation Masher. The Boundaries of Force.' John Prados. *The VA Veteran*. February/March 2002.

'Profile of Service. Edmond John Landers. Captain/Infantry. United States Army.' Walter S. O'Shea. 2006.

'Public Safety During Combat: A positive lesson from Vietnam.' Col Frank L. Miller, Jr. 2003.

'Spoils of War.' David McNeill. *The Irish Times Magazine*, 14 May 2005.

'The Battle for Saigon.' David T. Zabecki, *Vietnam Magazine*.

'The First Marines in Vietnam.' Timothy J. Kutta. Ospreypublishing.com.

'The Jungle Doctor.' Edward T. O'Donnell. *The Irish Echo*. April 9-15 2008.

'Time Heals Almost Everything.' Mike Flood. *We Remember II. The Vietnam stories of the men of the 2nd Battalion, 1st Marines*.

'The Marine War: III MAF in Vietnam, 1965-1971.' Jack Shulimson, U.S. Marine Corps Historical Center.

'The Star and the Sickle. A study of Soviet-Vietnamese Relations during the Vietnam War.' Austin Williams.

'Vietnam Revisited.' Brian Finch. *Vietnam Newsletter*.

**Newspapers**

*Evening Herald*, Dublin.
*Connaught Tribune*, Galway.
*The Enniscorthy Echo*, Wexford.
*The Irish Times*, Dublin.
*The Irish Echo*, New York.
*The Irish Examiner*, Cork.
*The Western People*.

**TV**

'The Green Fields of Vietnam.' TV documentary. Ann Roper/RTE. 2003.

**CD**

'Airborne All the Way.' Radio documentary. Vanessa Connolly. 2002/3. Irish Veterans Memorial Project.

**Internet sites**

air-america.org
1st Battalion, 22nd Infantry homepage.
12th Tactical Fighter Wing Association homepage.
173rd Airborne.com.
174ahc.org.
B/2/501 Airborne.
Brownwater Navy Vietnam.com.
Helis.com. Helicopter History Site. Hueys in Vietnam.
Irish on the Wall: Irish Born Killed in Vietnam.
James Webb.com.
Medal of Honour Citations.
Merchant Navy Association, MNA.org.uk
Ray Smith.com
Swiftboats.org.
The 9th Infantry Division Index.
The Australian involvement in Vietnam.
The Vietnam Veterans Memorial Wall Page.
The Virtual Wall. Vietnam Veterans Memorial.
The Wild Geese.com.
Tim O'Brien.net.
Vietnamtripledeuce.org.

# IRISH VIETNAM VETERANS AS POSTED ON THEIR ROLL OF HONOUR

## IRISH WHO LOST THEIR LIVES SERVING WITH US FORCES, VIETNAM

**Sgt Patrick Christopher 'Christy' Nevin, Army**
Date & Place of Birth: 25 April 1937,
Claremorris, Co. Mayo, Ireland.
Home of Record: East Chicago, Indiana.
Date & Place of Death: 23 February 1966, SVN.
Vietnam Memorial: Panel 5 East, Line 67.

**L/Cpl Paul Ivan Maher, Marine Corps**
Date & Place of Birth: 6 July 1945, Dublin,
Ireland.
Home of Record: Hauppauge, New York.
Date & Place of Death: 5 March 1966, Quang
Nam.
Vietnam Memorial: Panel 5 East, Line 120.

**SP4 Timothy Daly, Army**
Date & Place of Birth: 21 July 1945, Limerick,
Ireland.
Home of Record: Edgewater, New Jersey.
Date & Place of Death: 3 February 1967, SVN.
Vietnam Memorial: Panel 14 East, Line 111.

**L/Cpl Bernard Anthony Freyne, Marine Corps**
Date & Place of Birth: 13 May 1945,
Ballaghadereen, Co. Roscommon, Ireland.
Home of Record: Woodside, New York.
Date & Place of Death: 10 March 1967, Da
Nang.
Vietnam Memorial: Panel 16 East, Line 52.

**SP4 Michael Francis Smith, Army**
Date & Place of Birth: 25 November 1945,
Ballyconnell, Co. Cavan, Ireland.
Home of Record: New York, New York.
Date & Place of Death: 18 March 1967, Tay
Ninh.
Vietnam Memorial: Panel 16 East, Line 107.

**SP4 John Coyle, Army.**
Date & Place of Birth: 03 January 1946, Kilcogy,
Co. Cavan, Ireland.*
Home of Record: Hackensack, New Jersey.
Date & Place of Death: 29 March 1967, SVN.
Vietnam Memorial: Panel 17 East, Line 67.
* Born Birmingham, England of Irish-born parents, prior to emigration to US at circa.4 years of age.

**Cpl Patrick 'Bob' Gallagher, Marine Corps**
Date & Place of Birth: 1 February 1944,
Ballyhaunis, Co. Mayo, Ireland.
Home of Record: Lynbrook, New York.
Date & Place of Death: 30 March 1967, Quang
Nam. Vietnam Memorial: Panel 17 East, Line
71.

**Sgt/FC Edward Michael Howell, Army**
Date & Place of Birth: 21 June 1937, Dublin,
Ireland.
Home of Record: Cleveland, Ohio.
Date & Place of Death: 17 April 1967, Long An.
Vietnam Memorial: Panel 18 East, Line 41.

**PFC Maurice Joseph O'Callaghan, Marine Corps**
Date & Place of Birth: 27 December 1946,
Dublin, Ireland.
Home of Record: Iselin, New Jersey.
Date & Place of Death: 21 April 1967, Quang
Nam.
Vietnam Memorial: Panel 18 East, Line 62.

**Cpl Terence Patrick FitzGerald, Army**
Date & Place of Birth: London, England. *
Home of Record: California.
Date & Place of Death: 26 May 1967.
Vietnam Memorial: Panel 20 East, Line 114.
* Father born Kerry, mother born Galway.

**PFC John Patrick Collopy, Army.**
Date & Place of Birth: 06 July 1946, Limerick,
  Ireland.
Home of Record: Dorchester, Massachusetts.
Date & Place of Death: 15 July 1967, Long
  Khanh.
Vietnam Memorial: Panel 23 East, Line 74.

**SP4 Edward Anthony Scully, Army.**
Date & Place of Birth: 25 June 1945, Cork,
  Ireland.
Home of Record: West Point, New York.
Date & Place of Death: 13 Nov 1967, Kontum.
Vietnam Memorial: Panel 29 East, Line 92.

**Capt Edmond J. Landers, Army.**
Date & Place of Birth: 07 July 1937, Oola, Co.
  Limerick, Ireland.
Home of Record: Vacaville, California.
Date & Place of Death: 15 May 1968, Gia Dinh.
Vietnam Memorial: Panel 60 East, Line 24.

**1/Lt Anthony Paul O'Reilly, Army.**
Date & Place of Birth: 01 June 1938, Galway,
  Ireland.
Home of Record: Kettering, Ohio.
Date & Place of Death: 03 June 1968, Kien
  Tuong.
Vietnam Memorial: Panel 60 West, Line 3.

**2/Lt Pamela Dorothy Donovan, Army
  Nurse Corps .**
Date & Place of Birth: 25 March 1942, Wirral,
  Merseyside, UK. *
Home of Record: Brighton, Massachusetts.
Date & Place of Death: 08 July 1968, Gia Dinh.
Vietnam Memorial: Panel 53 West, Line 43.
* Irish-born parents and siblings, Irish citizen and
  Irish educated until emigration to US.

**Cpl Philip Sean Bancroft, Marine Corps.**
Date & Place of Birth: 11 June 1949, Belfast,
  Northern Ireland.
Home of Record: Pittsburgh, Pennsylvania.
Date & Place of Death: 30 Sept 1968, Quang
  Nam.
Vietnam Memorial: Panel 42 West, Line 45.

**SP4 Brian Francis McCarthy, Army.**
Date & Place of Birth: 5 Oct 1945, New York. *
Home of Record: New York City, New York.
Date & Place of Death: 15 March 1969, Binh
  Long.
Vietnam Memorial: Panel 29 West, Line 47.
* Born in U.S. to Irish Father from Cork.

**Cpl Sean T. Doran, Army.**
Date & Place of Birth: 9 October 1948, Dublin,
  Ireland.
Home of Record: Lennox, California.
Date & Place of Death: 28 March 1969, Tay
  Ninh.
Vietnam Memorial: Panel 28 West, Line 68.

**L/Cpl Peter Mary Nee, Marine Corps.**
Date & Place of Birth: 15 August 1947,
  Connemara, Co. Galway, Ireland.
Home of Record: Cambridge, Massachusetts.
Date & Place of Death: 31 March 1969, Quang
  Nam.
Vietnam Memorial: Panel 28 West, Line 99.

**1/Lt John Cecil Driver, Army.**
Date & Place of Birth: 16 May 1936, Dublin,
  Ireland.
Home of Record: Dublin, Ireland.
Date & Place of Death: 17 April 1969, Thua
  Tien.
Vietnam Memorial: Panel 27 West, Line 99.

**RD3 Martin S Doherty, Navy.**
Date & Place of Birth: 8 April 1949, New York.*
Home of Record: New York.
Date & Place of Death: 4 Dec 1969, Vietnam.
Vietnam Memorial: Panel 15 West, Line 23.
* Father Born, Mayo, mother born Galway,
  buried in Kilkerrin Cemetery, Galway along-
  side her.

**Sgt Arthur Fisher, US Marine Corps.**
Date & Place of Birth: 31 July 1942, Portrush,
  Co Antrim, Northern Ireland
Home of Record: North Tonawanda, New York
Date & Place of Death: 20 November 1970,
  Quang Nam.
Vietnam Memorial: Panel 6 West, Line 73.
Buried in St Pancras, Islington and Finchley
  Cemetery, London.

## IRISHMAN WORKING WITH AIR AMERICA

**Patrick Factna McCarthy.**

Date & Place of Birth: Dunmanway, Co. Cork, Ireland.

Home of Record: New York City.

Date & Place of Death: 7 December 1968, Laos.

Air America Memorial, University of Texas, Dallas.

## IRISHMAN IN CANADIAN UNIFORM

**James Sylvester Byrne.**

Sgt, Royal Canadian Army Service Corps.

Date & Place of Birth: 17 April 1929, Dublin, Ireland.

Current Status: Missing, 18 October 1965.

Plane was lost over Laos.

## IRISHMAN WORKING FOR USAID

**Michael Murphy.**

Office of Public Safety, USAID, attached to South Vietnamese Police Field Forces.

Date & Place of Birth: 9 Feb 1928, Cork City, Ireland.

Home of Record: Alaska (on leave from Alaska State Troopers).

Date & Place of Death: 23 May 1968, SVN.

## IRISHMEN KILLED SERVING WITH AUSTRALIAN FORCES

**Rifleman George Nagle, 9th Royal Australian Regiment.**

Date & Place of Birth: 1946, Clonmel, Co. Tipperary, Ireland.

Home of Record: Australia.

Date & Place of Death: 6 Jan 1969, Phuoc Tuy Province.

**Driver/Signalman David G Doyle, 3rd Cavalry Regiment.**

Date & Place of Birth: 1950, Dublin, Ireland .

Home of Record: New South Wales, Australia.

Date & Place of Death: 31 July 1970.

**Sgt Robert Fleming, 1st RAR and 1st Australian Reinforcement Regiment.**

Date & Place of Birth: 1946, Northern Ireland.

Home of Record: Melbourne, Australia.

Date & Place of Death: 9 Nov 1970, South Vietnam.

**Sgt Thomas Birnie, 2nd Royal Australian Regiment.**

Date & Place of Birth: 1940, Belfast, Northern Ireland.

Home of Record: Townsville, Australia.

Date & Place of Death: 25 March 1971.

List compiled by Declan Hughes, Irish Veterans Memorial Project, and James Durney. List valid as at July 2008.

## VETERANS INTERVIEWED AND FEATURED

Tom Kelly, US 173rd Airborne Brigade.

Ed Somers, 1st Royal Australian Regiment.

John Dullahan, US 1st Cavalry Division.

John Barnicle, US 9th Aviation Battalion.

Pat O'Leary, US 101st Airborne Division.

Dan Danaher, 1st Royal Australian Regiment.

Pat Landers, 5th and 7th Royal Australian Regiment.

Michael Cahill, British Merchant Navy.

Mike Flood, US 1st Marine Division.

Rory O'Connell, US 1st Marine Division.

Gerry Duignan, USAF.

Sean McGovern, USAF.

Michael Coyne, US 11th Armoured Cavalry Regiment.

Canice Wolahan, US Navy, HQ Support Activity.

Martin Hennigar, US Army Engineers.

Sean Levins, US 15th Artillery Regiment.

John O'Sullivan, US 174th Assault Helicopter Company.

Pat Nee, 3/4th US Marines.

John Barrett, US 1st Infantry Division.

Joe Hennessey, Air America.

John Dobbin, British Merchant Navy.

# APPENDIX I

**Run For The Wall.**
The man who led the identification of the Irish who lost their lives in Vietnam is Declan Hughes (currently Coordinator of the Irish Veterans Memorial Project). Here he explains how it all began, and how he ended up travelling overland from Los Angeles, California, to Washington DC with several hundred motorcycle-riding Vietnam Veterans in May 1999. Following this preface is the diary he kept of that journey.

"In late 1997, while working with the Vietnamese community in Dublin, a ring came into my possession that had been removed from the finger of a dead GI after a battle in Vietnam, and over 30 years later, I was asked if I could find the family of that GI. In early 1998, I brought the ring to Washington, to the late Libby Hatch, Special Projects Officer of the Vietnam Veterans Memorial Fund (VVMF) – the organisation that, against all the odds, built America's National Memorial to the American dead in Vietnam. They also commissioned a half-scale replica of the Memorial, designed to tour communities all across America – bringing the Memorial to people who otherwise would never be able to visit the original. "While there I attended a VVMF Media Launch on the Mall, and at the close of this event, I asked the dumbest question of the year: when would the Travelling Memorial travel to Ireland? To say the least, the reaction was one of surprise. Why, I was asked, should the Vietnam Memorial travel to Ireland – a country politically 'neutral' throughout the 20th century? A country that had never been involved in the World Wars, Korea, and especially Vietnam. My response at the time was that if you consider that the 40 million or so Americans who claim Irish ancestry are correct, then you must take that assumption to some further conclusions: a percentage must have served in the military; a percentage must have served in Vietnam; and a percentage must have died in Vietnam.

"When Libby and I dug deeper into official statistics, we discovered that – officially – only one Irish-born was killed in Vietnam – John Driver, from Ringsend in Dublin, who gave as his Home of Record his Home of Birth. However, looking at Irish immigration patterns throughout the 50s and 60s into America, coupled with compulsory military service, thousands of Irish must have served at this time. A percentage must have served in Vietnam. A percentage, sadly, must have died.

"We worked on, dug deeper, followed leads and clues, and I walked through cemeteries, posted messages on web-sites, etc. We worked out a tentative tour of Ireland for the Memorial, and convinced the powers that needed convincing, until eventually, Jan Scruggs, President of VVMF and original inspiration behind the creation of the Memorial, agreed that The Wall should travel to Ireland. After doing some media in Ireland, the solitary figure of John Driver was soon joined by others who, up to this, had remained unidentified as anything other than more American casualties.

"By late 1998, the decision to bring The Wall to Ireland had been made, and preparations were proceeding apace in Ireland, with myself and Monica Worth (acting as Irish and

US Tour Coordinators respectively), meeting and organising with a range of individuals and organisations. It was during one of these cross-country journeys that we learned of Libby's tragic death in a motorcycle accident back in the US. This served to make us redouble our efforts to see the memorial in Ireland as a tribute, not only to those Irish who lost their lives in Vietnam, but to Libby, without whose energy and creativity such a tour would never have come off.

"On Remembrance Sunday (Veterans Day) 1998, the 50,000 Irish who lost their lives in World War I while serving in British Army regiments, were officially recognised by the Irish State. At a ceremony in Belgium, the President of Ireland and Queen of England stood side by side in official remembrance – 80 years after that war had ended. At the same time, in Washington DC, a wreath was laid by Vickie Curtin of the Irish Centre, at the Vietnam Memorial, for the first time giving recognition and respect to the Irish-born who died in Vietnam while serving with United States forces – some 23 years after the fall of Saigon.

"Work to identify more Irish killed in Vietnam continued, culminating in the visit of The Wall That Heals, the half-scale travelling replica, to the four historic provinces of the island of Ireland, through April/May 1999. On public view in Collins Barracks Cork, Dublin Castle, Queens University Belfast, and NUI-Galway, the tour ended with a stay at Adare Manor, Limerick, where Prime Minister Bertie Ahern met many family members and laid a wreath. Earlier, the President of Ireland Mary McAleese paid her respects to all who died when she visited The Wall at Queens University, Belfast.

"As the tour wound down in Limerick, The Wall's travelling managers John and Linda Anderson, suggested I follow up my research by flying to Los Angeles and connecting up with Run For The Wall (RFTW), and travelling with them cross-continent to Washington DC in time for Memorial Day at the end of May. They explained that RFTW was a very large 'family' of Veterans, most of whom rode motorcycles, and that every year they completed this marathon bike ride in remembrance of all who died, and all those who were POW (prisoners of war) and MIA (missing in action), and to call on the authorities for a full accounting. The decision to fly 6000 miles to LA, followed by another 3000 across America, in the company of hundreds of bikers was made on the spur of the moment, and without giving it much serious thought. But the experience was unique, and to give something back to strangers who had given me so much, and taken care to take good care of me while on the road, I jotted down my daily journal of the trip. It follows as it was written back in May 1999."

Meanwhile, the work of identifying Irish who died in Vietnam continues, though now as part of a wider project. The Irish Veterans Historical Research Centre, (aka Irish Veterans Memorial Project) has been established as a charity in Ireland, and the search goes on for Irish men and women who served in forces throughout the 20th century, up to the present day. The Project has plans to renovate an old disused church in south Roscommon for use as a research centre and memorial, and is busy looking for funds to do this. Declan Hughes is Coordinator of the project.

**Run for The Wall 1999**
**Day 1**
… Today we departed Ontario, California. … It seems like hundreds of motorcycles, sup-

port vehicles and chase trucks departed Ontario, and luckily I was among them. Not being too well up on the golden rule – if ya snooze, ya lose – I came very close to not being among them. Thankfully, Deekin takes my stupidity into account, and I get a ride to the truck stop from Side-Car, to whom I'm eternally grateful. Then the wonderful Wally took over, and with gear safely stashed, registration complete, obligatory RFTW band on my left wrist, and much egg on my face from nearly flunking in the first hour, I became an official member of this amazing Run for the Wall Family.

## Day 5

... Also especially installed for our arrival, and courtesy of the New Mexico Army National Guard, was a Huey – one of the infamous helicopter trademarks of Vietnam. Many of these guys rode to the LZs in Hueys, were pulled out in Hueys, were covered by Huey door-gunners, were brought out wounded in Hueys, loaded their eternally-covered buddies aboard Hueys. Many were also Huey pilots and door-gunners themselves, and it didn't take much to see what they saw in their mind's eyes.

And what did I see? Young guys who went to America in the 50s and 60s to escape an economic depression that seemed to last for centuries in the Irish gloom. When 'Sam' came calling, they could so easily have turned round and come home, or moved on elsewhere, but instead they put on the uniform. Many never mentioned Vietnam in their first letters home, not wanting to alarm their parents, brothers and sisters. One even went so far as posting his letters home to the States first, and having them sent on to his family in Ireland. He finally had to come clean when he was due to be awarded the Navy Cross, and the media got wind of what he'd done to get it.

Patrick 'Bob' Gallagher, Cpl, USMC, in a defence post at Cam Lo on the 18th July 1966, had kicked the first grenade back out, and jumped on the second one. As his buddies escaped, two more grenades exploded, and with a hair's breadth to spare, Gallagher had managed to fling the one he was lying on out into the river, where it exploded on impact. In January '67, he heard about the award he was to receive, and decided to inform his parents. He would be home in April, and he'd receive it then, he told them. However, it was not to be, and the media that descended on the little village in the West of Ireland for the hero's return, covered his funeral instead. Patrick Gallagher was shot dead while on patrol in Da Nang on March 30th 1967.

For most of the guys, the last kind word probably came from a Huey door-gunner, as they jumped down into elephant grass a million miles from the shores of Connemara, or Cork, or Dublin. Having met so many of the surviving parents, brothers, sisters, uncles, aunts and in some cases, children of my 16 Irish guys who fought and died alongside their American cousins, I was fine until I was asked if I was alright. Thanks for standing beside me this day, Dragon Joe.

## Day 6

... Since beginning this trip, I've been giving out lapel pins from The Wall's visit to Ireland as I get talking with individuals. Most appear genuinely fascinated to hear that The Wall went to Ireland in the first place, and somewhat taken by the revelation that Irish-born fought and died in US uniform beside them in Vietnam. I should add that Irish-born fought and died alongside them in Australian uniform also, and up to very recently no-one knew a thing about any of these guys.

So as I was walking through the grounds, I passed a little stall which was giving away soaps and toiletries to anyone who needed – a pattern repeated all along the route, and for which thoughtfulness we should be really grateful. However, what I spotted was Irish Mist soap, and passed a suitable comment along the lines of "they must have been expecting me". I handed an Ireland pin to the girl on the stall as a thank you, and was quite taken aback when she nearly cried. She told me she'd give it to her Dad, who was in a wheelchair, saying he would really break down when he saw it. I tried to find out why, but couldn't, and she went off to find her father and, I guess, made him cry. The longer I live, the less I understand.

## Day 9

… Back down in the parking lot, where they were still feeding and watering us, and giving out commemorative patches to mark the visit, an announcement came over the tannoy. "Will the Irishman travelling with Run for the Wall please come to the podium. The Irishman travelling with Run for the Wall, please come to the podium."

Not having any idea what this was about, I made my way through the crowd, all the time wondering if I'd paid the hotel bill at Corydon, or had I left something unspeakable behind in the room, or perhaps Immigration were enforcing a crack-down? Or had I really gotten up someone's nose, and this was now pay-off time!

However, when I got there, I was introduced to a lovely lady called Francis Turley, from De Soto, Missouri, who had heard there was an Irishman with the group, and wanted to tell me that the Travelling Wall had just been to Ireland. As a Gold Star Mother, Francis was one of the Moms who had written a personal letter to Irish families who had lost a son in Vietnam. She was as surprised to meet me as I was to meet her, especially when I explained that I was the one who actually organised The Wall going to Ireland. I told her about the tour, and gave her an Ireland pin. She had Irish connections, as did the woman next to her, who also wanted to say hello – as did the Director of the VAMC, who also got a pin (in return for a patch!). A really unexpected and ironic visit for me. Interesting to have such feedback while travelling through this extraordinary country.

## Day 11

… From here we hike further into the interior, with another group shot at the Lincoln Memorial. Something of a frightening event for the hordes of tourists who, up to that moment, were simply unsuspectingly inspecting the "must sees" and "must dos" of Washington. Old Abe however, I'm sure felt a warm tingle flood through his marble veins as we spilled over his steps, and gazed out across the Reflecting Pool, all the way down The Mall, the Washington Monument looking pretty damn snappy in it's new overalls.

And every time I see the Capital Dome, in my mind's eye I still see the black and white procession past the steps, the riderless horse with boots reversed in the stirrups, and the casket draped in the Stars and Stripes. If only we knew then how many would follow on that journey to Arlington, and all the other "Arlingtons" from November 63 to May 75. So many lifetimes away in a very literal sense. JFK was, of course, the "first Irish President" –

which equally of course, he wasn't. Irish blood ran through the veins of so many US Presidents, it's amazing that Ireland never actually signed up to become an extra US State.

He was the first Catholic President, and probably because he'd been in Ireland only months before his death, and wowed them in the aisles, US recruiting sergeants began having a never-ending field day, with many young kids trying to sign up in the Embassy in Dublin. Everyone it seemed, wanted to "bear any burden, meet any hardship, support any friend and oppose any foe to assure the survival and success of liberty". You can't fault the sentiments, and you can't tell what he would have done had he lived.

... I didn't go to Arlington. In one way I was sorry not to go, but in another I wasn't. Over the past two and some years, I've searched through enough graveyards to convince me of the benefits of cremation. I've read down headstones of all kinds and, ironically in Ireland, so many graves of Irishmen who served in various British Regiments. World War I saw 35,000-50,000 Irishmen killed in action, all in British Army uniforms, and the great irony for me was the obvious link between these guys, and the Vietnam Veteran. In *We Were Soldiers Once . . . and Young*, Col. Hal Moore writes that "the country that sent us off to war was not there to welcome us home. It no longer existed ... and we went to ground in the cross-fire ... "

The Irish who went to war in 1914, wearing their British Army uniforms because there wasn't any "Irish" army, returned in 1918 (those that did), to a different country. The Easter Rebellion of 1916 had taken place, and the Irish wanted their freedom. Men who had endured the slaughter of the trenches to secure the freedom of others, were treated like traitors in the ensuing years, and "went to ground in the cross-fire".

In November 1998, they were finally recognised and honoured as the Irish who served, and the Irish who died. After 80 years, very few "old soldiers" were left to take the salute. At the same time, on Veterans Day in Washington DC, a wreath was laid at The Wall for the Irishmen who fought and died in Vietnam – the very first wreath laid to officially recognise and honour these men, and "only" 23 years after the war.

Since that wreath-laying, the Travelling Wall has been to Ireland, more men have been identified, the President of Ireland has walked the Travelling Wall. The Prime Minister of Ireland has laid a wreath, and spent an evening with the families. The families, each of whom for 30 years believed themselves to be the sole Irish family to lose a son in Vietnam, have met with, photographed, telephoned, and laughed and cried with each other. Only 23 years after the war.

And having flown 3,000 miles across the Atlantic, and 3,000 across the continent to California, and another 3,000 back to DC, I carried my 16 names, and 16 sets of relatives, with me to The Wall. I laid an Ireland pin at the apex, and a laminated list of the 16 at the Soldier's Statue.

Declan Hughes © 1999.

In reference to the above or any queries on Irish war veterans Declan Hughes may be contacted at dectwth@eircom.net

# APPENDIX II

Gerry Duignan, from Rinn, Co. Roscommon, served with the USAF from 1968-72 in Binh Dinh province, where he befriended the nuns and children of a local orphanage. In November 2006 he wrote this piece, for *Vietnam The Irish Experience,* on the fate of the orphanage as South Vietnam finally fell to the communists.

"We veterans have many stories of our war, but my greatest is as follows. In January 1968 whilst on a mission with a fellow airman, I came across an orphanage in a remote area of the Binh Dinh province. Here was home to about 100/120 children from infants to early teens, mostly girls. There were five nuns and lots of community help. They existed mostly on charity and on the wits of the nuns. In those early days after Tet, they adopted me and I became part of that little group. In 1973 their world was turned upside down when the NVA drove into Binh Dinh province.

"The sister and the children fled before the advance with thousands more and in a harrowing ordeal, they made it to the coastal city of Nha Thrang. There they stayed for six months until it was safe to return home. They came back, cleaned up the orphanage, and settled into life once again. But it was short-lived. After Tet in 1975, the NVA were on the move again and this time it was final! In early March, there was a two-pronged attack on the coastal city of Qui Nhon along Highways 1 and 19. The sisters were faced with a grave situation, evacuate or stay? They decided to stay, but to send the American-Vietnamese orphans to Saigon in the hope of getting them out of the country. There were ten of these children in the orphanage. The task fell to the youngest sister, a twenty-six year old women called 'Thanh.' She took the children and ten other girls as helpers and started this perilous journey.

"It was 300 miles to Saigon with roads full of refugees and retreating soldiers. They had no transport and carried what provisions they were able. They left early in March and it took them until 25 April to reach Saigon. When they arrived, they were exhausted, tired, hungry and dirty, but the road was not yet over. Here Thanh sent eight of the girl helpers back home and keeping two with the children, she hoped to get the Amer-asians to America. They were never heard of again. That week was the last week before the fall of Saigon. On 4 April a C5-A loaded with as many as 1,000 children and helpers crashed on take-off from Ton Son Nhut.[1]

"The eight girls now returned to an orphanage that no longer existed. By the time they reached home, the nuns were evicted and had gone off to live in a small annex of the local church. These girls were now homeless and had no families. They had to accept unpaid work in the kitchens and laundries of the victorious NVA. Later, many of them married ex-soldiers and settled in the general area.

"One, in particular, was luckier and married a man she had known before the final attack. They have four children and are now grown up and in education in university. A credit to their Mum and Dad. Others have not fared as well. The victorious army of the North were also poor and those who married and reared a family today live in generally poor conditions. At Tet celebrations, they tend to come home again to the place of the orphanage and celebrate the feast. We are aware of each other's lives and they are proud to have a 'brother' who still remembers them. (The names and places are omitted or changed for safety reasons.)

"And so Vietnam lies in the past, a storybook of beauty as it grows rich in the 21st Century. For we who survive and tell stories, it will always be the Vietnam War. The words of Mai Van Hang, an NVA soldier killed near Pleiku (in the last letter to his wife) probably shares the sentiments of many of us — on all sides:

"How devastating and poignant this war is! It has stolen the vernal springs of our lives. We fledglings who knew nothing except our schoolbooks! I didn't expect to be so wretched. If I see you again in the future, I will tell you everything in detail. If not, please calm your grief and do not mourn me." [2]

Gerard Patrick Duignan, November 2006.

### Notes to Appendix II
1  During Operation Babylift 127 children, including seventy-six babies, fifty-nine civilian women and eight military crew were killed in the crash of a C5-A Galaxy on 4 April 1975 near Saigon.
2  Bernard Fall, Street without Joy, Harrisbury, PA, 1961.

# INDEX